Commons, Community and Collective Action

Abhilas K. Pradhan
27.03.1976 to 05.03.2021
Dedicated
to the departed soul...

Preface

Ever since thinking on 'inclusive development' was sparked by 'investing in countries lagging behind in development' in the 1950s and the United Nations World Commission on Environment and Development coined the term 'sustainable development' in 1987, the theology of management of common property natural resources has moved towards sector wide approaches. In these new perspectives there has been a continued focus on supporting sustainable livelihoods of rural people and tribal communities with their active involvement in utilization and conservation of common natural assets by formulating and implementing participatory policies and programmes.

In the context of management of forests in India and its states and union territories, participatory management policies such as Joint Forest Management have provided for developing participative, collaborative and people-centred authority to manage forests sustainably. The Joint Forest Management approach in Odisha involves sharing of products, control, responsibilities and decision making in the context of common forests covered under JFM that is based on a formal institutional agreement between the Forest Department of Government of Odisha and the local user groups in the forest fringe villages. The broad objective of JFM is to provide an active participatory role to the local communities in the production, use, management and protection of forests on the 'care and share' principle.

But in practice, people's active role in forest management is largely undermined or grossly ignored and emphasis has rather been placed on increasing forest cover outside forests by planting trees. Needless to say, sustainable management of forests continues to remain the most challenging task.

The threat of destruction and degradation confronting the forests due to demographic pressure, inadequate investment and inappropriate management on the one hand and displacement of the conventional saviors of forests, the tribals and rural people, in the name of development on the other still loom large on the horizon. This has necessitated a focused rethinking and deliberation on 'how can we integrate various contrasting motives for exploiting forests and managing this vital part of the commons sustainably'.

This book is a revised and updated version of the doctoral thesis of the lead author titled 'Heterogeneity, Common Property Resources and Collective Action: An Empirical Study of Linkages in Villages of Odisha' prepared with the active involvement of the second author for which the former was awarded a Ph.D. Degree by Utkal University in 2012. Although publication of the work was suggested in the viva-voce examination of the thesis, it could not be effected due to his over busy engagement with teaching and other assignments in the Indira Global Business School, Pune.

The book successfully integrates the emerging issues of forest usage and management on the basis of the findings of an empirical survey conducted in three districts of Odisha state, India. The book is one of its kinds, which focuses on four contemporary interlinked themes: Dependence, Heterogeneity, Collective Action, and sustainability all integrated into the frameworks of the theory and practice of Joint Forest Management implemeted through the Vana Sanrakhyana Samities/ Vana Surakhya Samities in the state.

I strongly feel that this book will be quite useful for researchers and policy makers and will encourage further research in emerging areas of forestry and environment.

Rabi N Patra

Acknowledgements

Commons, Community and Collective Action has evolved from the doctoral dissertation titled "Heterogeneity, Common Property Resources and Collective Action: An Empirical Study of Linkages in Villages of Odisha". The book owes its birth to the generosity of a number of people who have seen us through the research Odyssey culminating in the dissertation. We believe, expressing gratitude to them is no recompense for their contribution, but we would like to extend our sincere gratitude and heartiest thanks to all of them for their help.

We owe the greatest debt of gratitude to all those scholars whose work we have consulted in preparing this book. We are thankful to the officials of the J.N. Library, University of Bombay; National Library, ICSSR Library & ISI Library, Kolkata; Ratan Tata Library, Delhi University; J.N.U. Library, Teenmurty Library and ICSSR Library, New Delhi; NIRD&PR Library, Hyderabad; and SPISER Library and IIM Library, Ahmedabad for ungrudgingly making available to us the requisite books, reports & journals and accessing data relating to our work.

We are extremely grateful to Late Prof. Adwait Kumar Mohanty, Former R.B.I. Chair Professor, Department of Analytical and Applied Economics, Utkal University for introducing us to this exciting field of research and for his insightful comments, dedicated help, advice, inspiration, encouragement and continuous support in writing the book. We put on record our special thanks to Prof. Arabinda Mishra, Theme Leader Livelihoods at the International Centre for Integrated Mountain Development (ICIMOD), Kathmandu (Nepal) for his insightful and innovative motivation for the work.

Our special thanks are due to Sri Tarakanta Mohanty (Retired Divisional Manager, *Odisha* Forest Development Corporation Ltd.) for his support in acquainting us with the personnel of the Forest Department of Government of Odisha and the key persons in the study area for field investigation. We owe a lot to the investigators Mantu Babu, Lalit and Debendra for their unstinted help in collecting primary data for this work. We are also thankful to the sample households who have spent their valuable time and provided us with information for conducting our research work.

We gratefully acknowledge the support of our survey respondents and forum participants who spared valuable time to provide us necessary information for this work. It is also our good fortune to have benefited from consultations with them.

We are very much thankful to Mr. J.K Singh of Abhijeet Publications, New Delhi for his personal efforts in bringing out the book in quick time.

We acknowledge with much pride and delight our debts to Smt. Janaki Jena, Mr. Rabindra Kumar Pradhan and Sasmita who have been the perennial source of encouragement and spiritual support behind this work.

We are exclusively responsible for the errors, if any, in the work.

Rabi N. Patra
Abhilas K. Pradhan

Contents

Acronyms and Abbreviations

CFA - Community Forest Association
CFM - Community Forest Management
CFR - Community Forest Resource
CHg - Central Plateau & Hills
CIFOR - Centre for International Forestry Research
CPR - Common Pool Resource
DP - Southern Plateau & Hills
DPF - Demarcated Protected Forests
EG - East Coast Plains and Hills
EHg - Eastern Plateau & Hills
EHm - East Himalayas & Brahmaputra Valley
EKC – Environmental Kuznets Curve
FFV - Forest Fringe Village
FPC – Forest Protection Committee
FSI - Forest Survey of India
FUG - Forest User Group
GC - Gujarat Coast Plains & Hills
GoI - Government of India
IFRI - International Forestry Resources and Institutions
IPCC - Intergovernmental Panel on Climate Change
ISFR - India State of Forest Report
IsI - All Islands
JFM - Joint Forest Management
LG - Lower Gangetic plains
MDF - Moderately Dense Forest
MG - Middle Gangetic plains
MoEF - Ministry of Environment &Forests
MoEF&CC - Ministry of Environment, Forests and Climate Change
MPCE - Monthly per Capita Expenditure (also Monthly per Capita Consumer Expenditure)

NDMA	-	National Disaster Management Authority
NF	-	Non-Forest
NSO	-	National Statistical Office
NSSO	-	National Sample Survey Office (previously National Sample Survey Organisation)
NTFP	-	Non-Timber Forest Products
OF	-	Open Forest
PCP	-	Public-Community-Participation
PPP	–	Public Private Partnership
PF	-	Protected Forests
PFM	-	Participatory Forest Management
REDD	–	Reducing Emissions from Deforestation and Forest Degradation
RF	-	Reserved Forest
RFA	-	Recorded Forest Area
RGI	-	Registrar General of India
SDG	-	Sustainable Development Goals
SFR	-	State of Forest Report
TD	-	Western Dry Region
ToF	–	Treecover outside Forests
TG	-	Trans- Gangetic plains
UDPF	-	Undemarcated Protected Forests
UF	-	Unclassed Forests
UG	-	Upper Gangetic plains
UNFCCC	-	United Nation Framework Convention on Climate Change
UNFF	-	United Nations Forum on Forests
UNFI	-	United Nations Forest Instrument
UNGA	-	United Nations General Assembly
UNSPF	-	United Nations Strategic Plan for Forests
UT	-	Union Territory
VDF	-	Very Dense Forest
VP	–	Van Panchayat
WCED	-	World Commission on Environment and Development
WHg	-	Western Plateau &Hills
WC	-	West Coast Plains & Hills
WHm	-	Western Himalayas

1

Introduction

Natural resources are the mainstay of a rural economy all over the world. Changes in the technique and rate of their extraction, utilization pattern and management practices have substantially impacted their substantially, the people and their living standards as also intra- and- intergenerational resource allocation and the environmental basis of sustainable economic development. Contemporary globalization and growing market orientation of human activities, even in the ordinary business of life and statecraft have led to exploitation of the natural resource base with commercial motive and their consequential degradation through a sequence of deleterious environment-economy interactions. In the process, new challenges to meeting the bonafide needs of the people and the economy, and management and sustainability of natural resource systems have emerged at the local, regional, national and global levels.

1.1 Natural Resources and Economic Development

The role and significance of natural resource assets in the process of economic growth and development is increasingly recognized by mainstream development economists in recent years. They have asserted that natural and environmental resources are the ultimate support of much of the economic activities. They are a direct life support to a large part of human and livestock population, a store house of material provision for the pharmaceutical sector and a major source of genetic pool and biodiversity. By acting as a sink for residual wastes generated by the production and consumption processes, they play an important assimilating role and help in nutritional recycling. These resources are crucial for climatic regulation and watershed protection, balancing among various living organisms, maintaining natural stability of the eco-system, preserving global environment and addressing various socioeconomic issues across countries irrespective of their stages of development and are vital to the cause of sustainable development. There are country specific evidences indicating sizable contribution of natural resource bodies to their national income and livelihood support system.

1.2 Problems of Overexploitation

A retrospection into the past seventy years of human civilization suggests that human beings have changed the eco-system extensively and more rapidly during this period in the human history. These changes have enabled various nations to achieve remarkable economic growth and bring about substantial net gain in human welfare. However, such benefits have accrued at the expense of enormous environmental costs. The spread of mechanization driven by energy intensive technology, reckless consumerism and adoption of unsustainable activities to satisfy the craze for faster economic growth and ever-increasing material enjoyment have caused massive depletion and serious degradation of natural resources. Over extraction of minerals and ground water, conversion of farm lands and common lands into concrete structures, ruthless urbanization, indiscriminate use of bio-nondegradable products, irrational waste disposal practices and mismanagement of natural resources have posed serious problems. The major concern is that natural resources are irreversible. Exploitation of ecological resource system beyond the carrying capacity leads to degradation of land and forests, extinction of rare species, loss of biodiversity and water bodies, fresh water scarcity, air and noise pollution, ozone layer depletion and emission of greenhouse gases, and creates environmental disasters beyond the control of any man-made technology so as to threaten the very life of people and other living organisms on this planet. A proper understanding of the dynamics of economic growth-ecological resource system linkages is absolutely imperative for achieving steady economic growth with environmental sustainability as well as mitigating the emerging socio-economic challenges.

1.3 A Taxonomy of Natural Resources

Natural resources are not a homogeneous lot. They can have four different configurations depending upon the nature of the property rights regime and of the institutional management mechanisms governing their extraction and use.

1. There are scarce natural mineral resources like coal, bauxite, iron ore, petroleum etc. which are owned, managed and exploited by the government to raise revenue or for use in some productive activities.
2. There are some natural resources which are under the ultimate ownership of the state but are managed and used by private individuals / parties such as mines and forests secured by them on temporary long-term lease from the government.
3. Another type of natural resources which are familiar to economists are those to which access is open and free for all. In such cases property rights are not assigned and enforced and the users have access but they do not enjoy ownership. These resources are subject to free riding and overexploitation. Gordon (1954) noted that open access resources are overused and the eminent biologist Hardin (1968) termed that overuse "The Tragedy of the Commons" ascertaining that "freedom in the commons brings ruin to all". The atmosphere and the open seas can be taken as the examples of open access resources.
4. A very important and popular kind of environmental resources are those which are geographically located, managed by local institutions, not open access, but accessed and used by a well-defined group of local users. These are widely known as common property resources or simply CPRs. Village tanks, forests, common pastures and grazing lands are the examples of CPRs.

1.4 Common Property Resources: Basics and Formalization

Feeny *etal.* (1998) define (institutionally managed) CPRs as those resources which are owned, managed and used by an identifiable community of interdependent users who exclude outsiders and are themselves governed by well-understood explicit/implicit rules of resource extraction and use, and rights and duties to one another. Thus viewed, CPRs have a healthy combination of the properties of non-exclusion and subtractability. Members enjoy rights of equal access and use (access is open and free for users), and exclusion is difficult and costly. Secondly, members use CPRs jointly which involves subtractability. i.e., if one uses more, less remains for another and the use by one lowers the welfare of the other users. Thus, CPRs share their first property (non- exclusion) with public goods and second property (subtractability) with private goods and hence are both public and private property for the community of co-owner-users (Bromley, 1991). In another sense, CPRs are neither public nor private property, but communitarian property. Stevenson (1991) identifies the following seven characteristics of CPRs.

1. The resource unit is well defined by physical, biological and social parameters.
2. The resource has two groups associated with it: a well-defined included user group and excluded persons.
3. The resource has multiple (more than two) users.
4. The user group operates within the boundaries of a set of well understood rules regarding their rights and duties about resource extraction,
5. The users share joint nonexclusive entitlement (they enjoy simultaneous claims) on any particular unit of the resource.
6. The users compete for the resource and hence impose negative externalities on one another. They make mutual investment and assist each other in resource management.
7. Users and owners are not always coincident. The owner may rent his right of use to someone.

Olson (1965) and Ostrom (2002) talk of some salient attributes of commons like low value of output per resource unit, economies of scale by using a large size/ area and by building infrastructures to use them, lack of accuracy of information about the resource, low returns from investment in the area, users' perception of potential benefits and risks and their norms of reciprocity and trust etc. These salient attributes of commons affect the incentives of users and optimality of outcomes.

1.5 Economics of CPRs

The seminal contributions of CPRs to sustainable rural livelihood systems have been widely established in the literature on development economics. But despite high dependence of the people, especially of those at the lower echelons, unequal benefit sharing among the users is a cause of concern. Efficient management of CPRs and adopting the most appropriate institutional mechanism for the same are all the more important. However, the applicability and effectiveness of collective action vis-a-vis other forms of management for ensuring resource sustainability is still debated.

1.5.1 Dependence on CPRs

In 2022, more than 90 crore of India's 140 crore population live in the rural areas. They are critically dependent upon the community-owned local resource base or common property resources such as forests and mangroves, common pastures and grazing lands, village ponds and tanks, streams and rivers, and nullahs and canals for their livelihood. CPRs are sometimes the only assets to which poor people have access and these resources act as insurance against risk for them especially during the time of non-availability of wage employment. In villages with abundant CPRs, the wage income of the workers is usually high probably because the opportunity cost of labour is high. Further, since the CPR system consists of self-renewing assets, it provides continuing livelihood support and services to the people at no/nominal additional extraction costs. In the ongoing process of globalization, opening up of new markets, privatization and urbanization, production and demand patterns are changing very fast even in the rural sector. The process is likely to have serious effects on the exploitation of CPRs and their management. It is possible to argue that CPRs are overexploited and have suffered a quality deterioration affecting the rural people in general and the rural poor in particular by causing further worsening off of their resource position and economic status. A reduction in the dependence on CPRs, problems of resource sustainability and management inefficiency, and a lack of community concern over these resources can be other possible outcomes.

1.5.2 Heterogeneity and CPRs

Market arrangements, inherent to the mainstream growth process, favour social stratification and the dissolution of ethnic bonds and customs (Seeland, 1991). Along with social stratification, economic heterogeneity arises from the uneven income distributional effects of developmental interventions by the state. Inequalities in economic status in the community tend to increase due, among other things, to (i) uneven distribution of knowledge and skills required for new employment opportunities created through the development process; (ii) flow of disproportionately greater benefits to large farmers from measures leading to increased agricultural productivity; (iii) growing intersectoral differences in factor productivity and per capita income in a dualistic economy (Kant, 2000) and (iv) unequal ownership of productive assets.

Conventional policy interventions by the state tend to follow the neo classical treatment of natural and socio-economic systems as independent of each other. However, due to the presence of strong real-world interactions among these systems, developmental efforts that ignore the linkages are likely to create serious distortions or end up as failures (Norgaard, 1989). In the case of CPRs, particularly in the less developed countries, socio-economic characteristics of user population play an important role in defining the management regime. Change in the socio-economic forces, through either the normal growth process or sharp policy interventions, can significantly influence individual behaviour within the user population and hence, on the community level institutions related to resource management. Two important socio-economic factors capable of causing significant shifts in CPR management practices are the socio-economic heterogeneity of the user population and its dependence on common resources (Kant, 2000). Heterogeneity may lead to inequalities in the access to

CPRs and hence to unequal sharing of benefits therefrom.

1.5.3 Management of CPRs and Collective Action

CPRs being scarce, their efficient management assumes critical significance. The nature of management in turn, depends upon the prevailing state laws or conventional practices and customs. Three possible alternative management regimes have been recognized in the literature on CPRs. They are: the private property rights regime, the state property rights regime and the decentralized collective management regime.

1.5.3.1 Private Property Rights Regime

Under the private management system, property rights in CPRs are assigned to private individuals/proprietors in parcels. Each owner is able to protect his property rights. Privatization is intended to internalize the externalities. But it may enable some users to secure strategic locations/positions in the CPR, (e.g., proximity to water in common grazing pastures) and thereby to obtain a disproportionately greater share of the overall benefits. This result stems from the impersonal character of the functioning of markets. A second problem with the private property rights regime is that it increases the individual risks, affecting the economic position of the poor adversely. A further defect is that dividing the CPR into parts is likely to lower its overall productivity and output/returns therefrom. This defect arises from the element of indivisibility in the CPRs. A more serious and damaging impact can come in terms of conversion of CPRs to other productive assets which cause a deterioration of physical status and resource quality. Such deleterious outcomes are not likely to arise under community ownership and use of CPRs.

1.5.3.2 State property rights regime

In a state property rights regime, the government owns, manages and uses the CPR. The government may follow a policy of sustainable extraction/harvesting and take punitive action against the intruders. But common experience shows that the government can be an inefficient harvester and at the same time coercion may not be effected because ever since at least the days of Kautilya, government machinery is blatantly corrupt and characterized by laxity. Further, even with state ownership, control and vigil, locals can maintain a certain degree of access without any responsibility to manage the resource. Government's limited capacity to monitor the use and management of the common resource leads to a de-facto open access situation. Everyone who can access has an incentive to extract the maximum amount of resource/output. The individual garners the value and the state bear the cost of the CPR resulting in what Hardin (1986) termed "The Tragedy of the Commons".

1.5.3.3 Collective Management Regime

Economists and the social scientists consider collective management of CPRs as an effective alternative to impersonal markets and inefficient states. It operates in decentralized settings where agents interact freely with minimal intervention by any regulatory authority. Collective action in the context of a CPR involves provisioning of the resource as a public good for the user group, its sustainable extraction and management, and protecting the resource against outsiders. This system claims three distinct advantages: (i) CPRs being heterogeneous in terms of location, productivity, access etc., individual risks are lower due to risk pooling; (ii) CPRs being mobile (grass and plants grow, fishes swim) and /or indivisible (a tank, a village forest, a grazing pasture), their division into parcels will lower productivity and output while their use in totality yields better dividends; and (iii) if reasonably abundant, their community management augments the income of the people in the community (Dasgupta, 2005). Besides, collective action can better internalize the ecological externalities compared to the markets (Baland and Platteau, 1996). But it can have a dark side too. Richer households may enjoy a larger share in the benefits, heterogeneity of the user group may cause cracks in reciprocal behaviour and collective co-operation may breakdown, and all these may cause resource degradation (Dasgupta, 2005).

As it obtains, collective action can take two forms. One is a co-management system in which the state and the community co-operate in a formalized institutional setting for the maintenance, growth and sustainable extraction of the resource. It has developed in many countries in terms of the public-community-participation (PCP) model in line with the PPP mechanism. It is a hybrid of state property rights regime and collective management regime. In this form of management, the common resource is owned by the state but used by the community and is managed by a committee comprising representatives of community and state. The Joint Forest Management (JFM) institution in the context of CPR forests is a case in point. It has the advantages of state patronage and motivation based efficient governance of the resource system. But it has the disadvantage of unnecessary bureaucratic interference which turns the regime into a state management institution characterized by inefficiency, corruption and unsustainable practices. The second is a purely community management regime in which the community of co-users, say of the forest resource, voluntarily join hands, form a group and work towards raising trees, preventing illicit felling and promoting sustainable extraction. It is mostly informal in nature and is found in the remote parts of different countries of the world.

1.6 The Research Problem

Over the years, significant economic growth has been accomplished in India and the same has percolated at least partially, into the countryside in terms of proliferation of alternative livelihood systems. Along with this development the men-environment relationship might have changed considerably particularly in the rural hinterlands in Odisha, as elsewhere in the world, impacting on people's dependence on common resource systems, the adoption of innovative resource management practices and sustainability of the resource base to cater to the needs of future generations. In this backdrop the contours of our research problem may be drawn along three inter-related lines such as dependence, heterogeneity and collective action, vis-à-vis the ownership, use, management and sustainability of Common Property Forest Resources in the context of villages of Odisha.

1.7 Review of Literature

There has been a spate of research on CPRs in recent years (Bromley, 1992). The literature has grown more rapidly in the last 2-3 decades. Concerns about the conflict between ecology and economic development; and between environmental degradation, natural resource depletion and CPR dependence and sustainability have stimulated such a swift growth. A brief review of the recent studies and their research findings which are relevant to the present work has been presented here. The basic objectives of such a review are:

i. to understand the different aspects of the problem studied so far;
ii. to perceive the gaps, if any, in previous research; and
iii. to attempt an in-depth study of the problem to overcome some of the deficiencies.

For a comprehensive analysis the review has been made in respect of four major issues viz; dependency, management, heterogeneity and collective action, and sustainability.

1.7.1 Dependency

Studies from round the world provide substantial evidence on the extensive use of environmental resources by rural households in key economic activities such as consumption, production and asset formation. Forest is one of the most productive natural capital assets which supports life (Soman and Anitha, 2020) and a clear and passionate understanding of forest dependence at the households level is imperative for long-term conservation and sustainable management of the forest (Garekae et al., 2017). This is because forest sustains life and provides for the subsistence needs of about around 25 per cent of the global population (SOFO, 2016). The various products procured from forests remarkably contribute to the shelter of 18 per cent of the population of the world, improvement in quality of life, income and employment generation from the forest sector along with meeting their daily livelihood needs (SOFO, 2014). Forests make a significant contribution to the household economy with the level of dependency estimated to vary in the 14-45 per cent range

(Anitha and Muraleedharan, 2002; Uberhuaga, 2020; Kalaba et al., 2013; Mukul et al., 2016), fuelwood collection from the forest being approximately 80–90 per cent and the dependence on timber and Non-Timber Forest Products (NTFPs) being as high as 90 per cent (Gautam, 2006). Vinodan and Manalel, (2011) found that 26.4 per cent of the tribal community gets regular employment from ecotourism activities (Vinodan and Manalel, 2011). It may be noted that the extent of dependence on forest and other natural resources varies across communities over space and time (Beckley, 1998). About a decade back, a MoEF (2010) estimates showed that more than 35 crore people lived in close proximity with the forests and secured their subsistence needs from the forests in India with the income from forest produce accounting for 40-60 per cent of their total household income. Needless to say, the tribals, who are considered as the most vulnerable population groups, largely depend on forests to meet their livelihood requirements. In such view of the matter, conserving these resources assume crucial significance (Verma et al., 2015., Verma et al., 2019; Ninan and Kontoleon, 2016; Ninan and Inouea, 2013a; Ninan and Inoue, 2013b; Ramachandra et al., 2017). But there is excessive forest dependence which leads to overexploitation and diversion of forestland to other uses (Soman and Anitha, 2020) and more often than not hinders the working of conservation strategies (Anitha and Muraleedharan, 2002; Jain and Sajjad, 2016; Bhandari and Jianhua, 2017).

Micro-analytical research studies on common property forests in Odisha reveal that people are highly dependent on forest resources. Mallik's (1994) study shows that income from sale of NTFPs constitutes 38.8 per cent of total income of a household and accounts for as high as 40 per cent of income from all forest sources. His second study (1996) estimates income from sale of seasonal Kendu leaves and minor forest produce at 13.9 per cent and 7 per cent of total income respectively. If income from all forest sources were considered, the share would come to 20 per cent per annum. Another study by Mallik and Panigrahi (1998) finds the income from all forest sources and that from sales of NTFPs to be 20 per cent and 10.6 per cent respectively of a household's annual income.

From his study of community participation through JFM in Odisha, Mohanty (2006) finds that the poor people are very much dependent on CPRs. He argues that protection of CPRs is essential for reducing poverty. Samal (2009), in his study of dependency of rural tribal households on common property forest resources in Keonjhar district of Odisha, also observes that the tribal people are critically dependent on forest resources. He has found the share of forest income in the household total income to have marginally risen during 1995-2000 suggesting that forest dependence of tribals has increased over the years. Sarap and Sarangi (2010) found very high forest dependency among the poor and tribal households in Odisha.

Jodha (1986) found a negative relationship between the total income of the household and the share of the total environmental income in it, thus indicating that poorer households' dependence on environmental resources are more than that of the rich. His study found income from the CPRs comprising between 9 and 26 per cent of the total incomes of the poor households, and between 1 and 4 per cent of the incomes of the rich households. Cavendish (2000) has arrived at even larger estimates from a study of villages in Zimbabwe: the proportion of income based directly on CPRs is 35 per cent for the people as a whole, the figure for the poorest quintile being 40 per cent. Adhikari (2001) finds considerable agreement among researchers on the issue of a direct relationship between poverty and CPR dependency and observes that poverty is likely to lead to a remarkably high dependence on CPRs.

Balasubramanian and Selvaraj (2003) examined the interconnections among poverty, private coping mechanisms and collective action for tank degradation and management in Ramanathapuram district of Tamilnadu. They observed that the poor are critically dependent on CPR tanks for agricultural operations, livestock rearing, and fuel wood and fodder.

The study by Meinzen-Dick et al. (2006) on the dependence on CPRs reveals that apart from fulfilling religious, cultural and recreational functions, commons play a major role in the livelihoods of the poor and marginalized groups in the society. In India, the contribution of community forests to the income of the poorer households is nearly 29 per cent.

The study by Pathania et al. (2008) relating to the system synergy of farming system and CPRs in the hilly region of Himachal Pradesh shows the crucial importance of CPRs for sustaining livelihoods of people. The channels emanating from common property water resources are the main source of irrigation in the hilly region. The consumption of various CPR land products has been found to be very high for marginal farmers than for the small farmers. The results indicate strong forward linkages of CPRs with livestock and agriculture and significant dependence of households on CPRs for provision of fodder, grazing, leaves for litter, fuel wood, farm implements, stacking material, fencing, soil collection, mining materials and NTFPs.

Pathania etal. (2010), from their study in Himachal Pradesh noted an inverse relationship between land holding size and dependence on common property land resources for grazing livestock and collection of stones and sand, fuel wood, timber, stacking sticks, NTFPs and leaves indicating that relatively poorer households depend more on forests for their livelihood than the rich.

The studies by Hardin (1968) and Ostrom (1990) show that in developing countries forest resources play a crucial role in providing livelihood and subsistence to a large majority of population.

A study by Jumbe et al. (2005)in Zambiarevealed that forest income constitutes around 20 per cent share in the total household income and the result was very similar to those of earlier studies by Cavendish (1999), Campbell et al. (2001) and Fisher (2004) in some of the neighbouring countries. The study also found that for the poorest quartile, the share of forest income in the total household income was 60 per cent whereas for the richest quartile its share was about 20 per cent. The study shows the high relative importance as well as a high degree of dependency of the Zambian rural household on forests. Sapkota and Oden's (2008) study on community forests in Terai of Nepal reveals high forest dependency, particularly in the case of poor households.

The study by Turkelboom et al. (2001) in Bhutan Himalayas found that dependence on CPRs varies across regions. CPR dependence decreases due to the cash crop focus in agriculture and substitution of some CPR products. In remote less developed areas CPRs are more important to sustain rural livelihoods.

Inoni (2009), in a study in the delta state of Nigeria examined the correlation between the socioeconomic characteristics of the rural households and dependence on the common pool forest resources. The findings show that poor households are heavily dependent on the non-timber forest products (NTFP) because they are resource constrained. Income from forest resources contributed in the range 41.3per cent to 67.2 per cent to the households' total income. The proportion was even greater for poorer households than those in higher income groups.

The study by Fisher et al. (2010) in Malwa reveals that households with low income rely more on forests than those with high income. For the poor households, forests are an important source of food and cash earnings and they act as safety nets to survive famine and weather related crop failure.

Mishra (2020) examined the interrelationship between poverty and forest dependency on the basis of a household-level data collected through a primary survey in Paikmal block of Bargarh district Odisha, India. Her findings suggest significant heterogeneity in the nature and extent of forest dependency across households and a strong linkage between forest dependency and household-level poverty. She argued that the levels of poverty would have been much higher had there been a lack of access to forest produce for the households surveyed. But, contrary to perceived knowledge, it has been found from the study that the households with relatively larger holdings not only derive high absolute income from forests, but also a high share of their income comes from forests. She concludes observing that destruction of forests itself may act as a poverty-generating mechanism.

According to Saha and Agarwalla (2021), forest, as a rich ecosystem, is the source of livelihood of a large number of people residing in its fringe areas. For them the forest dwellers' dependence on the forest varies across forest zones depending on various factors, such as the natural features obtaining in the area and the socio-economic-demographic characteristics of the people in the forest fringe habitats. The authors' study, based on application of econometric tools to primary data in constructing an index and determining key factors affecting the extent of the forest dependence, evaluates the forest dependence of people residing in and around the Similipal Biosphere Reserve in India. Results indicate that forest-zonal characteristics have significant impact on the extent of the people's forest dependence; people's forest dependence is likely to be higher in the periphery compared to the core zone.

1.7.2 Management of CPRs

The importance of CPRs for the livelihoods of rural households is universally recognized, more so in a developing and village dominated country like India inhabited by millions of tribals in and around forests. But in the ongoing process of growing commercialization and reckless consumerism, significant damage has been done to the natural resource system particularly in the developing countries like ours. In such countries these resources are vulnerable to tragedy of commons due to their over-exploitation and lack of effective institutional mechanisms for their governance (Hardin, 1968; Ostrom, 1990). It has now been increasingly accepted that the damage has been too serious to result in climate change and loss of biodiversity threatening the very survival of human beings. In such view of things, prudent management of the natural resource base assumes considerable significance. Further, management of CPRs gets precedence over their use mostly because efficient and effective management are a fundamental pre-condition for achieving equity in access and in distribution of benefits from the resource system.

Research on CPRs emerged in the 1980s in response to the incorrect presumption that the tragedy of the commons was inevitable. The growing body of research on commons share the conventional thesis that all commons may not be well managed but at the same time boldly argue that projects for protecting CPRs and preventing their degradation can succeed with collective action despite unfavourable conditions and can help to preserve these resources, raise productivity and alleviate poverty.

The large body of CPR literature on institutional arrangements to manage CPRs and prevent the occurrence of the tragedy of commons can be put in four schools of thought. They are: the private property rights school, the state property rights regime school, the decentralized co- management school and the informal community management school. The private property rights school advocates creation and enforcement of private property rights to solve the problem of CPR degradation (Cheung, 1970; Demsetz, 1967; Johnson, 1972; Smith, 1981). The state property rights regime school postulates that a state property rights regime can avoid the tragedy of commons (Hardin, 1968). The system of co-management is a variant of collective action and is suggested on the grounds that it combines the benefits of active state patronage, efficient human resource development, appropriate utilization of rural skills and effective local participation to secure optimum value addition and resource conservation (Ojha, 2006; Vemuri, 2008). The community management school of thought argues the case for voluntary compliance-based assurance approach operating through decentralized collective management by users to avert the degradation of CPRs (Jodha, 1986; Wade, 1987; Berkes, 1989; Chopra et al.1989).

It is no gainsaying that management of CPRs is closely linked to governance arrangements. However, there is considerable disagreement among researchers regarding the definite nature of institutional arrangements vis-à-vis effectiveness in achieving of pure community ownership compared to other institutional arrangements. But others such as Grafton (2000), Antinori and Bray (2005) and Bray et al. (2006) have shown that the different forms of the desired goals of conservation of CPRs, their sustainability and improvements in resource institutional arrangement are interdependent. It appears that they do not consider condition. Researchers like Netting (1976), Agrawal (1996), Arnold (1998) and Somanathan et al. (2005) examined the performance private, community and government as distinct domains of governance but as mixed forms.

Recent literature on CPR management arrangements highlight the failure of private property to internalize the externalities arising out of CPRs as also of the state institutions in ensuring sustainable management of CPRs. Economists, anthropologists, sociologists and political scientists broadly agree on the credibility and compatibility of collective action mode of management of CPRs with a local focus and establish the primacy of local level collective action as an effective mechanism for realizing enduring and successful CPR management (Ostrom et al., 1988; Ostrom, 1990). The collective action problem in respect of CPRs arises because an individual does not internalize the full consequences of his or her own actions. In other words, it is the presence of crowding externalities in the CPRs which calls for some kind of collective management regime.

The collective action management system is preferred to the other two forms of common property resource management regimes because it overcomes the problems of inefficiency in a state management regime, inequity associated with the private property regime and over bureaucratization of the co-management system, while containing the benefits of all these systems. Collective action can also strike a balance between rules and appropriation, ensure desired representation of interests and equity, administer conflict resolution, empower resource users, provide effective monitoring, contain transaction costs, enable congruence between ecosystem and governance, strengthen organizational capacities and adopt processes at appropriate scale (Ostrom, 1990; Bromley, 1991; Eggertsson, 1990; Hanna, 1992; Hanna and Munasinghe, 1995).

Several studies focus on the role of institutional arrangements and collective action in shaping CPR related outcomes. For example, Agrawal and Yadma (1997) lay emphasis on the nature of institutional mediation; Ostrom (1999) on the principles of institutional design; Ribot (1999) and Dietz et al. (2003) on the need for compatibility between institutions and their politico-ecological context; Ribot (2002) on the importance of broadly based groups in institutionalized governance; Mc Carthy (2004), Agrawal (2005) and Gibson et al. (2005) on the crucial significance of local enforcement; Nygren (2005), Wittman and Geisler (2005) and Lemos and Agrawal (2006) on the need for extending governance rights in respect of natural resources to a large number of actors; Anderson et al.(2006) and Brooks et al.(2006) on the ongoing process of decentralization leading to increase in community control over forests; and Agrawal and Chhatre (2006) on the role of local variation in determining CPR related outcomes. Guha (1989) and Peluso (1992), however, have focused on the likely social resistance to collective action for CPR management.

While pure community ownership of CPRs is not very difficult to be found, what is more popular is a co-governance kind of arrangement in which governments are observed to have entrusted the responsibility and right of governance to a number of actors (Nygren-2005; Wittman and Geisler, 2005; and Lemos and Agrawal, 2006). Some of the important forces which have led to the spread of co-governance arrangements include the need of limiting fiscal deficits, tied aid from institutional donors demanding involvement of local actors, pressure from communities and groups for gaining control over CPRs and the observed greater efficiency of local actors in protecting CPRs at lower cost and using them more sustainably relative to government agencies. Marothia (2010) also does not favour pure state, pure community or pure privately-owned structures for the development of CPRs as each one of them has more negative outcomes than positive impacts. He suggests distributed or polycentric governance as the most appropriate mechanism for CPR management.

As stated earlier, collective action mode of managing CPRs has two variants-formal co-management system and informal community management system. The most popular form of formal institutions designed for managing common property forest resources is Joint Forest Management (JFM). In this system the management committee is manned by officials of the forest department of the government and some locals selected by the officials. Though the decision-making power is vested in the committee, the authority, in practice, is exercised by the forest department through their officials. It is thus joint in form but authoritarian in spirit.

A good amount of research has been done on the JFM system in India and other countries. While some of them show that the system is doing well, some others find faults with it and recommend corrective action. Studies by Kumar (2002), Sarker and Das (2006), Tacconi (2007), Behera (2008) and Tiwari (2010, 2010-A) indicate the effectiveness of JFM in managing common forests. Kumar's (2002) study in Jharkhand however, suggests that the JFM has succeeded in halting forest degradation but failed in realising the poverty reduction objective because it prefers the rural non-poor. He recommends the adoption of suitable compensatory mechanisms to improve the effectiveness of JFM system. The study by Sarker and Das (2006) highlights the positive role of JFM program in protecting forests and higher developmental outcomes of women headed Forest Protection Committees (FPCs) which are a part of the JFM system. Such differential outcomes are found to be due to the presence of higher social capital base of the female headed FPCs.

Behera (2008) assessed the social and economic (livelihood), institutional (participation), and ecological (conservation) outcomes of JFM in a fringe village in Kadapa district of Andhra Pradesh. The study reveals a strong positive role of voluntary community participation in JFM leading to substantial growth of forests. This has been attributed to the benefits of employment generation in forest-based activities and income from collection of NTFPs accruing to the locals from the working of the JFM led forest protection through involving the beneficiaries. The inherent attitudes of the people towards forests and their adoption of indigenous conventional methods have been found to be powerful forces in promoting forest regeneration. If they can be provided with appropriate technical knowhow and better management practices, the result would be better.

Tiwari's (2010) empirical study in Jharkhand reveals that the JFM is effective in forest protection. He suggests greater decentralization in decision making particularly with regard to funding, streamlining the flow of benefits of forest management to the communities without upsetting the arrangements provided in the government resolution relating to JFM and promoting management partnership between the village communities and the state with focus on socio-economic and ecological objectives.

In another study Tiwari (2010-A) made a comparative analysis of forest management practices during pre- and post-JFM periods in some sample villages in Jharkhand. The results show remarkably better management in the post-JFM period with respect to protection of forests from grazing, illicit felling, revival of grass cover and canopy of trees, fire control, plantation as well as awareness of coherence among village. The village community also benefited substantially in terms of greater employment opportunities, higher participation of women and livelihood generation. The study laments dominance of the government forest department over control of resources, fundings and decision making. He suggests a more viable community-state partnership in the strategy of decentralized management for ensuring balance among social, economic and ecological objectives of JFM.

Tacconi's (2007) study is suggestive of a strategy similar to Tiwari's (2010-A). It reveals that decentralization of management, though important, is not a sufficient condition for effective forest conservation. Policies in respect of incentives, monitoring and evaluation are suggested as these are central to a more meaningful decentralized pattern of JFM.

Scholars like Reddy et al. (2001), Sundar (2001), Ojha (2006) and Ali et al. (2007) observed problems with the JFM system. Reddy et al. (2001) in their study found that forest degradation in India is more of qualitative nature than quantitative. Qualitative decline in Indian forests are reflected in declining value addition of the forest sector to the economy. Although JFMs are successful, their achievement is at much lower level than expectation. In their view a comprehensive policy has to be formulated in respect of JFM practices to check quality deterioration.

Sundar (2001) made a study of participatory forest management in Bastar district of Madhya Pradesh. The study found state appropriation of forests from community, illicit felling by private capital and repression of movements to stop this. The state is alien to community action in the sense that it serves interests of the rich and the powerful, and the government exerts tight controls on participatory committees. The author recommends scaling up of local level positive social capital and state's accountability for improving the performance of the participatory management committees.

On the basis of his study on the working of Joint Forest Management in Odisha, Ojha (2006) argues that the system has not been successful because of its target-oriented approach. The forest officials, to fulfil target, have been found to have persuaded one of the villages from the collective to form Van Sanrakhyana Samiti (VSS)-a JFM type institution, leading to disintegration of the collective. In some cases, they demarcate a patch of forest from the area protected by the collective and allot the same to the VSS giving rise to conflicts.

Ali et al. (2007), in their study on the system of participatory forest management in the North West Frontier Province (NWFP) of Pakistan observed that the local community was not motivated in forest protection owing to mismatch between local level needs and objectives of Joint Forest Management Programme. Their results indicated that the priority of the local people was financial and food security, whereas the NWFP model of JFM emphasized forest protection and regeneration. Such mismatch has a negative impact on the working of participatory management of forest resources.

The most conventional and time-honoured forest management system on this planet has been the community forest management regime. It is an informal system run in terms of traditional practices and unwritten conversions which are carried forward to successive generations. Community action mode of managing CPRs is inherent in the very attitudes of the rural and tribal folk who benefit from them and have been taking steps for their sustainable management and regeneration from time immemorial.

Klooster and Masera (2000) in their study in Mexico demonstrated that Community Forest Management (CFM) is quite effective as it offers tangible local benefits while conserving forests and sequestering carbon. They also suggest that adequately designed and properly implemented community forest management projects can avoid deforestation and restore forest cover and forest density.

A study by Lise (2000) in Haryana, Uttar Pradesh and Bihar found that voluntary people's participation is induced by good quality of forests and social factors are more important than economic considerations in encouraging community participation in resource management. The state, however, has a clear role to motivate people's participation. For that matter it should act as a facilitator and motivator for promoting broad based participation and effective forest management by improving resource quality.

Mallik (2000) in his study on sustainable management of NTFPs in the state of Odisha suggests that secure and enforceable user rights are pre-conditions for successful collective management and conservation of common property forest resources. He, however, adds that security of tenure and resource rights are necessary, but not sufficient conditions for resource sustainability and advocates community-based self regulating institutions with effective and transparent mechanisms for sustainable forest management and equitable benefit sharing for ensuring sustainability of forest resources.

A comparative case study of Van Panchayats (VPs) in Uttaranchal and Forest Protection Committees (FPCs) in West Bengal by Ballav et al. (2002) reveals that these institutions are more effective for management and protection of forests compared to the conventional JFM system. Collective action survives, flourishes and promotes sustainability when the users themselves devise, apply and monitor rules to use and manage resources. They can effectively counteract opportunism and overcome constraints of cooperation. The community should be given sufficient flexibility (fines and sanctions for offensiveness) in day to day operations rather than being imposed from above. The authors found reduction of such flexibility over time and unnecessary over interventions by government authorities on the functioning of local level management. Such excessive intervention is seen to be accompanied by rent seeking and corruption on the part of the government officials. There is a need of freedom for micro planning and a free hand for VPs/FPCs for forest protection at the grass root level without undue interference of Forest/ Revenue departments of the government.

Mukhija (2005) argues the case for group interest and collective action on three grounds. They have positive social outcomes and promote equity; people can be rational fools (Sen, 1977), put the common good ahead of self-interest and co-operate; and self-interested behaviour can lead to successful collective group behaviour and common interest solutions in respect of CPRs.

Matta and Alavalapati (2006) in their analysis of JFM programme in Tamilnadu, India highlighted the cost-benefit considerations of members of the collective action group. These considerations have considerable influence over the group participation, performance and success of collective action in respect of forest management.

Ojha (2006) pleads for community-based forest management in the context of Odisha. He observes that although these informal institutions have proved effective in managing local forest resources, they are yet to get recognition within a public law framework with which they can perform better. A growing consensus among researchers on the issue of better community management of common forest resources has also been noted by him. In his opinion self-organization of forest users can be more effective because they are more likely to devise their own rules to protect a forest that is starting to deteriorate. But community management suffers from democracy deficit in terms of participation of women and marginalized sections in managing common property forest resources. At the same time he considers co-management as a threat to collective action form of community management regime.

Rishi (2007), in her study on JFM in Madhya Pradesh found both the rural management committees and forest officials to have a positive attitude towards each other and towards forest protection and management. But while the committees were unable to express a clear attitude towards their functioning and role of women, the forest officials wanted more operational freedom and limited government control. JFMs need to be more institutionalized for collaborative efforts among stakeholders.

Ostrom (2010) argues that individuals attempt to solve efficiently and sustainably common pool resource problems on their own in diversity of settings. Building trust, developing rules consistent with ecological systems and the quality of resources are important considerations in this regard. Common resources in good condition motivate trust building for both management and resource sustainability.

Sarap and Sarangi (2010) observed that deforestation and mining activities have caused deterioration in forest quality which has threatened the livelihood support systems of the people depending on forests. They hold that the existing forest management institutions are not effectively working due to their poor democratic structure and suggest that working of the existing institutions can be enhanced by ensuring effective participation of different groups including women and the poor, in the decision-making process. Democratization of the institutions would not only increase effectiveness in management but also would provide them with better opportunities in strengthening their livelihood options. Decentralized participation helps in managing various types of conflicts prevailing in forest dependent villages as well as long term development of natural resources.

Ameha et al. (2014) examined the working of five of the pilot participatory forest management (PFM) programs undertaken in Ethiopia basing on the Forest User Group (FUG) members' analyses of the programs and using data collected by means of group discussions, key informant interviews and transect walks through the PFM forests to assess four selected outcome variables viz. forest income, change in forest conditions, forest ownership feelings and effectiveness of FUGs as forest managing institutions at three points in time—before the introduction of PFM, during implementation of the projects and after the projects ended. The results show that the state of the forest has improved with the introduction of PFM in all of the five cases, while in four of the five cases, the improvement was maintained after projects ended. Forest income was perceived not to have been negatively affected owing to regulated access to the forests following introduction of PFM. The study expressed serious concern about the long-term institutional effectiveness of the FUGs particularly after projects ended.

Iqbal et al. (2021) conducted a study in purposively selected Six forest ranges having maximum number of JFMCs from the "East Forest Circle" of Jammu division of J&K following the multistage sampling plan for the selection of respondents. Twenty-four committees, four from each selected ranges of East circle, and 192 respondents, eight from each selected JFMC, were selected through random sampling technique. The perception measurement consisted of 26 items. Results of quasi-experimental research design showed that respondents had favourable perception towards Joint Forest Management

Programme and its efficacy in improving the condition of forest and contributing towards assets development in villages situated close to forests, helping in proper utilization of degraded land, promoting participation of local people in implementation of different government schemes for the conservation of different forest resources and in improving socio-economic condition of villagers. Forest officers and JFMCs members were observed to be very active having very good relations with the local people. Extra efforts are to be directed to strengthen the JFM platform to increase forest tourism for enhancing the employment opportunities and income of the communities residing in close proximity of forests.

The binding forces of people's myth, belief and tradition significantly contribute to the management of natural resource systems. The existence and survival of a community institution largely depends upon whether it was born out of the need and necessity of the people or an outcome of the project.

1.7.2.1 Collective Action and the Role of State

It is wrong to postulate that community management of CPR-forests are autonomous non-formal institutions operating in isolation of the help of the government or the state. While in most cases they operate as autonomous units, a positive and proactive government/state can add to their effectiveness.

While justifying state intervention in community-based CPR management systems, Sekar (2001) cautions against excessive state intervention in community-based CPR management and argues that state involvement should be restricted to provision of guidance for community participation. He holds that the government should guide community participation, act as a facilitator and counselling unit and should take the responsibility of refining and updating the technical inputs. Such arrangements would boost the moral responsibilities and duties of the user group and help arresting free-rider behaviour in respect of resource use and their sustainability.

While examining the role of state in institutionalizing community-based watershed management (CBWM) in three Indian states, Sarvanan (2002), emphasizes the need of state support for improving the effectiveness of collective action. His study suggested community-based management of watershed projects with the state sharing power with multiple sets of other institutions for ensuring efficient CPR management.

1.7.2.2 The Facilitating Conditions

The effectiveness of community-based forest management is determined by some factors. Agrawal (2003) synthesises the facilitating conditions identified by Ostrom (1990), Wade (1994), and Baland & Platteau (1996) into four groups for examining the effectiveness of local community-based management systems. They are as follows.

(i) The CPR System

The size of the resource system, its boundaries, resource mobility, possibility and extent of storing the resource units, rate and predictability of flow of benefits from the resource system, and ease of monitoring the resource conditions are the biophysical and edaphic factors represented by resource system characteristics.

(ii) The user groups

Among the user group characteristics, he mentions the size of the group and its boundaries, the nature of heterogeneity (of gender, religion, wealth, caste etc. defining heterogeneities of endowments, interests and identities) and extent of interdependence among group members, their dependence on CPRs and the availability of resources with the group to meet the costs of initiating and maintaining collective actions. These are indicative of socio-political and economic variables which shape the resource governance outcomes. It is, however, quite possible that similar group heterogeneities may produce different outcomes depending on circumstances (Neupane-2003), Adhikari and Lovett-2006, and Baland and Platteau (1996) argue that heterogeneities of endowments have a positive effect on resource management while those of identity and interests may pose problems for collective action and thus may affect the effectiveness of governance. In Agrawal's (2003) view variations in forms of property rights cause differences in resource management outcomes. If the management is politicised, then specific individuals/groups reap disproportionately higher benefits and efficiency gains are not percolated to the ordinary members and to the society as a whole.

(iii) The institutional arrangements

The governance related variables which define institutional arrangements are represented by rules of user incentives and behaviour. Locally devised simple rules that are transparent, easy to enforce and deal with conflicts, and can hold the users and enforcers accountable, enhance the effectiveness of governance.

(iv) The external environment

Demographic, market, cultural and technological factors; the nature of government agencies and the level of involvement of NGOs etc. constitute the nature of external environment and are the critical factors determining resource governance and shaping resource conditions.

Dietz et al. (2003) supplement the four clusters of variables stated above by incorporating adaptive governance into the analysis. They postulate seven requirements of adaptive governance such as (i) availability of necessary information; (ii) capacity to deal with conflict; (iii) compliance with rules; (iv-vi) provision of technical, institutional and physical infrastructure; and (vii) ability to adapt and change for ensuring effective management of CPRs in respect of group action.

Dasgupta (2005) has discussed six important aspects of a community-based CPR management system. (i) Communitarian management allows risk pooling and hence minimizes individual household risk. (ii) CPRs are mobile and indivisible and on account of the externalities created by components and the premium attached to indivisibility, parcelling would prove inefficient and community management would be more productive. (iii) Trust, mutual affection and bond of long-term relation make community management more sustainable. (iv) When the user group is very large, the CPR becomes unmanageable and reduces to an open access resource ending in overexploitation and the tragedy of the commons.

(v) Even when they are managed by the community, CPRs may degrade if social norms of behaviour are fragile, and on account of political instability and population pressure and when state authority damages local institutions tending the CPRs into open access regimes. (vi) Heterogeneity in the group is a fair reason of failure of community management.

Available research has typically focused on locally situated small user groups and communities. There are many cases of such successful local management of CPRs. Community management compares favourably with private and state ownership on grounds of equity, sustainability and efficiency.

1.7.3 Heterogeneity and Collective Action

CPRs yield multiple outcomes over which diverse stakeholders assert competing claims and are characterized by community accessibility, ownership and management. In many cases accessibility and benefit sharing may not be equitable and management may not be broad based. Such inequality is attributed largely to socio-economic heterogeneity of the users and of the members of the group looking after the management of the common resource. Discussions over the differential impact of group heterogeneity and the role of collective action have generated a large flow of research work on this aspect of common property resources.

Poteete and Ostrom (2004) found a lack of consensus among scholars as to the role played by heterogeneity and group size on the basis of a survey of research on the interrelations among group size, heterogeneity, and institutions in the International Forestry Resources and Institutions (IFRI) research network. Collective action for sustainable management among resource-dependent populations has important policy implications. The existence of non-linear relationships was observed in that some forms of heterogeneity do not negatively affect some forms of collective action. While institutions can affect the level of heterogeneity or compensate for it, group size appears to have a non-linear relationship to at least some forms of collective action. Moreover, group size may be as much an indicator of institutional success as a precondition for such success.

Sullivan et al. (2017) explored differences in governance relationships and community efforts to remove the-mile-a-minute weed (Mikania micrantha), an exotic, rapidly spreading invasive plant, on the basis of five case study community forests in the subtropical region of Chitwan, Nepal. Examination of the de jure (formal) versus de facto (on the ground) institutions and actor relationships relevant to Mikania removal efforts revealed heterogeneous governance relationships in Mikania management across community forests which run contrary to the expectations set by the de jure situation. Regular discussion of distrust of government and non-government officials among the members help explain collective action efforts and management decisions. Results indicate that understanding differences between the de facto and the de jure institutions and collective action problems may be vital in structuring successful efforts to manage invasive species and other social-ecological threats. We present data-informed propositions about common pool resource management and invasive species.

Employing in-depth qualitative and quantitative research methods Flanery et al. (2020) investigated the role of community interaction in the village of Fabe near the Korup National Park in Cameroon, in reducing emissions from deforestation and forest degradation (REDD+) program. Accepting community integration as a function of three structures: geographical, social and hierarchical, the authors applied differentiation along three categorical variables: age, gender and place of origin (locals vs. non-locals) in order to establish hierarchy. The existence of diversity in terms of education, age, gender, occupation, religion, land tenure and place of origin was found to exist within the sample. For example, youth had greater levels of education compared to the old, and women had lower levels of education than men. Women and strangers were observed to be less involved in decision-making due to obvious constraints. The authors argue for the existence of potential among the groups for recognising generalized interests which could help improving collective action and reaping desired outcomes in respect of controlling deforestation and forest degradation. Educating community members about risks, opportunities, and rights were taken as the favourable factors for promoting collective action.

In their study on community-based forest management in the inner Terai region of Nepal, Negi et al. (2018) explored the role of community and user attributes such as group size, social heterogeneities, forest user's perception on forests, and affiliation to the user group, in the collective action of managing community forests. Results of a survey of 180 households spread across twelve community forest users' groups conducted by the authors show that group size (number of forest users affiliated to the community forests) and perception of the management of their community forests are strong predictors of forest user participation in community forest management. Income inequality and ethnic diversity were found to have no significant association. Land inequality, however, was found to decrease participation in the management and use of community forests. These community and user attributes play a crucial role in the success of collective action and may vary from community to community. The findings also suggest a more diagnostic approach involving a clear understanding of these community characteristics and application of a quasi-experimental research design before contemplating any community-based project interventions for stimulating successful collective action in diverse community forest management (CFM) arrangements.

Applying land use data from Guatemala Fortmann et al. (2017) estimated the impact of a community forest concession policy on avoided deforestation relative to a matched control area when accounting for group heterogeneity. Results revealed that the concession policy reduced deforestation throughout the study region.

Gehrig et al. (2019) explored the effect of socio-cultural heterogeneity among user fisher groups on resource extraction in lab-in-the-field Common Pool Resource (CPR) experiments in Zanzibar, Tanzania. According to them, collective action of resource users is essential for sustainability and where user groups are socio-culturally heterogeneous, establishing cooperation across salient group boundaries is required. Their analysis of between-village differences in extraction behaviour in the heterogeneous setting has not shown any aggregate effect of heterogeneity on extraction. It has also come out that the effect of heterogeneity on pure cooperativeness can be inconsistent across two communities from the same social-ecological system.

Okumu and Muchapondwa (2017) analysed the factors influencing household level of participation in Community Forest Associations' (CFAs) activities and the determinant of success of collective action in community forest management as well as the link between households' participation levels and success of collective action. The empirical results drawn from a study of CFAs in Kenya by using SES framework suggest that while devolving forest management to local communities, a more diagnostic approach and consideration of employment status, household size, education level, residential status, ownership of private woodlots, precipitation, and distance to nearest main road and nearest market are important. The role of factors such as; average age of household heads, distance an household is from the nearest edge of the forest, the institutional quality i.e. level of institutional organization in terms of implementation of Ostrom design principles, salience of the resource (level of dependence on the resource), number of households within a CFA jurisdiction (group size), proportion of males in the executive committee, education level of the CFA chair, level of interaction with the various government departments in terms of frequency of meetings, intensity of social interaction, structure of the group and whether officials are selected competitively should also be understood. It has been found that CFAs are more likely to be successful in collective action if they are initiated by the communities themselves with frequent interactions with government departments and in in presence of incentives. CFM and collective action have the potential to increase efficiency and equity.

The study by Luswaga. & Nuppenau (2020) was an attempt to explore communities' participation in the participatory forest program in Tanzania involving 159 households, randomly sampled from four villages bordering state and community-managed forests, in the West Usambara Mountains. Applying the factor analysis technique and using three components of participation viz. training attendance, trust in institutions, and location as predictors of participation intensity of the households a participation intensity index was formulated to assess economic, decision-making, and protection activities. The study observed significantly higher levels and intensity of participation in the villages around the state forest as compared to those around the community forest. The study concluded moderate perceived performance of the participatory programs in achieving the participation aims with better results in the state forest jointly managed with the community. Raising awareness and improving communication with villagers, fulfilling promises for the communities, and provision of more forest-linked interventions are recommended to improve the situation.

Drawing on collective action theory and their empirical research from six cases in in the American West, Charnley et al. (2020) attempted to identify practices for promoting collective action to restore fire-resilient forests in western landscapes. They analysed wildfire risk reduction through a collective action lens, and compared and contrasted collective action theory for creating an environmental public good (fire-resilient forests) versus managing common pool resources. Results indicate that diverse landowners coordinated planning and implementation of wildfire risk reduction across property boundaries. Collective action to reduce wildfire risk has potential to catalyse forest restoration to protect values at risk and promote the ecological benefits of fire; it can also lead to relationship-building and partnerships among landowners and other stakeholders, providing a strong foundation for future collective action to conserve and restore large landscapes. In order to promote collective action to reduce wildfire risk and restore fire-resilient forests in the American West, the authors suggested landowner coordination in planning and implementing strategically-designed restoration treatments to optimize their effectiveness.

Contrary to the theoretical supposition that heterogeneity, economic heterogeneity in particular, influences the likelihood of collective action for forest management, field research indicates that heterogeneity, whether in economic, social, or other dimensions, presents a challenge for collective action with variations in perceptions of costs and benefits amongst different groups, high transaction costs faced by the disadvantaged, decrease in trust because of differences in power hierarchies, and differences in resource access Nagendra (2011). While the costs of collective action tend to be disproportionately borne by the poor, by women, and artisanal castes who are especially dependent on forest products, the elite capture of benefits of community action can also further exacerbate relative poverty and inequity. The author argues that these challenges can be dealt with effectively by strong local institutions and federations.

Somanathan et al. (2007) examined the role of heterogeneity in asset ownership and ethnicity in the success of community management of Himalayan forests. The question as to whether heterogeneity hinders collective action has also been studied. According to them reaching an agreement about the sharing of benefits or costs of collective action is difficult due to heterogeneity among group members. The study found no correlation between caste heterogeneity and indicators of collective action or forest cover, but some evidence of a link between land equality and forest cover in pine forests and lack of any link between land equality and forest cover in broadleaved forests. Results suggest no evidence of ethnic heterogeneity and gender hindering collective action.

In an earlier study, Somanathan et al. (2002) examined the effects of village-level heterogeneity in caste and land ownership, and of female membership in the Panchayats on collective action for forest conservation in the context of community management of forests by Van Panchayats to meet local needs in the Indian Central Himalayas. The study found no evidence as to any effect that caste heterogeneity or female membership of the Panchayat have on forests but some evidence that greater equality in land ownership may enhance collective action and forest conservation in pine forests and not in broadleaved forests. This is surprising because villagers' interest in conservation is greater in broadleaved than in pine forests.

Srinivasan (2005), in his study on heterogeneous (community to which they belong, legal status, educational levels, type of equipment used for fishing etc.) users' decision to participate in co-management (roles for both the state as well as users) in the context of Cochin estuarine fisheries in

Kerala, found that heterogeneous fishermen's decision to participate in collective action under co-management was dependent on the distribution of benefits from cooperation. His study also found that the members anticipating disproportionate benefit from collective action are likely to take a lead role.

Baland and Platteau (1996-A), have discussed certain important issues relating to inequality and collective action in respect of CPRs. Their analysis throws light on the impact of inequality on the success of collective action i.e. whether inequality promotes/discourages collective action to prevent overexploitation. They found that distribution of wealth among the users influences the access to CPRs. Some people having a large amount of factors of production such as capital, skills, network of relations, market information and credit may enjoy better access to the CPRs. Therefore, they reap a greater share of the benefits. In the presence of heterogeneities, relation between the poor and rich become unstable and hostile and the rich exploits the resource as intensively as possible without any regard for the viability of the resource base (Boyce, 1994: Baland & Platteau, 1996). The level of wealth of the poorer households may be too low to pursue efficient use of CPRs as that may threaten their survival. In such case they may seek off-CPR employment. Rich may have better access to other outside opportunities and they expect to shift out in future for which they overexploit the CPR.

The effect of inequality on the success of collective action is, however, not certain. Inequality may produce two opposite effects. First, as Olson (1965) emphasized, when the 'large' member benefits more, he may bear the costs of managing the CPR and encourage the 'small' users to free ride. Second, since the 'small' users have a tiny share of the benefits, they may not think it wise to participate in collective effort and may quit. The net effect will depend on the respective strengths of these opposite effects. But there is also the evidence that the rich members act as patrons concerned with the subsistence of the poor to see that the collective effort works and benefits all (Wade,1987).

Bardhan (1984) and Boyce (1988) have argued that collective action is quite effective in a more egalitarian agrarian structure.

For example, group effort is more fruitful in a CPR like irrigation water. However, inequality in private resource endowments such as land and wealth may bring failure to a community-based CPR management. Libecap's (1995) study of collective action in marketing by orange growers shows a strong negative impact of heterogeneity on the effectiveness of collective action. An econometric study by Bardhan (2000) in south India revealed that inequality in land holding among irrigators were negatively related to cooperation on water allocation and field channel maintenance. A similar finding was reported by Dayton-Johnson (2000) from a study of farmer managed surface irrigation systems in Central Mexico. Adhikari (2000), too, argues that inequality among resource users has negative impact on the local level collective action. Equity impact is also not positive as a result of inequality among resource users.

From their study of Indo-German Watershed Development Program in Maharashtra, Srigiri et al. (2003) found a remarkable improvement in the livelihood position of the people in the project area. The impact has been uneven in favour of the marginal farmers who derived greater benefits from the improved natural resource base in terms of higher productivity gains and adoption of economically better cropping pattern due to their access to land in comparison to the landless. Hence heterogeneity has been strengthened and issues of poverty and inequality could not be effectively addressed.

Vemuri (2008) finds faults with the co-management system of CPR governance. In her opinion the co-management institution no doubt, confers benefits of human resource development, skill development for value addition but is largely a political entity and restricts the involvement of the poor and marginalized sections of the society who draw a disproportionately smaller share of the benefits but make greater physical contribution in regeneration of resources. The effects of inequality on the sustainability of collective action very much depends upon the factors like, free rider problem and sharing of benefits among group members. In a highly heterogeneous environment, group effort towards CPR management is very difficult to achieve and sustain.

Balasubramanian & Selvaraj (2003), from their study on the collective action to overcome tank degradation and ensure efficient management in Ramanathpuram district of Tamil Nadu, found that the poor extended double effort in terms of labour towards tank management relative to non-poor and collective action had a positive impact on the rice productivity. A noteworthy finding of the study is a U-shaped relationship between inequality and collective action to maintain tanks-collective action decreasing first with growing disparity between the rich and the poor and then increasing. The study also reveals that increase in the number of beneficiaries has negative effects on incentives for co-operation.

On the issue of heterogeneity, Dasgupta (2005) views that in the benefit sharing process richer households enjoy a greater access and a larger share compared to the poor. Therefore, presence of group heterogeneity is one of the major causes of the failure of collective actions in CPRs.

Ojha (2006), on the strength of his study in Odisha, argues that community management suffers from democracy deficit in terms of participation of women and marginalized sections in managing common property forest resources. The access to the forest resource by these groups is limited.

Recent research has established the paramount superiority of collective action in managing common property resources. But the results are varied in respect of the impact of heterogeneity on the efficacy of collective action in ensuring equity. While some studies argue that collective action is effective in the context of an egalitarian structure others lament its failure in addressing the issues of inequality. It has even been argued that in the presence of heterogeneity, collective action leads to an accentuation of existing inequality. Given the complexities of the inequalities-collective action interlinkage, it may be fair to conclude that a homogeneous group may better succeed in collective effort for designing and enforcing conservation of CPR than a heterogeneous one.

1.7.4 Sustainability

Concern for sustainability is of recent origin and is still in a nascent stage. Sustainability of resources and management systems for promoting enduring growth and achieving intergenerational equity has gained currency since WCED's publication of the seminal book titled 'Our Common Future'

(1987). Emphasis has been led on such use of natural resources by the present generation as would enable the future generations to experience at least the present generation's level of well-being (Sengupta, 2001).

Ever since the appearance of WCED's 'Our Common Future', a vast literature on sustainability has developed in respect of both sustainable use and sustainable management of common resources. A review of some of this literature is presented here. As an illustrative starting point reference may be made to Babu (1988), Raj (2006) and Samal (2009). Babu (1998), in his study on common lands in the Haryana state has argued that resource base has undergone substantial degradation due to unsustainable management practices. Raj (2006), in his study in the Indian Central Himalayas, found that overexploitation of CPRs poses a serious threat to the longevity of such resource system. The findings of the study focus on the need of appropriate management practices to conserve the common property land, forest and water resources. A people-centered approach to management has been advocated by him for realising sustainable, balanced and equitable sharing of CPR benefits and development in the area. Samal (2009) observes that more time is required and more distance needs to be covered than before to get the same quantity of forest produce indicating that the forest has depleted and sustainability is jeopardised. The role of traditional environmental knowledge and community tenure systems in promoting sustainable CPR management and inter-generational equity is well established.

Wade (1988, 1994), Ostrom (1990), and Baland and Platteau (1996) postulate that members of small local groups can design institutional arrangements to help manage resources sustainably (Agrawal, 2001). However, if agents are not fully aware of ecological processes or are unable to protect the common resource against intruders or are inclined to overharvest it due to their poverty, state intervention may be needed (Baland and Platteau, 1996). They have also raised doubts about the ability of user groups to manage resources efficiently and lay down four conditions for successful group management. These include a) characteristics of the resource, b) nature of users' group that depends on the resource, c) features of the institutional regime for management and d) the nature of the relationship between a group, and the external forces (markets and technology) and authorities (state and government).

Kellert et al. (2000) suggest community based natural resource management systems for increasing the participation of marginalized groups and ensuring both resource-and-management sustainability. Ojha (2006), while focusing on the positive aspects of community ownership and management of common property forest resources, advocates a well-defined benefit sharing mechanism within the broad contours of collective action to ensure equity and resource sustainability.

Sonak et al. (2006), from their study of Khazan ecosystem of Goa, lament the ecological unsustainability of Khazans due to disruption of the self-regulating coastal tribal peasant communities.

Turkelboom et al. (2001) argue the case for locally agreed arrangements and strong local leadership for promoting CPR sustainability albeit with a caveat. When the CPR is scarce, households think it irrelevant to agree upon sustainable management practices. They use the resource base by hit-and-run and cause degradation to the common resource system.

Adhikari (2001) emphasizes the need of an appropriate property rights regime as a vital determinant of the economic and environmental sustainability of CPRs, and the social sustainability of the people dependent on them.

Some researchers have linked sustainability to group heterogeneity. They have found that resource sustainability and management sustainability are difficult to achieve in the face of inequality in benefit sharing, social heterogeneity in group composition and disparities in asset position among them (Bardhan, 2000; Dayton-Johanson, 2000; Balasubramanian and Selvaraj, 2003). Olson (1965) visualizes greater possibilities of enforcing CPR conservation when the user group is homogeneous than when it is heterogeneous.

Adhikari's (2001) concept paper highlights considerable disagreement among researchers on the issue of the relationship between poverty and resource management sustainability. At the one extreme scholars like Baland and Platteau (1996) are observed to have argued that absolute poverty threatens the survival of the poor and with future holding no hope for them, they are inclined and rather forced to make unsustainable use of CPRs through a hit-and-run process of exploitation. At the other extreme scholars like Jodha (1986) Reddy (1999) and others have observed that poor people being critically dependent on CPRs view their degradation as survival risk and attach significant attention to their conservation through adoption of sustainable CPR management practices. It is no gainsaying, therefore, that poverty does influence the quantity and quality of CPR base.

Sarker (2009) found that co-management of common forest resources would sustain rural livelihoods and that the poor and very poor categories of households who are most dependent on these resources manage the resource base sustainably. He laments that illegal collection of timber products from forest have an adverse effect on the sustainability of forest resources. On the other hand Sapkota and Oden (2008) observed overexploitation of community forest resources by poor households and urged upon the authorities to provide alternative livelihood options for transforming group of over extracting poor people into a conservation group. Contrary to this Mahanty et al. (2006) found a trade-off between equitable access right to CPRs and sustainable management.

Sarvanan's (2002) study of community-based watershed management in Himachal Pradesh, Madhya Pradesh and Uttaranchal States in India focuses on participatory local institutions for managing CPRs in contrast to delivery-based functioning of government programs. Ability to address community needs, accountability and transparency in management have been cited as the key factors in ensuring sustainability of local institutions and arresting resource degradation. The important role of NGOs in promoting resource sustainability has also been highlighted in the study. For improving environmental quality and sustainability of CPRs, Mohanty (2006) suggests decentralized participatory governance, and a strong political will and commitment. He also emphasizes protection of CPRs for ensuring their sustainable regeneration.

Tábara and Pahl-Wostl (2007), emphasize the need to overcome dualism between the individual and collective, between human and natural systems, and between human agency and natural conditions through a holistic understanding of human-natural interactions, mutual self-organisation and resilience. In their opinion resource and management sustainability calls for the construction of a self-ware society that transcends existing dualisms to create a self-sustaining humanity on a life supporting planet.

Chisika and Yeom (2021) focused on the need for ecologically sustainable management of natural forests using the case of Kenya's natural forests in the wider context of biodiversity conservation and climate change action. They argued the case for identification of deadwood, a critical component of natural forests, which performs a vital function in forest biological and ecological functions but has received little attention around the world both in academic discourses and policy making. Apprehensions are that forest degradation through the removal of deadwood, even though widely neglected, results in considerable biodiversity loss and might alter natural forest ecosystems, thereby exacerbating the impacts of climate change. The reason being, these have outcomes that run contrary to the wider provisions of ecologically sustainable forest management. In their view, deadwood management appears to be affected by many complex biological, technical, policy, and socio-economic factors that appear to be acting together against sustainable deadwood management. Findings suggest the restoration of deadwood and increasing consciousness on the value of deadwood through more research studies for improving the sustainable management of natural forests.

He et al. (2021) probed into the conditions for the success and sustainability of community forestry in terms of environmental conservation and local livelihood benefits. The paper explores the link between local conceptions of environmental justice and sustainable community forestry by using a combination of qualitative and quantitative approaches on the basis of a case study in a thickly populated and culturally heterogeneous village in southwest China. Findings show a significant increase in village forest cover that has made a remarkable contribution to improvements in local livelihoods because of the villagers' ability to align forest management with local justice norms and practices for establishing effective and durable local institutions for collective action and efficient community forestry.

Community ownership and local systems of CPR management are crucial. Local management and group ownership offer checks and balances to prevent overharvesting by stealing and other illegal means, provide incentives and motivations to protect CPRs, ensure effective management and have positive effects on resource productivity, equity and sustainability. There is need of identification, recognition and patronization of local area community management agencies for the purpose.

1.8 Gaps in Past Research and Importance of the Study

It is clear from the above discussion that since the mid-1980s there has been an unprecedented growth of literature on different issues pertaining to CPRs. But the findings of these studies are increasingly diverse. While there is a near consensus among researchers on the critical dependence of rural households, and poor and tribals in particular on CPRs, quite a good number of studies have found massive depletion of these resources leading to their reduced availability to the people, unequal access to them and disproportionate benefit sharing resulting from heterogeneity, and the need of appropriate management mechanisms for improving sustainability.

The available literature on CPRs, as evidenced from the above review, is exhaustive no doubt, but it suffers from three limitations. Most of the previous studies deal largely with the nature and extent of CPR dependency, socio-economic heterogeneity and CPR management, and sustainability of common resources and management regimes. They are fragmentary in nature undertaken more with a view to suggesting corrective measures than with the objective of understanding the problems at large at the micro level and evolving a total strategy of CPR development. Second, the conclusions of these studies are derived from the experiences gathered in specific regions for which they cannot be generalized for other areas with different and rather opposite socio-economic background.It is pertinent to note that region, user group and institution specific studies on the dependency, management and sustainability of CPR systems are of great interest in India, a country known for its large and varietal diversities. The significance of such research is of far greater interest in a poor but resource rich state like Odisha which has a vast rural population (85.03 per cent), tribal concentration (22.13 per cent) and regional variations in development. Third, among the various common resources available in the state, forest resources are very important in terms of dependence of both tribal and non-tribal rural households. However, no comprehensive in-depth study has yet been undertaken in the state to examine the various interconnected issues of dependence, management, heterogeneity and collective action in respect of common property forest resources. The studies by Mallick (2000), Ojha (2006), Mahanty et al. (2006), Mohanty (2006) and Samal (2009) have been based largely on secondary data and have failed to delve deep into these issues at the micro level. It may be noted that with a gradual shift in emphasis from macro level planning for resource use, management and sustainable development to regional planning for local area development and village level democracy the seminal importance of primary studies at the grassroots level assume vital significance.

In view of the above, the present study proposes to investigate into the complexities of common property resources with special reference to forest resources at the village level in the state of Odisha.

1.9 Objectives of The Study

The following are the objectives of the study.

1. To study the dependence of rural households on CPRs, compute the rate of their depletion and workout their current status at the national level.
2. To estimate the levels and extent of dependence of households on common property forest resources in

relation to their economic heterogeneity in villages of Odisha.

3. To examine the role of socio-economic heterogeneity in the existing institutions and incentives for collective action and participatory management of common property forest resources in villages of Odisha.
4. To identify the trends in status of common property forests and their sustainability in Odisha at the village level.
5. To derive lessons from the survey and suggest appropriate policy measures that can facilitate sustainability of common property forest resources, their use and management.

1.10 Hypotheses

The hypotheses tested in the present research are the following

1. Dependence on common property forests is related directly to household size but inversely to the income and agricultural land holding status of the households.
2. Socio-economic heterogeneity among the members of the management institutions has a negative bearing on its effectiveness in managing common property forests.
3. Common property forest resources are becoming less sustainable over the years.
4. The greater the sustainability of the management institutions the higher is the prospect of sustainability of the common property forest resources and vice versa.

1.11 Study Area, Data and Methods

The present study aims at examining the dependency, management, heterogeneity and collective action in the context of CPR forests on the basis of a sample survey conducted in six villages of three blocks in three districts of Odisha. It is a micro level study of 210 sample forest dependent households selected in the study area. A broad outline of the materials and methodology used in the study is presented in this section. The standard methodology of making an empirical research on the basis of a sample survey has been adopted in the present study.

1.11.1 Study Area and Sample Households

As stated above, the study area comprises six villages in three blocks of three districts in the state of Odisha.A four stage simple random sampling procedure has been followed and is considered to be efficient, the sampling units being the districts, the blocks, the villages and the households. The details of the sampling frame are discussed below.

a) Selection of Sample Districts

The NSSO 54th Round Survey on "Common property Resources in India (January 1998-June 1998) has divided the country into 15 major agro climatic zones. In this classification the state of Odisha comes under two zones viz., East Coast Plains and Hills (EG) and Eastern Plateau Hills (EHg). Out of the total 30 districts in Odisha, 19 districts come under the EHg (Bargarh, Boudh, Deogarh, Jharsuguda, Koraput, Malkangiri, Nawapara, Nawarangapur, Rayagada, Sonepur, Balangir, Dhenkanal, Kalahandi, Keonjhar, Mayurbhanj, Phulbani Sambalpur, Sundargarh and Angul) and 11 districts fall under EG (Gajapati, Jagatsinghpur, Jajpur, Kendrapara, Khurda, Nayagarh, Balasore, Cuttack, Ganjam, Puri and Bhadrak). The ratio of the districts under the two agro climatic zones EG and EHg is roughly 1:2. We have purposively limited our study to three districts selecting one district from EG and two districts from EHg by using the ratio and following a random approach. Accordingly, Balasore and Mayurbhanj districts have been selected from the EHg zone and Keonjhar district has been selected from the EG zone.

b) Selection of Sample Blocks

The selection of blocks from the three districts has been done on the basis of availability of CPR forest area. For this purpose, a complete list of blocks having high CPR forest coverage has been prepared for each of the three selected districts on the basis of information obtained from the forest department officials and one block has been picked up at random from the list for each district. The three blocks so selected are Nilagiri, Jashipur and Patna from Balasore, Mayurbhanj and Keonjhar districts respectively.

c) Selection of Sample Villages

From each block two villages were randomly selected on the basis of information on the availability of CPR forest provided by the Revenue Inspector of the respective blocks. In total six sample villages have been covered in the present study. The two sample villages from the Balasore district under Nilagiri block are Tenda and Banthiapada, the sample villages from Mayurbhanj district under Jashipur block are Ramasahi and Mandam, and the villages from Patna block of Keonjhar district are Ghatabalijodi and Tanda.

d) Selection of Sample Households

A total of 210 sample households have been selected from six villages with equal number of households (35) from each village selected at random for intensive investigation. This size can be accepted as reasonably good for a standard primary survey. The sampling method adopted in the survey is considered appropriate to minimize bias factor and for more representative results.

1.11.2 The Data-Nature, Sources and Methods of Collection

The present study is based on both secondary and primary data. The information on Common Property Resources in India brought out by NSSO's 54th Round Survey (January 1998-June 1998) forms the major data source of this research. In addition to this, other secondary sources such as the population Census for Odisha, Economic Survey of Government of Odisha and official publications of concerned departments have been tapped to obtain secondary data for the research. For the analysis of institutions and incentives for collective action in the management of CPRs, three case studies have been conducted in the six sample villages.

The primary data have been collected by using both the case and survey methods. Data relating to village profile, availability of CPR forests, land scenario etc., have been collected from the offices of the Revenue Inspectors. Under the survey method, a household has been taken as the unit of investigation.

The relevant information and data have been collected with the help of a pre-tested specially designed schedule canvassed in person among the sample households.

A pilot field survey was conducted in the month of March, 2010 for five selected households in Banthiapada village of Nilagiri block in Balasore district whereafter the schedule was redrafted in the light of the experience gained. The major field survey was conducted between April and June, 2010.

1.11.3 Methods of Data Processing and Tools of Analysis

The data drawn from various sources have been subjected to statistical treatment. After necessary editing and processing, standard statistical tools and econometric techniques have been applied to study CPR forest dependency, heterogeneity and collective action.

Household level CPR forest dependency has been linked to economic heterogeneity among the user group. The effectiveness of local level institutions on collective action for management of CPR forests has been analyzed in terms of social and economic heterogeneity among the members of the informal management committee. Multivariate regression analysis has been conducted to study the determinants at the household level CPR forest dependency. Simple statistical techniques such as percentage, average, maximum, minimum and standard deviation have been used for interpreting results of field survey.

1.12 Relevance of the Study to The Present-Day Problems and Need of The Society

Odisha is one of the least developed states in India. The state is characterized by grinding poverty, staggering unemployment and widespread economic backwardness. Around 85 per cent of the state's total population reside in village areas. Economic backwardness, underemployment situations and lack of adequate gainful off farm employment opportunities in rural areas have led them to depend heavily on agriculture and CPR systems for their livelihood and income generating activities. Common Property Resources such as rivers, ponds, grazing area, village pasture, village land and village forests etc. play a major role in the lives and economy of the rural population of the Sate. Round the year the rural households are critically dependent on them in varied ways.

Particularly from CPR forests they collect Non-Timber Forest Products such as sal seeds, kendu fruits, mahula, honey, sal leaves, tendu leaves, mango, tamarind, jack fruits, khejur, jhuna, lakha and variety of other fruits. Similarly, they also depend heavily on fuel wood for cooking, heating and lighting purposes. For house construction and fencing they collect timber from the CPR forests. Sales proceeds from fuel wood and non-timber products constitute a significant portion in households' annual income. The CPR forest system thus is important for the rural people, especially the tribals and other economically weaker sections of the rural population.

However, owing to growing commercialization of the means of livelihood even of the rural households, the CPR base of the state is depleting at an alarming rate. In the interests of the livelihood security of the rural folk and ensuring sustainability of resources and their management so vital for enduring overall development of the state economy CPR forest resources need to be managed properly.

Keeping in mind the role and importance of CPR forest resources in the state, this research has made a sincere attempt to study the degree and extent of village level dependence on CPR forest resources in Odisha. An assessment of the future sustainability of the existing CPR forests and effectiveness of village level local management institutions for ensuring both resource and management sustainability in the villages of Odisha has also been made in the study. The role of heterogeneity in influencing forest dependency and managerial efficiency has been examined too.

In view of the primacy of CPR forest resources in the state Odisha, and in the consumption, employment and income generation activities of the common men, the findings of the study will be a guide to the planners and policy makers for evolving effective policy planning for management and sustainable use of CPR forests in the state.

1.13 Limitations of the Study

The present study is based on a micro level sample survey covering 210 sample households conducted over a period of two months during the year 2010. The area of investigation of the study is limited to 6 sample villages from Balasore, Keonjhar and Mayurbhanj districts in the state of Odisha. The work is confined to household level dependency on CPR forests, sustainability of the CPR forest system and functioning of existing village level institutions for management of such resources in the state. Analysis is based on the field level information collected from the sample households in six villages. Their capacities to memorize facts and their willingness to furnish correct information have, therefore, a direct bearing on the accuracy of data. In spite of best efforts to elicit accurate information from the respondents by cross questioning and convincing them to apply their experience and personal judgment while furnishing information, there might be some errors. Further, being a micro level field study based on sample technique and confined to six villages in three districts, the results and findings of the study may not claim generalizability with respect to time, space and activity.

1.14 The Structure of the Study

The Study is designed in seven chapters.

Chapter 1 is introductory. The basics of CPRs and the research problem, review of related past research, importance of the study and its objectives, the hypotheses tested through the study, relevance of the study, data and methods, limitations and the structure of the study are discussed in this chapter.

Chapter 2 is devoted to analysis of common property land resources in India with reference to dependence, depletion and projected status on the basis of secondary data obtained from the NSSO 54th Round survey on Common Property Resources in India.

Chapter 3 describes the economic profile of Odisha, the sample districts and the villages.

Chapter 4 deals with household level dependency on common property forest resources and its links with user group heterogeneity.

Chapter 5 examines community management of common property forest resources and its relation with socio-economic heterogeneity of the members of management committee at the village level.

Chapter 6 studies the issue of sustainability of CPR forests in the selected villages.

Chapter 7 concludes with a summary of major findings and some policy suggestions.

2

Common Property Resources in Rural India: Dependence, Depletion and Current Status

2.1. Introduction

India is a land of villages. According to the National Commission on Population, the population of India is projected at 137.6 crore for March 2022 of which 65.5 per cent or about 90 core live in the rural areas (GoI, 2019). A vast majority of them are partially or wholly dependent on CPRs for their livelihood. But with the spread of liberalization, privatization, globalization and market orientation even to the ordinary business of people's lives, the CPR base of the country is depleting very fast. If the present rate of depletion is assumed to persist, it could be alarming. A modest attempt has been made in this chapter to estimate the extent of dependence of rural households on CPRs at the macro level. A second objective is to compute the depletion of these resources across agro-climatic zones of India and to workout projected depletion so as to find out their current status. The National Sample Survey (NSS) 54th Round (January 1998-June 1998) data on "Common Property Resources in India" (1999) form the data base of the exercise, this being the only source of authentic data in India so far.

2.2 Concepts and Definitions

The concepts and definitions used by NSSO have been adopted to analyse dependence, depletion and current status of CPRs in India.

2.2.1 *Definition of CPRs*

NSSO defines CPRs as those resources which are accessible to and collectively owned/held/managed by an identifiable community and on which no individual has exclusive property rights. The rules governing the use of these resources are well defined and followed universally. A CPR implies the existence of an institutional arrangement for its management. The terms "accessibility", "collectively owned/held/managed", "identifiable community" and "exclusive property rights" are explained below.

2.2.1.1 *Accessible*

Accessibility to a resource system is determined by either legal system or convention. By the former approach if the community has a legal right of ownership or possession on the resource, then it is clearly 'accessible' to the community. Following the later approach, resources for which customarily accepted user rights exist are treated as 'accessible' to the community of users.

2.2.1.2 *Collectively owned/held/managed*

The term "collectively owned /held" presumes a legal status. A resource system that is collectively owned/held (by legal sanction or official assignment) by a community is considered to be a common property resource. A resource nominally held by a community is treated as "collectively managed" when the group of people who have the right to its use are governed by a commonly accepted set of rules. In most cases the rules are unwritten.

2.2.1.3 *Identifiable community*

The user group consists of a well-defined group of individuals. For example, all inhabitants of a village or one/more settlement(s) of a large census village form an identifiable community. Besides, a community may be a caste based or religion based or occupation-based group of people. It can also be a group in terms of the traditional social order.

2.2.1.4 Exclusive property rights

Exclusive property rights mean rights of resource ownership vested in a unit. In the case of CPRs, an individual/ family/company/corporation is not granted exclusive property rights. Even co-operative societies are not given such rights. However, a resource held by a co-operative society constituted of co-users of the resource prior to its formation, is treated as a CPR. In this sense co-operative irrigation societies, farmers' co-operatives, fishermen's co-operatives, etc. may be considered as CPRs.

2.2.2 Resource Taxonomy

NSSO considers three broad forms of CPRs viz., common village land, government forests and common water resources.

2.2.2.1 Common village land or 'commons'

These refer to common property land resources within the boundary of the village which are formally (i.e. by legal sanction or official assignment) held by the village panchayat or community of the village. They include the following.

(i)Village panchayat grazing land/pasture land

This is a well-defined category of commons used in official land-use records and is the most important constituent of CPR land. Traditionally, many villages have land earmarked as permanent pasture land/grazing land. These have region specific names like *gauchar, gochar, gairan, gomol,* etc. Villagers have user right on permanent pasture by legal sanction. Village woodlots which may have come up on the grazing land/pasture land are not considered under this category.

(ii) Village forest & woodlot (not under Forest/Revenue Department) and van panchayat forest

This category includes all land under village forest and woodlots including the area notified as forest within the village which may belong to the forest department, or any other government department (like Revenue /Public Works department) but is formally under the management of village panchayat or a community of the village. *Van panchayat* forests in the hills of Uttar Pradesh, which are formally managed by village communities, are also included in this category.

(iii) Village sites and threshing floor

They include village sites and all area of land which is earmarked for common use of the villagers for economic activities, such as (a) processing of agricultural produce, (b) storing of grains, other agricultural produce, firewood, etc., and (c) use for other household enterprises.

2.2.2.2 Government forest

On the basis of legal status, forests in India are classified into following three categories, viz., Reserved forests, Protected forests, and Unclassified forests. They include all state-owned area of land classed as forest whether or not they are actually under forest. However, land under social and farm forestry, village forests, *Van Panchayat* forests and forests owned by individual households are excluded.

2.2.2.3 Common water resources

Common water resources are those which are not held by individuals but are held by the whole village community or a caste/religion/occupation/traditional social order/geographical location-based community. Some common water resources are also constructed by or lie within the jurisdiction of a government department.

2.3 Data and Methods

The analysis and results presented in this chapter are based solely on secondary data contained in the NSS 54th Round Report on CPRs in India and in the India State of Forest Reports for various years published by the Forest Survey of India. Since the survey was confined only to common property land resources in rural India and forests in particular, our discussion relates to dependence, depletion and current status of CPRs in land and forests only. For collection of data on CPRs the NSSO used both *de jure* and *de facto* approaches.

Even though both these approaches were applied by the NSSO for collecting data on area of CPRs, data collected using the *de jure* approach was used in the NSS Report and the same was adopted here to ascertain the size of CPRs, and estimate their depletion and current status. In this approach common land which were within the boundary of the village and were formally held by the village community/panchayat by legal sanction or official assignment were treated as CPRs. The NSS used *de facto* approach for collecting data on the use of CPRs. It considered all lands which were practically used as common resources even if individuals enjoyed exclusive ownership rights on them or the resources were located outside the village boundary. In this sense grazing of cattle on private land between two crops and fishing in privately owned agricultural land submerged during flood may be taken as CPRs.

Dependence of rural households on CPRs has been analysed by looking mainly at data on collections of fuel wood, fodder and other materials from CPRs. Depletion of CPRs across different agro-climatic zones in India have been computed at the compound rate using the status of these resources in 1993-94 and 1998 as given in the NSS Report (1999). The same has been used to work out the projected depletion of CPRs in various zones for the period 1998-2010 and to obtain the status in 2010.

2.4 Dependence on CPRS – NSS Data

The vital link between CPRs and rural livelihood systems is as old as civilization itself. The burgeoning literature on CPRs point to the importance of these resources for fulfilment of the continuously growing human wants, more so, wants of the poor people living in the villages.

2.4.1 Contribution of CPRs

Rural households in India collect a variety of materials from CPRs. These include green grass & leaves and shrubs to feed livestock, dry leaves and fuel wood for cooking and heating, bamboo and timber for construction, roots, fruits and fish for consumption, and a host of other non-timber forest products like sal and kendu leaves, mahua, tooth sticks, honey, tamarind, resin, ak and seeds to meet their needs. Besides, they use streams, ponds, rivers and canals for irrigation, livestock rearing and household enterprises, and medicinal plants and herbs to get relief from diseases. A comprehensive picture of dependence of rural households on CPRs is presented in *Table-2.1*.

Table 2.1: Dependence of Rural Households on CPRs

Sl.No	*Description*	*Magnitude*
1	Households reporting collection of any material from CPRs (per cent)	48
2	Average value of annual collection per household (Rupees)	693
3	Households reporting grazing of live stocks on CPRs (per cent)	20
4	Households reporting use of common water resources (per cent) for	55.8
	i) Irrigation.	23
	ii) Livestock rearing	30
	iii) Household enterprise	2.8

Source: NSS (1999), Common Property Resources in India, 54th Round, Jan 1998-June 1998.

It can be read off the table that 48 per cent of the rural households are dependent on CPRs in one way or the other. They collect a variety of materials from CPRs. These include fuel wood, fodder, manure, weeds, grass, medicinal herbs and edible oil etc. In addition to collection of materials, the rural households are dependent on CPRs in varied ways. One fifth of the rural households use CPRs for grazing their livestock and 23 per cent use various common property water resources like tanks, wells, tube wells, canals, rivers and springs etc. for irrigating their land. Similarly use of common property water resources (CPWRs) for livestock rearing is found to be quite high. 30 per cent of the households have been reported using CPWRs for this purpose. Only 2.8 per cent of the households have been found using CPWRs for household enterprises suggesting that their dependence on these resources for running enterprises is marginal.

NSSO (1999) classifies the materials collected by the rural households from CPRs into three broad categories, viz, Fuel wood, Fodder and 'Other'. The third category (other) comprises materials used as manure, roots & fruits, tubers & vegetables, gums & resins, honey & wax, medicinal herbs, leaves & weeds, and fish. *Table-2.2* gives the estimates of percentage shares of different materials collected from CPRs in the annual value of collections per rural household across agro-climatic zones of India.

Table 2.2: Collections from CPRs across Agro –Climatic Zones

Agro -Climatic Zone	*Percentage Distribution of value of Collections*				*Average value of Collection*
	Fuel Wood	*Fodder*	*Other*	*All*	*(Rupees)*
Western Himalayas (WHm)	59	39	2	100	1939
East Himalayas & Brahmaputra Valley (EHm)	53	8	39	100	1219
Lower Gangetic plains (LG)	48	5	47	100	408
Middle Gangetic plains (MG)	52	39	9	100	464
Trans- Gangetic plains (TG)	44	51	6	100	528
Upper Gangetic plains (UG)	31	69	0	100	1070
Eastern Plateau &Hills (EHg)	64	4	31	100	845
Central Plateau &Hills (CHg)	62	18	20	100	744
Western Plateau &Hills (WHg)	68	25	7	100	674
Southern Plateau &Hills (DP)	72	18	10	100	628
East Coast Plains & Hills (EG)	65	18	17	100	559
West Coast Plains & Hills (WC)	49	13	38	100	715
Gujarat Coast Plains & Hills (GC)	61	30	9	100	658
Western Dry Region (TD)	71	29	0	100	230
All Islands (Isl)	79	3	18	100	467
India 58	25	17	100	693	

Source: Same as Table-2.1

The estimates indicate that at the all India level, value of fuel wood collection forms a major part (58 per cent) of the total collections from CPRs followed by fodder (25 per cent) and others (17 per cent). It also shows that the share of fuel wood in total collections from CPRs is predominant in all the agro-climatic zones except TG and UG. In these two regions the share of fodder in total collection value from CPRs are 51 per cent and 69 per cent respectively. Since these two are agriculturally developed zones, collection value of fodder from

CPRs dominates collection value of fuel wood and other products. However, the category 'other' accounts for a significant proportion of the collections in the agro-climatic zones LG (47 per cent), EHm (39 per cent), WC (38 per cent) and EHg (31 per cent).

2.4.2 Collection from CPRs, Consumption Expenditure and Household Size

The rural households collecting materials from CPRs can use them directly to meet the household needs and/ or sell them to earn livelihood. The money value (explicit & implicit) of these materials can be linked to household size and to consumption expenditure for estimating the extent of dependence on CPRs. Data relating to value of annual collections from CPRs and annual consumption expenditure per household, and average household size are presented in *Table*-2.3.

Table 2.3: Value of Collections, Consumption Expenditure and Household Size across States

State	*Value of Annual Collections from CPRs per Household.*	*Annual Household Consumption Expenditure (Rupees)**	*Average Household Size*	*Ratio of 2 to 3 (Per cent)*
(1)	(2)	(3)	(4)	(5)
Andhra Pradesh	554	386	4.3	2.78
Assam	1071	338	5.4	4.89
Bihar	519	289	5.4	2.77
Gujarat	663	416	4.8	2.77
Haryana	1174	546	5.8	3.09
Karnataka	635	365	5.0	2.90
Kerala	390	604	4.6	1.17
Madhya Pradesh	984	326	5.1	4.93
Maharashtra	799	384	4.8	3.61
Odisha	929	301	4.6	5.59
Punjab	1057	614	5.2	2.76
Rajasthan	266	452	5.4	0.91
Tamil Nadu	667	381	4.0	3.65

Uttar Pradesh	690	373	5.6	2.75
West Bengal	450	358	5.0	2.09
India	693	382	5.0	3.02

Source: Same as Table-2.1

*Computed from MPCE and average household size data given in Table-T8 of NSS 54th Round Report No.452 (54/31/4)

Table-2.3 makes interesting reading. It exhibits a positive correlation between the average value of annual collections from CPRs and average household size. The correlation coefficient works out to be 0.28 and is indicative of the fact that larger the average household size, greater is the annual average value of collection. This seems reasonable because large sized rural households are likely to collect more materials from CPRs for their livelihood purposes. Poor income and low opportunity cost of labour may be taken as a further explanation for this state of affairs.

The ratio of value of collections to consumption expenditure is estimated to be 3.02 per cent at the all India level. The ratio is the lowest for Rajasthan (0.91 per cent) probably because a large area of the state is under desert. It is the highest in Odisha (5.59 per cent) and relatively high in Madhya Pradesh (4.93 per cent) and Assam (4.89 per cent) because of high forest cover, poor income and low opportunity cost of labour. The correlation coefficient between the value of collections from CPRs and household consumption expenditure is also positive. It works out to 0.2 indicating that rural people are dependent on CPRs.

2.4.3 Collection and Use of Fuel Wood

It is widely accepted that rural households in India depend substantially on non-commercial sources of energy, particularly on fuel wood for cooking and heating purposes. Needless to say, CPRs are a major source of fuel wood for them and for a large many household they are the only source too. Since the share of fuel wood in the total collections from CPRs is predominant (58 per cent), it can be taken as an indicator of dependence of rural population on CPRs. Agro-climatic zone wise relevant data are presented in *Table*-2.4.

Table 2.4: Fuel wood Dependence of Rural Households across Agro-Climatic Zones

Agro Climatic Zone	*Percentage of Rural Households*		*Annual Collection Per Household (Kg)*
	Using fuel wood	*Collecting fuel wood from CPRs*	
Western Himalayas (WHm)	73	67	1203
East Himalayas & Brahmaputra Valley (EHm)	57	43	911
Lower Gangetic plains (LG)	50	34	260
Middle Gangetic plains (MG)	46	32	338
Trans- Gangetic plains (TG)	53	26	283
Upper Gangetic plains (UG)	54	24	415
Eastern Plateau & Hills (EHg)	78	71	848
Central Plateau & Hills (CHg)	62	45	485
Western Plateau & Hills (WHg)	69	57	516
Southern Plateau &Hills (DP)	80	64	565
East Coast Plains & Hills (EG)	69	48	465
West Coast Plains & Hills (WC)	59	27	358
Gujarat Coast Plains & Hills (GC)	73	55	480
Western Dry Region (TD)	45	11	219
All Islands (Isl)	74	64	822
India	62	45	500

Source: Same as Table-2.1

The table reveals that rural households depend heavily on fuel wood energy sources and for that matter on the CPRs. On the whole 62 per cent of the rural households are dependent on fuel wood energy and 45 per cent on fuel wood collections from CPRs. A further investigation into the data brings out that more than 60 per cent of the rural households in the four agro-climatic zones viz, EHg, WHm, DP & ISL reported collection of fuel wood from CPRs and their dependence is higher than that at the national level. This may probably be due to the fact that large parts of these areas are covered by forests. The annual collections per household remains very high for four agro-climatic zones such as WHm (1203 Kg), EHm (911 Kg), EHg (848 Kg), and IsL (822 Kg) which are substantially higher than the national average collection (500 Kg). Less than 40 per cent of the households in six zones, viz, LG, MG, TG, UG, WC and TD have reported collecting fuel wood from CPRs. Obviously, the quantity of collections in these zones is lower than the national average. However, these figures suggest high dependence on CPRs, of course with the exception of TD due to low forest coverage.

The Environmental Kuznets Curve is popularly used as a rough approximation of the likely relationship between economic growth and degradation of environmental resources. It postulates that in the early stages of economic growth, environmental degradation is faster but it recedes with economic growth later gaining momentum after a peak as can be seen from the following *figure*.

Figure 2.1: Environmental Kuznets Curve

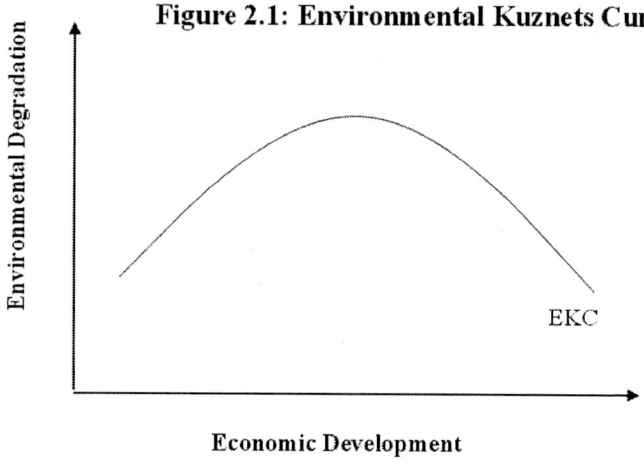

In view of this it can be hypothesized that villages with large population sizes may have a lower level of dependence on CPRs than those with smaller population sizes. The estimates of percentage of households using and collecting fuel wood from CPRs across size class of villages have been used to examine the dependency syndrome in the rural areas. Such estimates are given in *Table-2.5*.

Table 2.5: Fuel wood Use and Collection by Population Size Class of Villages

Population Size Class	*Percentage of Households Reporting*	
	Use of fuel wood	*Collection of fuel wood from CPRs*
Less than 100	93	88
100-200	78	71
201-600	66	53
601-1200	64	48
1201-2000	61	45
2001-5000	60	41
5001 and Above	55	37
All	62	45

Source: Same as Table-2.1

The table shows an inverse relationship between the population size class of villages and percentage of households reporting use of fuel wood and collection of fuel wood from CPRs. The correlation coefficients between population size class of villages and percentage of households reporting use of fuel wood, and its collection from CPRs have been found to be very high at -0.67 and -0.72 respectively[1]. The percentages of households reporting use and collection of fuel wood from CPRs are estimated at 93 and 88 respectively for villages with population up to 100. For villages with population exceeding 5000 these percentages are 55 and 37 respectively.

Size class of population in a village can be taken as a proxy indicator of the level of economic development and availability of alternative employment opportunities as also the opportunity cost of labour. It can be reasoned that villages with large population sizes have a higher level of economic development, better employment opportunities outside collection from CPRs and high opportunity cost of labour leading to lesser dependence on CPRs.

1. The correlation coefficients have been estimated considering the mid points of population-size class of villages. However, in calculating correlation coefficient, the last class has been ignored because of its open-end nature.

Household dependence on fuel wood as the major source of energy in the rural areas gives an approximation of dependence on CPRs. It is held that collection and use of fuel wood in the rural sector tend to decline with economic growth over time. NSS Reports 404 (50th Round-1993) and 452 (54th Round -1998) contain valuable information and provide deep insights into this issue. Available estimates are presented in *Table-2.6*.

Table 2.6; Dynamics of Collections and Consumption of Fuel wood in States

State Average	*Percentage of Households Using fuel wood*		*Average Quantity Collected*	*Quantity Consumed*
	54th Round (1998)	*50th Round (1993-94)*	*54th Round*	*50th Round*
Andhra Pradesh	81	94	545	950
Arunanchal Pradesh	85	96	5448	3786
Assam 60	97	614	1411	
Bihar 58	70	446	623	
Gujarat 73	83	483	877	
Haryana41	90	306	1013	
Himachal Pradesh	59	91	1080	2346
Jammu & Kashmir	51	89	553	2234
Karnataka	79	96	484	1446
Kerala 53	95	204	1301	
Madhya Pradesh	76	96	621	1673
Maharashtra	67	82	522	776
Manipur	75	96	1157	1635
Meghalaya	93	94	2558	2282
Mizoram	98	99	6688	1532
Nagaland	98	99	2972	2816
Odisha 75	91	944	1290	
Punjab 69	74	550	841	
Rajasthan	34	94	267	1368
Sikkim 69	74	1805	1832	
Tamil Nadu	70	93	497	816
Tripura 51	97	427	1417	
Uttar Pradesh	51	88	416	813
West Bengal	51	73	324	742
India	62	87	500	1015

Source: Same as Table-2.1.

The table shows that the percentage of rural households reporting the use of fuel wood is much lower in the 54th Round survey than in the 50th Round for all the states in India as well as for the country as a whole. The estimated quantity of fuel wood collection from CPRs per household per annum also indicates similar results. This may be taken to mean that the dependence of rural population on fuel wood and for that matter on CPRs for the supply of fuel wood has reduced during the period 1993-1998. The reduced collections and dependence may be attributed to depletion of common property land and forest resources leading to declining availability of fuel wood and/or a greater distance than earlier to be covered or alternatively, more time to be spent in collecting fuel wood from CPRs. However, the quantity of fuel wood collected annually from the CPRs, as evidenced from the 54th Round survey, is still high, particularly in the states under the EHm zone and in Odisha.

2.5 Depletion and Current Status – NSS Data

Human action for improving their living conditions has had both positive and negative effects on environment and natural resources including common property land and forest resources. A major part of the negative effects is manifested in resource depletion which has far reaching implications for livelihood sustainability and long-term growth. A good number of studies relating to natural resources indicate a rapid decline in the CPRs in terms of both size and productivity. Keeping this in mind we have attempted to estimate the depletion and current status of CPRs across agro-climatic zones in India for the period 1998-2010 on the basis of NSS data on reduction per 1000 hectares during five years preceding the 54th Round National Sample Survey (1999) and status of CPR land in 1998.The compound average annual rate of depletion has been computed by using the following formula.

$$CPR_{1998} = CPR_{1993}\ (1\text{-}r/100)^{5}$$

$$CPR_{2010} = CPR_{1998}\ (1\text{-}r/100)^{12}$$

Where

CPR_{1998} = status of CPRs in 1998

CPR_{1993}= status of CPRs in 1993

CPR_{2010} = status of CPRs in 2010.

r = compound average annual rate of depletion

Table-2.7 gives a summary picture of depletion and status of CPRs in different agro-climatic zones in the country.

Column-2 shows depletion of CPRs, column-3 gives CPR status and colmn-4 presents CPR per household as obtained from NSSO 54th Round Report. In column-5, status of CPRs in 1993 has been estimated using columns-2 and 3. Column-6 gives depletion of CPRs during 1993-98. Estimates of compound average annual rate of depletion of CPRs during 1993-98 are given in column-7. Status of CPRs in 2010 is estimated with 1998 as base (column-3) using the depletion rates (column-7) and is shown in column-8. Column-9 gives the projected area of depletion of CPRs during 1998-2010.

The table indicates higher rates of depletion for the agro-climatic zones MG (1.48), TG (1.46), EHg (1.02), DP (0.88), UG (0.57), and LG (0.53). Interestingly per household availability of CPR land in these zones are lower at 0.07, 0.07, 0.44, 0.18, 0.03 and 0.02 respectively suggesting a strong inverse relationship between availability and depletion. This may be due to lower return from CPRs due to their smaller size and poor quality, and base resource conversion to more productive uses. To the contrary, lower rates of depletion in zones like CHg (0.3), TD (0.04), GC (0.02), and WHm (0.04) are observed to coexist with high per household CPR availability of 0.65, 4.77, 0.71, and 0.49 respectively. Higher benefits from the resource and a more sustainable use and management system may be the possible explanation for the situation. It can be seen from the table that both the estimated size of depletion during 1993-98 (8138.80 ha) and the projected area of depletion during 1998-2010(18907.78 ha) are quite high suggesting the urgency of corrective and preventive action to counter the challenge.

2.7: Depletion of CPRs During 1993-2010 and Status of CPRs in 2010

etion of s during 93-98 100 ha)	Status of CPRs in 1998(in 100 ha)	CPRs Per Household in 1998 (in ha)	Estimated Status of CPRs in 1993 (in 100 ha)	Total Depletion During 1993-98 (in 100 ha)	Compound AverageAnnual Rate of Depletion During 1993-98 per cent)	Projected Status of CPRs in 2010 (in 100 ha)	Proj Deple CPRs 1998 (in 1
(2)	(3)	(4)	(5)	(6)	(7)	(8)	(
0.2	18279	0.49	18315.63	36.63	0.04	18191.38	87
2.3	11231	0.18	11495.39	264.39	0.46	10621.00	61
2.6	1536	0.02	1577.002	41.00	0.53	1441.89	94
7.2	13745	0.07	14811.42	1066.42	1.48	11488.41	225
7.1	7809	0.07	8405.813	596.81	1.46	6543.85	126
2.8	1717	0.03	1766.461	49.46	0.57	1603.87	11
5.0	55346	0.44	58258.95	2912.95	1.02	48935.37	641
1.5	82365	0.65	83619.29	1254.29	0.30	79430.93	293
1.3	35154	0.29	35617.02	463.02	0.26	34067.16	108
4.3	24007	0.18	25085.68	1078.68	0.88	21603.62	240
1.3	20468	0.15	20737.59	269.59	0.26	19835.20	63
0	12359	0.16	12359	0.00	0.00	12359.00	0.
0.1	39193	0.71	39232.23	39.23	0.02	39099.00	94
0.2	96941	4.77	97135.27	194.27	0.04	96476.33	46
0.5	57	0.12	57.28643	0.29	0.10	56.32	0.
1.9	420219	0.31	428357.8	8138.80	0.38	401311.22	189

le-2.1

umns 2,3,5,6,7,8 and 9 have been estimated on the basis of data obtained from NSS 54th round

2.6 CPR Forests, Status and Dependence- Revelations of FSI Data

2.6.1 *Status of Forests*

CPR forest refers to a group of plants, primarily of trees and other woody vegetation, that exist and grow on common land. They are determined not by the presence of trees alone but by absence of other dominant land uses. The most widely accepted way of assessing the status of forests is to look at forest data with respect to the dynamics of area under forests and the quality of the forests.

In India and for its states and UTs, forest area is assessed and forest data are published by two authorities using two approaches. The first is the forest area approach, technically known as 'Recorded Forest Area (RFA)' which refers to all the geographical area classified as 'forest' in government records and is used by the Forest Department of the State Government, that are the custodians of the recorded forests. In this view, forests have a legal status. The second one is 'Forest Cover (FC)' that denotes all lands more than one hectare (0.1 km^2) in area with a tree canopy density of 10 per cent and above irrespective of land use, ownership and legal status and is used in State of Forest Reports (SFR) published bi-annually by Forest Survey of India (FSI) since 1987. The FC is captured with tree cover and growing stock data using remote sensing technique i.e., satellite data.

2.6.1.1 Recorded Forest Area

From the RFA point of view, forest is a tract of land that is legally proclaimed to be forest under the Indian Forest Act, 1927 and, for the state of Odisha, under the Odisha Forest Act, 1972 (GoO, 2018). Three types of forests are specified by these Acts: Reserved forests (RF), Protected Forests (PF) and Unclassed Forests (UF).

The Reserved Forests refer to areas which are notified as such under the Indian Forest Act or the Odisha Forest Act i.e., in government gazette. These forests are the property of the government and the government is entitled to the produce of such forests. They enjoy a higher degree of protection and most of the human activities in the area are prohibited unless expressly permitted. The local population does not enjoy the right of using the products of a reserved forest but may be granted the privilege to use them in special cases. All forests declared as wild life or game sanctuary or national parks are treated as reserved forests and their conservation is a priority concern of the government.

Protected Forests are also notified under the afore stated Forest Acts and the government has proprietary rights over them and/ or is entitled to the forest-produce. These forests are protected from further depletion, but the restrictions are less stringent i.e., most of the human activities are allowed unless expressly prohibited. The local population enjoys privileges like grazing of cattle and collection of leaves, firewood, fodder and other minor forest produce etc. and is permitted to collect all produce of a protected forest except those which are specifically prohibited.

Any forest land or any other land 'recorded' in land records as 'forest' but not notified in government gazette as 'reserved' or 'protected' forests are termed as 'Unclassed Forests'. The tenurial status of such forests is not clearly defined. These include forest land owned by the Forest Department outside the reserve or protected forests, with the Forest Department having title to them and are used for forest roads, forest buildings, sites for nurseries, zoos, wild life parks and other miscellaneous purpose. These belong to both the individuals, and government and communities; some of them are owned by private entities, district councils, village community and even by individual households. Forests on revenue land, which are normally assigned to the forest department for management, are called revenue forests or Soyam forests.

2.6.1.2 Forest Cover

On the basis of internationally adopted norms of classification, FSI classifies forest cover into 4 types, namely very dense forest (VDF), moderately dense forest (MDF), and open forest (OF). Mangroves and scrubs have been separately classified.

All forest lands with tree cover (including mangrove cover) of canopy density of 70 per cent and above are included under VDF, those with tree cover (including mangrove cover) of canopy density between 40 per cent and 70 per cent come under MDF, the ones with tree cover (including mangrove cover) of canopy density between 10 per cent and 40 per cent come under OF, and those with poor tree growth, mainly of small or stunted trees, having canopy density less than 10 percent are denoted by scrubs. Any area not included in the above classes is termed non-forest area.

2.6.1.3 The Recorded Forest Area-Forest Cover Relationship

'Recorded Forest Area' and 'Forest Cover' define the extent of forest. Though seemingly similar, they may show different magnitudes. While 'RFA' measures extent of forest in terms of 'legal status' irrespective of actual forest canopy cover on the ground, 'FC' measures it in respect of 'forest canopy' on the ground irrespective of the legal status of land and species composition; 'RFA' may or may not have forest cover whereas 'FC' is bound by 'forest cover' but may not be a forest as per the legal tag and hence 'RFA' and 'FC' denote areas that may overlap with each other but may not show identical figures (GoI, 2019). The following figure depicts the RFA-FC relationship.

Figure 2.2 Forest Cover and Recorded Forest Area

(Adapted from GoI, 2020: India State of Forest Report 2019)

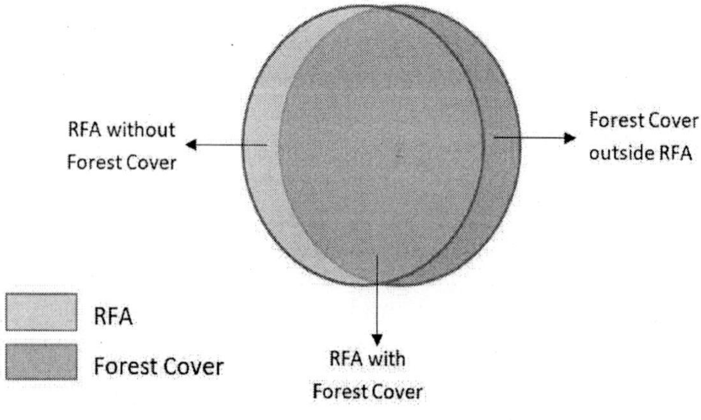

2.6.1.4 Why the RFA-FC Discrepancy?

'Recorded forest area' measures the land that is stated as 'forests' in the official record of a government forest department and it denotes the jurisdiction of the forest department. Alternatively, 'RFA' refers to land that is legally considered a forest, as per government records, regardless of the actual canopy density. 'FC', on the contrary, signifies all land that measure more than one hectare (0.01 km^2), and has a tree canopy density of more than 10 per cent, notwithstanding the legal status of the land. Obviously, in official records, some land that are not forests continue to bear the 'forest' tag simply because they are recorded as such. In such view of the matter areas where forests have been cleared and where the land has been diverted for developmental activities are included in 'RFA' and this is misleading. In India, close to 10 per cent of land classified as 'RFA' has no green cover and hence they may be justifiably termed as 'recorded forest area without forest cover'. The FSI explanation for the discrepancy is quite interesting. It says that some areas that are recorded as forest because these may be of ecological importance but may not have forest cover e.g., deserts, high altitude areas where trees don't grow, marshy lands and grasslands. Similarly, shifting cultivation lands and other lands that do not form part of 'RFA', might not have been actively used for shifting cultivation and are left as fallow lands over which a secondary forest has grown and such land could have possibly been shown as 'land having forest cover'.

2.6.1.5 Data Highlights

Category-wise extent of RFA for the States and UTs of India are given in Tables 2.8 and 2.9 and the magnitude of Forest Cover under different categories for each State and UT of the country are shown in Tables 2.10 and 2.11 for 1997 and 2019. These four tables are appended to this chapter.

Tables 2.8 and 2.9 make interesting points. The extent of Total RFA increased marginally from 765210 KM^2 in 1997 to 767419 KM in 2019. As a proportion of geographical area (GA) the increase is also not very substantial. RFA was 23.28 per cent of GA in 1997 and it rose to 23.34 per cent in 2019.

Looking from the lens of RFA classes, it may be seen that the share of reserved forests in total RFA has increased from 54.43 per cent in 1997 to 56.66 per cent in 2019 while the shares of protected and unclassed forests have come down from 29.18 per cent and 16.39 per cent respectively in 1997 to 28.53 per cent and 14.81 per cent in 2019. It means that some more forest areas have been taken to the 'Reserved Forests' category over this period. This shows the governments' concern for forest conservation and protection.

The FSI collects and publishes data on forest cover as well as scrubs and mangroves. Forest Cover (FC) data relating to 1997 and 2019 for the states, UTs and the country as a whole as given in Tables 2.10 and 2.11 suggest that the total area under forest cover in the country was 628570 KM^2 in 1997 that constituted 19.12 per cent of total geographical area of India has increased to 712249 KM^2 or 21.67 per cent of GA in 2019. During this period, area under scrubs lowered from 57211 KM^2 to 46297 KM^2. While the increase in FC has happened because of concerted afforestation programmes of the government(s) and increasing forest awareness among the public, the decline in area under scrubs (which consist of open woodland with thorny trees characterised by short trunks and low-branching crowns, dry grass land, xerophytic shrubs etc.) might have been caused by overgrazing and other human actions like fragmentation of the scrub jungle, plantation activities causing increase in canopy, degradation of scrub jungle etc.

Up to 2001, FSI was publishing FC data relating to Dense and Open Forests (OF), Mangroves and Scrubs. With effect from 2003, a more disaggregate analysis of Canopy Density with Dense forests comprising Very Dense Forests (VDF) and Moderately Dense forests (MDF) has been adopted. In 1997, Dense Forests constituted 58.43 per cent and OF accounted for 41.57 per cent of total area of FC of the country. As in 2019, OF have increased in share to 42.75 per cent while the share of Dense Forests has lowered to 57.25 per cent comprising 13.94 per cent of FC under VDF and 43.31 per cent under MDF. Thus, there has been a loss in Dense Forest Cover even when the total FC area has increased between the Forest Assessment years 1997 and 2019. This has created a paradoxical situation of 'Forest Cover Up and Density Down' and has serious implications for biodiversity.

It is heartening that for India as a whole, there has been an increase in area under Dense Forest Cover from 367260 KM^2 in 2019 in comparison to 1997. But the area under OF has also increased from 261310 KM^2 to 304499 KM^2 in this period and such increase has been little more than proportionate to that in dense forest cover. This proves that the various Acts to promote forests have not been as effective as desired; these have been, to some extent, toothless while the traditional custodians of forests, the tribals and wildlife have become clueless.

2.6.1.6 Status of Forests in Odisha in a Comparative Perspective

In order to have a clear understanding of the comparative status of forests in the state vis-à-vis the situation obtaining at the national level, it is imperative to look at the trend data. For this purpose, broad category -wise extent of RFA and FC for Odisha and India in different years are presented in Table 2.8.

The table reveals that RFA measured 58136 KM^2 or 37.34 per cent of Odisha's GA in 2001 has gone up to 61024 KM^2 or 39.31 per cent of GA of the state in 2019 while area under FC (FCA), that amounted to 49044 KM^2 (31.50 per cent) in 2001, increased to 51619 KM^2 (33.15 per cent) in 2019. In the case of India, while RFA declined from 774740 KM^2 (23.57 per cent) to 767419 KM^2 (23.34 per cent), FCA has increased from 653898 KM^2 (19.89 per cent) to 712249 KM^2 (21.67 per cent) between the 2001 and 2019 assessment years. Looking at the quality of forests, it may be seen that the shares of reserved, protected and unclassed forests in total RFA in Odisha that were 45.29 per cent, 26.70 per cent and 28.01 per cent in that order in 2001 have been estimated at 58.90 per cent, 41.06 per cent and 0.04 per cent respectively for 2019. For India, these figures were 51.62 per cent, 30.78 per cent and 17.60 per cent in 2001 and 56.66 per cent, 28.53 per cent and 14.81 per cent in 2019 respectively. From the stand point of quality of FC, it may be seen that the share of dense forests in FCA has come down from 57.45 per cent to 55.25 per cent for Odisha against a decline

Table 2.8: Trend of Recorded Forest Area and Forest Cover by Broad Types in Odisha and India *(KM^2)*

Year	Odisha/India	Recorded Forest Area					Forest Cover				
		RF	PF	UF	TOTAL	%	VDF	MDF	OF	TOTAL	%
2001	Odisha	26329 (45.29)	15525 (26.70)	16282 (28.01)	58136 (100.00)	37.34	28178 (57.45)		20866 (42.55)	49044 (100.00)	31.50
	India	399919 (51.62)	238434 (30.78)	136387 (17.60)	774740 (100.00)	23.57	395169 (60.43)		258729 (39.57)	653898 (100.00)	19.89
2003	Odisha	26329 (45.29)	15525 (26.70)	16282 (28.01)	58136 (100.00)	37.34	487 (1.01)	27712 (57.31)	20154 (41.68)	48353 (100.00)	31.05
	India	NA	NA	NA	NA	NA	54518 (8.04)	334056 (49.28)	289242 (42.67)	677816 (100.00)	20.62
2005	Odisha	26329 (45.29)	15525 (26.70)	16282 (28.01)	58136 (100.00)	37.34	7077 (14.52)	21241 (43.57)	20257 (41.55)	48755 (100.00)	31.31
	India	419028 (54.45)	216605 (28.14)	133993 (17.41)	769626 (100.00)	23.57	83472 (12.09)	319948 (46.36)	286751 (41.55)	690171 (100.00)	21.00
2007	Odisha	26329 (45.29)	15526 (26.70)	16282 (28.01)	58137 (100.00)	39.34	7073 (14.48)	21394 (43.79)	20388 (41.73)	48855 (100.00)	31.38
	India	NA	NA	NA	NA	NA	83510 (12.09)	319012 (46.17)	288377 (41.74)	690899 (100.00)	21.02
2009	Odisha	26329 (45.29)	15525 (26.70)	16282 (28.01)	58136 (100.00)	37.34	7073 (14.48)	21394 (43.79)	20388 (41.73)	48855 (100.00)	31.38
	India	430582 (55.96)	206212 (26.80)	132711 (17.25)	769512 (100.00)	23.41	83428 (12.05)	320238 (46.25)	288728 (41.70)	692394 (100.00)	21.06
2011	Odisha	26329 (45.29)	15525 (26.70)	16282 (28.01)	58136 (100.00)	37.34	7060 (14.44)	21366 (43.69)	20477 (41.87)	48903 (100.00)	31.41
	India	422536 (54.91)	213982 (27.81)	133020 (17.29)	769538 (100.00)	23.41	83471 (12.06)	320736 (46.35)	287820 (41.59)	692027 (100.00)	21.05

26329 (45.29)	15525 (26.70)	16282 (28.01)	58136 (100.00)	37.34	7042 (13.99)	21298 (42.30)	22007 (43.71)	50347 (100.00)
425404 (55.13)	214086 (27.85)	131341 (17.02)	771831 (100.00)	23.48	83503 (11.96)	318745 (45.67)	295651 (42.36)	697898 (100.00)
26329 (45.29)	15525 (26.70)	16282 (28.01)	58136 (100.00)	37.34	6985 (13.84)	21470 (42.55)	22005 (43.61)	50460 (100.00)
[illegible] (55.59)	[illegible] (27.39)	[illegible] (17.02)	[illegible] (100.00)	[illegible]	[illegible] (12.63)	[illegible] (44.58)	[illegible] (42.78)	[illegible] (100.00)
36049 (58.90)	25133 (41.06)	22 (0.04)	61204 (100.00)	39.31	6967 (13.37)	21570 (41.62)	23008 (44.81)	51545 (100.00)
434705 (56.65)	219432 (28.59)	113881 (14.84)	767419 (100.00)	23.34	98158 (13.86)	308318 (43.53)	301797 (42.61)	708273 (100.00)
[illegible] (58.90)	[illegible] (41.06)	22 (0.04)	[illegible] (100.00)	[illegible]	[illegible] (13.50)	[illegible] (41.75)	[illegible] (44.75)	[illegible] (100.00)
[illegible] (56.66)	[illegible] (28.53)	[illegible] (14.81)	[illegible] (100.00)	23.34	[illegible] (13.94)	[illegible] (43.31)	[illegible] (42.75)	[illegible] (100.00)

– Relevant Years and Odisha Economic Survey – Various Years

parentheses indicate percentages to total RFA/ Forest Cover, NA- Data Not Available from 60.43 per cent to 57.25 per cent for India between 2001 and 2019.

It is thus evident that Odisha has a higher share of RFA and FCA in GA but a lower share of dense forests in FCA as compared to India in the assessment years. However, in terms of RFA, it is found that RF and PF had lower shares comparatively in 2001 but a higher share in 2019 in Odisha than in India. But in the case of unclassed forests (UC), Odisha's share was higher than India's in 2001 which has reversed in 2019.

Expectedly, RFA is greater than FCA in all the assessment years in both Odisha and India. RFA was 18. 5 percent higher than FCA or alternatively, FCA constituted 84.4 per cent of RFA in 2001 at the state and national levels. In the 2019 assessment year, RFA measures 18.6 per cent higher than FCA and FCA is 84.34 per cent of RFA in Odisha. The difference has moderated at the all-India level in 2019 relative to 2001 with RFA being 7.75 per cent higher than FCA and the former being 92.81 per cent of the latter.

A summary picture of RFA by broad types in Odisha and India for three years viz. 1997, 2001 and 2019 is given in Table 2.9 below to have a compressive view of the broad trends.

Table 2.9: Recorded Forest Area by Broad Types in Odisha and India (KM²)

Year	Odisha/ India	Geographical Area (GA)	Reserved Forests	Protected Forests	Unclassed Forests	Total RFA	Total RFA as % of GA
1997	Odisha	155707	27087 (47.37)	30080 (52.60)	17 (0.03)	57184 (100.00)	36.73
	India	3287263	416516 (54.43)	223309 (29.18)	125385 (16.39)	765210 (100.00)	23.28
2001	Odisha	155707	26329 (45.29)	15524 (26.70)	16282 (28.01)	58135 (100.00)	37.34
	India	3287263	423311 (55.09)	217245 (28.27)	127882 (16.64)	768436 (100.00)	23.38
2019	Odisha	155707	36049 (58.90)	25133 (41.06)	22 (0.04)	61204 (100.00)	39.31
	India	3287469	434853 (56.66)	218924 (28.53)	113642 (14.81)	767419 (100.00)	23.34

Source: India State of Forest Report- 2001, 2019.

Note: Figures in Parentheses are percentages of Total RFA in the respective years.

It may be seen that RFA as a percentage of total geographical area has shown a rising trend over the years for Odisha, increasing from 36.73 per cent in 1997 to 37.34 percent in 2001 and 39.31 per cent in 2019, while it has hovered around 23 per cent at the all-India level. However, looking at RFA component-wise no clear trend is discernible. The share of RF in RFA has increased from 47.37 per cent in 1997 to 58.90 per cent in 2019 for the state while it has gone up marginally from 54.43 per cent in 1997 to 56.66 per cent in 2019 at the national level. The share of PF has lowered both in the state as well as for the country as a whole, but the decline is observed to be very large in the state. The share of UF has not changed much at the state and national levels.

2.6.2 *Dependence*

The dependence of people living in FFVs on forests is judged by quantities of goods collected by them from forests per annum and by the amount removed from forest by them per capita per annum. A snapshot of dependence is presented in the following table.

Table 2.10: Annual Removal /Collection from Forests by the People Living in FFVs -2019

Odisha/ India	Population in FFVs (Projected)	Per Capita/ Total	Fuel Wood	Fodder	Small Timber	Bamboo
Odisha	19638249	Per Capita	0.468	5.823	0.019	0.01
		Total	9186	56035	376521	11079
India	306556264	Total	85290	1053039	5848204	1834.25

Source: FSI, MoEF & CC, Government of India; India State of Forest Report-2019

Note: The figures for Total Fuel Wood, Fodder and Bamboo are in '000 tons; those for Per Capita Fuel Wood, Fodder and Bamboo are in ton; and the figures for Small Timber are in Cubic Meter (CUM) or M^3.

The total removal from forests by the people (19638249 persons) living in Forest Fringe Villages (FFVs) have been estimated at 9186, 56035, 110.79 thousand tonnes and 376521 M^3 in the cases of fuel wood, livestock, fodder, bamboo and small timber for Odisha for 2019. The respective figures for India stood at 85290, 1053039, 1834.25 thousand tonnes and 5848204 M^3. In per capita terms, these have been estimated at 0.468 ton, 5.823 tons, 0.010 ton and 0.019 M^3 for Odisha. In terms of total removal, Odisha ranks second in fuelwood, 5th in small timber and bamboo, and 7th in fodder while in per capita collections it ranks 7th in fuel wood, 15th in fodder, 10th in Bamboo and 12th in small timber among the states and union territories in India (GoI, 2019).

2.6.3 Current Status: The State of Forests

Forest cover and change in forest cover between two assessment periods is an important indicator of state of forests in a State/UT or a country. The change in forest cover is analysed with respect to forest cover of previous assessment which signifies actual change in forest cover on the ground (GoI, 2020). A summary picture of forest cover in Odisha and India in 2019 vis-à-vis 2011 is given in the following table.

Table 2.11: Forest Cover in Odisha and India (KM^2)

Odisha/India	*Geog. Area (GA)*	*VDF*	*MDF*	*Open Forest*	*Total Forest Cover*	*% of Geographical Area*
			2019			
Odisha	155707	6970	21552	23097	51619	33.15
India	3287469	99278	308472	304499	712249	21.67
			2011			
Odisha	155707	7060	21366	20477	48903	31.41
India	3287263	83471	320736	287820	692027	21.05
			2001			
Odisha	155707	27972	20866	48838	31.36	
India	3287263	416809	258729	675538	20.55	
			Change in 2019 over 2011			
Odisha	0	-90	186	2620	2716	1.74
India	206	15807	-12264	16679	20222	0.62

		Change in 2019 over 2001			
Odisha	0	550	2231	2781	1.79
India	206	-9059	45770	36711	1.12

Source: GoI, 2020, GoI, 2012

It is seen that there is an overall gain in forest cover amounting to 20222 sq.km for India and 2716 sq.km for Odisha in 2019 in comparison to the assessment reported in the ISFR 2011.This improvement in forest cover may be attributed to better conservation measures, protection, afforestation activities, tree plantation drives and increase in agroforestry while loss in VDF forest cover in the case of Odisha and that in MDF at the national level may be attributed to shifting cultivation, forest fires, felling of trees, natural calamities, anthropogenic pressure and developmental activities. In the Odisha context, the increase in forest cover has been mainly due to effective forest protection by participatory management intervention committees and regeneration of shifting cultivation areas.

A comparison between 2019 and 2001 makes worth reading. The increase in forest cover in 2019 over 2001 is seen to be greater than in 2019 over 2011 both at the national and state levels. In the case of Odisha forest cover increased by 2781 KM^2 or by 1.79 per cent compared to 2716 KM^2 or by 1.74 per cent. In the case of India there has been an increase by 36711 KM^2 or 1.12 per cent in comparison to 20222 KM^2 or 0.62 per cent. A second important point to note is that the increases are largely due to increases in the area under open forests. In Odisha there has been an increase in area under dense forests by 550 KM^2 between 2001 and 2019 which is a good sign. But at the all-India level large tracts of dense forests have turned non-forests while the aggregate forest cover has gone up which is a matter of great concern for the biologists, biodiversity conservation activists and climate change experts, policy makers.

2.7 Conclusion

Common property resources are a major life support system, especially for the poor rural households. The study reveals that rural households, particularly the poor, collect a variety of materials from CPRs and are critically dependent on them.

The results indicate that collections from CPRs bear a direct relation with household consumption expenditure and that large sized households collect more materials from CPRs. The findings exhibit that a majority of rural households are dependent on fuel wood energy and on collections of fuel wood from CPRs. Fuel wood use and its collection from CPRs are observed to be higher (lower) in villages with smaller (larger) population sizes. It can be reasonably argued that villages with large population have diverse employment opportunities, high opportunity cost of labour and a higher level of economic development compared to those with smaller population. Such variations can be a possible reason for difference in fuel wood use and collections from CPRs across villages. Time series NSS data show a decline in the percentage of rural households using fuel wood suggesting a direct link between dependence on and availability of CPRs. However, the quantity of fuel wood collected from CPRs per household remains very high pointing to intense exploitation of these resources. A noteworthy conclusion of the study is that the CPR base of the country is depleting at a threatening rate and if the 1993-1998 depletion rates were assumed to persist, then they could be all the more alarming.

Since CPRs play the role of a sheet anchor in the Indian rural economy, their depletion will have serious negative effects on livelihood and long-term growth. Conservation and sustainable management of these resources is, therefore, our first imperative. Throughout recorded history, mankind has endeavoured to manage these resources for furthering its material standard of living. But proliferation of economic activities and application of liberalisation, privatisation and globalisation (LPG) policies particularly since the second half of the 20th century, have had strong adverse effects on the sustainability of these resources and people's dependence on them. Needless to say the rural poor are generally sensitive to such depletion. Hence the onus of controlling depletion lies essentially with the government and the rural populace. A reorientation of macroeconomic policy framework and a comprehensive CPR management policy with focus on fine tuning of policies and participation of broadly-based groups and their linkage with outcome oriented poverty alleviation schemes can help overcome the challenge.

The analysis presented above is based on data collected through sample surveys conducted by the NSSO covering a limited timeframe of only two years i.e. 1993 and 1998. The compound average annual rate of change estimated for the period 1993-98 have been assumed in estimating depletion between 1998 and 2010 and making projections for the year 2010. The 54th Round survey data for 1998 relating to the collection of fuel wood from CPRs and the 50th Round survey data for 1999 in respect of consumption of fuel wood have been used for comparison as well as for explaining dependence on CPRs. In such view of things our results are subject to the limitations of secondary data, sampling, short time frame, assumption of a constant rate of change and incompatibility of data, and hence may not claim generalisability.

3

Socio-Economic Profile of Odisha and the Study Area

3.1 Introduction

Human beings and the rural poor and tribal folk in particular are linked to the nature largely in terms of resource flows from the CPR system to make possible and supplement livelihoods. The way this relationship is effected and made enduring depends to a very great extent on the availability of alternative livelihood opportunities vis-a-vis the system of common property natural resources. From this point of view the geographical, demographic, production, infrastructure and such other features exert considerable influence on the use and management of these resources in a locality at a disaggregated level, and in a broader perspective, at the aggregate level. Any attempt at analyzing various issues relating to CPRs shall, therefore, remain incomplete without a proper understanding of the broad socio-economic characteristics which are specific to an area. In this chapter a brief profile of the state of Odisha and the study area is presented.

3.2 Socio-Economic Profile of Odisha

3.2.1 Geography and Location

The state of Odisha is an extensive plateau gently sloping into the coastal plains along the Bay of Bengal in the east. It is bounded by West Bengal in the north-east, Jharkhand in the north, Chhattisgarh' in the west and Andhra Pradesh in the south. With a total geographical area of 1, 55, 707 square kilometres (sq. km) it accounts for 4.7 per cent of the land mass of the Indian subcontinent. The land of the state is classified into low, medium and up-lands with shares 25.6 per cent, 33.6 per cent and 40.8 per cent respectively in the total. The land comprises red, yellow, red-loamy, alluvial, coastal alluvial, laterite and black soils. The annual normal rainfall of the state is 1451.2 mm of which monsoon rainfall (June-September) is 1144.3mm or 79 per cent of the total rainfall. The climatic condition of the state is usually hot with high humidity during March- July.

3.2.2 Demography and Employment

Census 2001 reveals a 14.0 per cent decennial population growth rate; population density of 270 per sq. km; 72.9 per cent effective literacy; 17.1 per cent and 22.8 per cent shares of SCs and STs in total population; a work participation rate of 41.8 per cent; a high share of marginal workers (39.0 per cent). Cultivators constitute 23.4 per cent and agricultural labourers account for 38.4 per cent of the total workforce. There is a heavy concentration of population in rural areas (83.3 per cent); and a demographic dividend in terms of a very large sized population (more than 65 per cent) in 15 to 65 years age group.

The employment situation in the state shows a gloomy picture. Irrespective of the category of workers, the unemployment rate in Odisha has always remained higher than the national rate. Secondly, the unemployment rate has generally shot up and the difference between that in the state and the country has widened. The Odisha Economic Survey 2020-21 shows the usual status (PS+SS) unemployment rate for 2018-19 to be 7.6 per cent for the 15-59-years age group in the state (Government of Odisha, 2021).

Due to heavy population pressure, lack of adequate alternative employment opportunities and backlogging of labour force, the unemployment and underemployment situation in the state has become very serious. The dependence of population on CPRs and CPR forests in particular, in their niche appropriation process has remained very high. Obviously, the rural poor and tribals who live in close proximity to these resources base exploit it more causing depletion and deterioration of the system. This is a cause of concern for the health of the state's CPR system.

3.2.3 *Mineral Resources*

Nature has blessed the state with abundant reserves of mineral resources like coal, iron ore, manganese ore, bauxite, chromite, graphite, nickel etc. The all-India Mineral Resources Estimates reveal that the mineral deposits in the state in respect of chromite, nickel, bauxite, iron ore and coal are about 97.93 per cent, 92.46 per cent, 50.98 per cent, 33.17 per cent and 24.61 per cent respectively of their total deposits in the country. The total reserve of high grade iron ore in Odisha has been estimated at 3,789 million tons which is about one-third of the country's deposit. Such huge deposit of high quality minerals attracts many national and international steel manufacturers to establish steel plants in Odisha. In addition to this, Odisha has a substantial deposit of limestone, china clay, quartz, precious and semi-precious stones, copper and vanadium etc. The rate of exploitation of mineral resources like iron ore, chromite and graphite, bauxite etc. remains very high. If such extensive exploitation takes place to supply raw materials to industries, a vast forest area has to be sacrificed in the process of mineral exploitation leading to serious livelihood, environmental and climatic problems.

3.2.4 *Power*

Odisha has tremendous potential for generation of hydro and thermal power. It is one of the major power surplus states in India. During 2019-20, the state's installed power capacity was 8597.5 MW (CPPs 1933.5 MW and GRIDCO664 MW). In the construction of power projects many villages have been submerged in water and many areas have been deforested causing serious stress on the state's CPRs.

3.2.5 *Industry and Tourism*

With abundant mineral resources and comfortable power situation, the state has high potential for industrialization. However, the rate of industrialization in Odisha has remained very low. During different Plan periods, large industries like Rourkela Steel Plant, National Aluminum Company, Indian Charge Chrome Ltd., Paradeep Phosphates and coal-based power plants at Talcher, Kaniha and Banarpal have been set up in the state. Keeping in mind the low rate of industrialization in the state, three nodal agencies namely, Industrial Promotion and Investment Corporation Ltd. (IPICOL), Industrial Development Corporation Ltd. (IDCOL) and Odisha State Electronics Development Corporation (OSEDC) are engaged in promoting large and medium scale industries. In order to attract large scale investment for mineral based industrial activities, the state government has signed MoUs with various reputed national and international business houses. Emphasis is also being laid on the growth of micro, small and medium enterprises sector. The handicrafts and handlooms products of Odisha have earned high reputation in and outside the state. However due to various reasons this sector is in sick condition.

In Odisha, tourism is one of the important sectors which has the potential to generate employment opportunities and stimulate growth. A large many of our tourist spots are in the proximity or within the CPR system. The linkage between the pace of industrialization of a state and its CPR and environmental systems are well known. Clustering of industries in the state has created various environmental hazards via large scale deforestation activities and industrial waste disposal and emission. In addition to these, many of the base CPRs is gradually being converted to other high value assets in the industrialization process. Industrialization led CPR depletion is therefore, a cause of concern. Natural resource systems such as dense forests, wood land, sanctuaries, rivers, beaches, lakes and lagoons etc. play a vital role in development of the tourism sector of the state as elsewhere. Odisha is one of the Indian states which has tremendous potential in its tourism sector. Development and proper management of its natural resource base would not only attract tourists from in and outside the country, it can also generate huge revenue and employment opportunities in the state through its backward and forward linkage effects.

3.2.6 Forest Resources

Odisha had a recorded forest area measuring 51618.51 sq.kms as in 2019 which constitutes 33.15 per cent of the geographical area of the state. It included 6969.71 sq. km. (13.5 per cent) of very dense forests, 21551.93 sq. km. (41.75 per cent) of moderate dense forests and 23096.87 sq. km. (44.75 per cent) of open forests. This status is assumed to have remained for quite some period of time. Table 3.1 provides information on district-wise recorded forest area as per this classification.

Table- 3.1: District-wise Forest Cover in Odisha (KM²)

District		*2019Assessment*					
	Geographical Area (GA)	*Very Dense Forest*	*Mod. Dense Forest*	*Open Forest*	*Total*	*%of GA*	*Scrub*
Anugul	6,375	371.01	1,380.00	1,031.62	2,782.63	43.65	84.18
Balangir	6,575	70.00	224.00	841.26	1,135.26	17.27	143.16
Baleshwar	3,806	23.00	133.38	226.18	382.56	10.05	46.59
Bargarh	5,837	175.01	374.14	501.31	1,050.46	18.00	40.57
Baudh	3,098	262.91	562.04	465.99	1,290.94	41.67	57.39
Bhadrak	2,505	0.00	8.70	69.30	78.00	3.11	0.00
Cuttack	3,932	53.00	226.00	525.38	804.38	20.46	67.80
Debagarh	2,940	191.00	667.41	618.75	1,477.16	50.24	14.08
Dhenkanal	4,452	173.99	420.38	851.24	1,445.61	32.47	83.88
Gajapati	4,325	84.16	1,490.09	947.12	2,521.37	58.30	262.88
Ganjam	8,206	164.39	1,074.32	866.69	2,105.40	25.66	655.00
Jagatsinghapur	1,668	0.00	4.64	131.64	136.28	8.17	0.00
Jajapur	2,899	6.00	71.99	228.09	306.08	10.56	49.78
Jharsuguda	2,114	3.00	173.82	155.82	332.64	15.74	29.21
Kalahandi	7,920	361.64	734.19	1,323.97	2,419.80	30.55	371.69
Kandhamal	8,021	660.95	2,593.23	2,143.53	5,397.71	67.29	385.51
Kendrapara	2,644	83.40	88.54	139.36	311.30	11.77	1.99
Kendujhar	8,303	288.78	1,420.07	1,513.31	3,222.16	38.81	53.24
Khordha	2,813	21.00	186.00	260.09	467.09	16.60	90.47
Koraput	8,807	94.48	740.41	1,263.38	2,098.27	23.83	947.86
Malkangiri	5,791	158.00	712.76	1,465.41	2,336.17	40.34	45.90
Mayurbhanj	10,418	1,334.95	1,717.24	1,041.98	4,094.17	39.30	37.57

Nabarangapur	5,291	172.63	447.04	527.08	1,146.75	21.67	48.62
Nayagarh	3,890	189.00	965.00	559.75	1,713.75	44.06	171.36
Nuapada	3,852	86.01	481.69	706.76	1,274.46	33.09	108.82
Puri	3,479	0.00	59.73	165.36	225.09	6.47	10.79
Rayagada	7,073	419.54	853.42	1,873.55	3,146.51	44.49	359.91
Sambalpur	6,624	498.99	1,696.32	1,096.98	3,292.29	49.70	40.55
Subarnapur	2,337	2.00	187.00	161.85	350.85	15.01	29.22
Sundargarh	9,712	1,020.87	1,858.38	1,394.12	4,273.37	44.00	88.89
Grand Total	**1,55,707**	**6,969.71**	**21,551.93**	**23,096.87**	**51,618.51**	33.15	**4,326.91**

Source: G o I (2019). India State of Forest Report – 2019. Forest Survey of India, Ministry of Environment, Forest & Climate Change, Government of India.

The four major forest types found in Odisha are (a) Tropical Dry Deciduous Forests (57.87 per cent), (b) Tropical Moist Deciduous Forests (39.88 per cent), (c) Tropical Semi Ever Green Forests (0.68 per cent) and (d) Littoral and Swamp Forests (0.48 per cent). Thus forests in Odisha are by and large tropical in nature. The actual forest cover of Odisha in 2007 was 48855 sq. km. which constitutes 31.38 per cent of the state's geographical area in terms of forest canopy density classes. It includes 7073 sq.km. (4.54 per cent) of very dense forest (VDF) with crown density above 70 per cent, 21394 sq.km. (13.74 per cent) of moderately dense forest (MDF) with crown density 40-70 per cent and 20388 sq. km. (13.09 per cent) of open forest (OF) with crown density 10.40 per cent. Tree cover outside forest (ToF) and Scrubs (SC) assessed reportedly amount to 4435 sq.km. (2.85 per cent) and 4858 sq. km. (3.12 per cent) respectively. The VDF, MDF and OF account for 4.54 per cent, 13.74 per cent and 13.10 per cent respectively, totalling 31.38 per cent of the total geographical area of the state. ToF, SC and Non-forest area constitute 2.85 per cent, 3.12 per cent and 65.51 per cent of the state's geographical area. This suggests that the present forest coverage of the state is little higher than the 33 per cent stipulation recommended by the National Forest Policy 1988 but is very low in terms of density parameters.

To maintain the desired percentage and improve quality, afforestation of wasteland and rejuvenation of degraded forests are being accelerated in the state. Emphasis is being laid on conservation of forests and peoples' participation through JFM committees to check illegal felling and removal of trees. As a result, the production and revenue receipt from forest produce has increased from Rs. 311.10 crore in 2007-08 to Rs.346.07 crore in 2008-09 which seems to be quite substantial. Kendu leaf is a major source of forest revenue and it generates 80 per cent of all revenues from forest products. The Odisha Forest Development Corporation is the nodal agency for trading of Kendu leaf. During 2008-09, revenue to the tune of Rs.304.76 crore was generated from Kendu leaf trade. The share of forestry sub-sector in GSVA of Odisha was estimated at 2.6 per cent in 2011-12, it rose to 3.14 per cent in 2015-16 where after it has been falling. The GSVA share of forestry was 2.44 per cent in 2019-20 and it rose slightly to 2.71 per cent in 2020-21 (Government of Odisha, 2021).

The role of forests in the life of rural population of the state cannot be gainsaid. Apart from the forest produces, collection of Kendu leaves has remained one of the major forest related activities of the people residing close to forest areas in Odisha. It provides employment to the local people and generates a fairly good amount of income for the state. However, there has been a quality deterioration of the forest resources in the state over the years due to various reasons like population pressure, urbanization, unemployment and poverty. More effective policy measures are needed not only to protect the forests but also for their sustainable exploitation.

3.2.7 Animal Resources

Next to crop production, animal resources play a major role in the rural economy of the state. It has been estimated that about 80 per cent of the rural households in Odisha possess livestock of one or more species which supplement their family income. Livestock census 2019 reveals that the state has a total livestock population of 182 lakh of which cattle population comprises 55 per cent. Apart from this the state has a poultry population of 274 lakh. The total milk production of the state during 2019-20 was 23.70 lakh metric tonnes with per capita availability of 148ML per day. Similarly, the egg production during this period has been estimated at 23824 lakh million with per capita availability of 55 nos. per annum in 2019-20. Keeping in mind the importance of livestock in the livelihood system of rural people, the state government of Odisha have formulated a Livestock Sector Policy (2002-03) to promote the livestock sector for stimulating economic activities of the rural poor and improving their living standards.

In order to feed such a huge livestock, the rural population in Odisha heavily depends on village forests, pastures and common grazing lands etc. Ever increasing livestock population has enhanced fodder collection activities and hence the pressure on CPR systems is increasing in the state. Overexploitation, lack of community interest and absence of proper management institutions have further deteriorated the status of such CPRs both in quality and quantity. This has not only reduced the expected returns from livestock rearing but also has increased the dependence of the rural households on market to feed their livestock. Therefore, there is an urgent need for management and rejuvenation of the degraded CPRs for providing food security to the livestock population of the state.

3.2.8 Irrigation

The economy of Odisha is dominated by agriculture. Irrigation perhaps is the most important input for agricultural production. It insures crop failure due to drought and also provides food security. It has been assessed that out of 61.65 lakh hectares of cultivable land of the state, nearly 62.58 lakh hectares could be brought under irrigation. Of this, 21.38 lakh hectares or 34.16 per cent was covered through major and medium irrigation, 8.22 lakh ha. or 13.14 per cent through minor (flow) irrigation, and 18.16 lakh ha or 29.02 per cent by minor (lift) irrigation, 1.25 lakh ha or two per cent by mega lift irrigation and the rest 13.5 lakh ha or 21.68 per cent per cent were irrigated through other sources like ponds, private tanks, wells, and water harvesting structures etc.

It is evident from above that about 22 per cent of total irrigated land of Odisha depend on irrigation from various other sources like ponds, tanks and other water harvesting structure which signifies the relative importance of nature based irrigation systems in the state. Therefore, their conservation as well as renovation is important to strengthen the irrigation base and to boost agricultural productivity in the state.

3.2.9 *Agriculture*

Agriculture and allied sectors, the mainstay of the state's economy, contributed 21.27 per cent to the Gross State Value Added (GSVA) in 2020-21 at current basic prices. The latest available Agricultural Census 2015-16) reveals that, the operational holdings in Odisha were 48.66 lakh with 46.19 lakh hectares of area. However, small and marginal holdings accounted for 93 per cent of the holdings with 75 per cent of total area. The remaining seven per cent of holdings belonged to semi-medium, medium and large size classes with 25 per cent of total area. The Average size of operational holdings has declined from 1.30 hectare in 1995-96 to 0.95 hectare in the 2015-16 Census. Due to population pressure, the per capita availability of land in the state has considerably gone down over the years. The state is frequently affected by natural calamities like cyclone, flood and drought which bring fluctuations in the production of agricultural output and in the growth rate of this sector. During 2019-20, 115.71 lakh million tons of food grains were produced in Odisha. Paddy, the major cereal crop, accounted for 83.29 per cent of the total food grain production in the same year.

Study on dependence on natural resource systems reveals that during the periods of crop failure and drought etc., environmental resources including CPRs provide insurance against risk to the rural population. Since agricultural outputs are vulnerable to monsoon, CPRs are expected to provide economic support especially during failure of monsoon and lean periods of the year. The reduced availability of land per person may further increase the dependence of rural population on the natural resources and CPR systems in the state causing their depletion and degradation in future. Therefore, conservation as well as sustainable use of such resources is imperative for providing economic support to the large majority of rural poor.

3.2.10 *Fisheries*

The geography of the state provides ample opportunity for commercially viable aquaculture in a big way. Odisha has a long coastal, brakish and riverine-ecosystem. The state has abundance of water resources with a chain of large rivers and rivulets (Baitarani, Brahmani, Budhabalanga, Mahanadi, Rushikulya, Subarnarekha etc.). Its long coastline extends over 480 kilometers continental self-area and a stretching up to 24,000 sq.kms with a depth of 200 meters. Besides the Bay of Bengal, the Chilika lake with a water spread area of 790 sq.km. provides huge potential for production of marine fish as well as production of prawn through brackish water prawn culture. Fish production during 2019-20 was around 8.16 lakh tons, comprising 5.43 lakh tons fresh water fish (66.54 per cent), marine fish 1.57 lakh tons (19.24 per cent) and brackish water fish (14.22 per cent). The per capita consumption of fish in Odisha was estimated to be 16.2 kg. for this year.

The state is endowed with rich water body systems. The Chilika lagoon is the largest in Asia and it provides livelihood to thousands of people through fishery. Almost all the villages in Odisha have water body systems like ponds and tanks etc. Such rich water body systems provide huge opportunity for commercial aquaculture in the state. However, lack of initiatives both at local and state levels and of proper awareness, group conflicts and inadequate funds have led to their inoptimal exploitation and absence of proper management regimes have led to their serious depletion and degradation over the years.

3.2.11 *Income and Poverty*

A study of the state income during the Plan period reveals that the average annual growth rates of net state domestic product (NSDP) and NSDP per capita have been low with wide fluctuations resulting largely from variations in monsoon dependent agricultural production. The Plan-wise annual growth rates of NSDP and NSDP per capita at constant (1999-2000) prices are given in Table-3.2.

Table-3.2: Plan-wise Annual Growth Rate in Odisha

Sl. No	*Plan Period*	*Growth Rate at 1999-2000 Prices*	
		NSDP	*NSDP Per Capita*
1	1st Plan	4.69	2.69
2	2nd Plan	2.94	1.12
3	3rd Plan	4.80	2.31
4	4th Plan	2.39	0.26

5	5th Plan	4.45	2.50
6	6th Plan	4.77	3.01
7	7th Plan	7.48	5.52
8	8th Plan	1.67	0.07
9	9th Plan	4.99	3.56
10	10th Plan	9.40	8.23
11	11th Plan (2007-10)	8.53	7.29

Source: Government of Odisha (2010): Economic Survey 2009-10

The growth rate of the state compares unfavourably with the growth rate in the Indian economy except during the 10th and 11th Plan periods. Secondly, the growth rate of NSDP per capita has been lower than that of NSDP due to population growth. The standard of living in the state has been below the national average for most part of the plan period and bottomed in 2002-03. However, the long term falling trend in real per capita income has been arrested and rather reversed in the recent years.

The annual average growth rate of GSDP at constant (2011-12) prices averaged 7.05 per cent during 2012-13 to 2019-20 against the GDP growth rate of 6.61 per cent at the national level. During this period per capita income (PCI) in the state increased from Rs.48499 to Rs.104566 registering an increase of about 116 per cent while per capita income of India surged from Rs.63462 to Rs.134226 or by 111.5 per cent. It is heartening to note that over about a decade, PCI-Odisha has grown faster than PCI-India. However, the state's real per capita income has consistently remained below the national average and worse still, the gap between PCI-India and PCI-Odisha has widened over the years. It swelled from Rs. 14963 in 2011-12 to Rs. 29660 in 2019-20 or nearly doubled. The good thing is that, PCI-Odisha, which was about 76.42 per cent of the national PCI in 2011-12, increased to 77.90 per cent in 2019-20, the highest over the period, despite some intermittent slowing during 2012-13 to 2015-16 (Government of Odisha, 2021).

Despite rich mineral deposits, valuable forests and long coastline, Odisha has remained one of the poorest states in the country. As per the analysis of data furnished by the Planning Commission in 2011-12, the poverty head count ratio stood at 32.59 for Odisha as against 21.92 per cent at the all-

India level. Poverty in Odisha is substantially higher than those for most of the states in India. A number of poverty alleviation programmes have been implemented in the state to fight out the grave problem. The Swarna Jayanti Gram Swarojgar Yojana (SGSY), a centrally sponsored self-employment programme, has been implemented in the State since 1999 and a number of wage employment programmes such as Sampoorna Gramina Rozgar Yojana (SGRY), National Food for Work Programme (NFFWP) and Mahatma Gandhi National Rural Employment Guarantee Scheme (MNREGS) have also been implemented in Odisha to tackle poverty in the state.

Studies round the world have established direct linkage between poverty and environmental degradation and grinding mass poverty is a cause of concern to the government. In the absence of livelihood earning activities, poor people are more likely to fall back on environmental resources. The obvious outcome has been a rate of resource exploitation much higher than its natural regeneration rate. Such a high percentage of population below poverty line in the state may pose a serious threat to the long run sustainability of its natural resource systems in general and CPRs in particular.

3.2.12 *Transport*

In Odisha surface road is the major means of transport. In the absence of adequate rail links the state is heavily dependent on the surface road connectivity. By 2005-06 the state had a total road length of 2.70 lakh kilometers which accommodates a vehicle population of 91.23 lakh. The total railway route length till the same year was only 2652 kilometers. Since the state is in the process of both urbanization and industrialization, transport and communication networks are increasing very fast in terms of road and railway infrastructure. This is likely to cause further deterioration in the forest coverage of the state.

3.3 Profile of the Sample Districts

Empirical studies with generalizable conclusions are not free from local colours. Therefore, a description of the study area is imperative. This section provides the general profile of the area covered under the study. The present research covers six sample villages from three districts of the state Odisha, viz., **Balasore, Mayurbhanj** and **Keonjhar**. A brief description of the socio economic profile of these three districts is presented below.

3.3.1 District Profile of Balasore (As per District Statistical Handbook, Balasore, 2018)

3.3.1.1 Location and Geography

Balasore is one of the coastal districts of Odisha. It lies between 860 20′ and 870 29′east longitude and between 210 03′ and 210 59′ north latitude. It is bounded by Mayurbhanj district on the north, the Bay of Bengal on the east, Bhadrak district on the south and Keonjhar district on the west. The general climatic condition of the district is hot with high humidity during April and cold during November-December. Usually, the monsoon breaks in the district during June. The district has a geographical area of 3806 sq km with a forest cover of 382.56 sq km accounting for 10.05 per cent of its area. The geographical area of the district is 2.44 per cent of that of the state. The district has 2 subdivisions, 12 blocks, 12 tehsils, 2932 villages and 533001 households.

3.3.1.2 Demography

The total population of the district, as per 2011 census, is 2320529 with SCs and STs accounting for 20.6 per cent and 11.9 per cent respectively. The district accounts for 5.53 per cent of the total population of the state and has a population density of 610 per sq km., more than twice that of the state (270). The worker-to-population ratio in the district is estimated at 40.19 per cent. The average daily wage rates for different categories of workers are given at Rs.450 for carpenters, Rs 476.39 for masons, Rs 550 for tractor drivers, Rs 295.6 for agricultural laborers and Rs 248.9 for female agricultural laborers.

3.3.1.3 Agriculture

The actual rainfall in the district in 2018 is 1838.6mm against the normal 1592.0 mm and the yield rate of paddy, the principal crop of the district, was 35.29 quintals per hectare for 2017-17. The total production of paddy in the district was 7478421 quintals followed by 5688 (2016-17) quintals of sugarcane and 6458 quintals of groundnut in the same year.During 2017-18, the total irrigation potential created in the district stood at 112083 hectares and 91013hectares during Kharif and Rabi seasons respectively.

3.3.1.4 Infrastructure

In 2017-18 the district had 143 agricultural co-operative credit societies, 02 specialized co-operative marketing societies, One central co-operative banks with branches, 468 post offices and 2633 of the 2635 villages electrified. It has 122.41 kms of national highway, 161.24 kms of state highway, 122.91 kms of major district roads, 454.47 kms of other district roads, 116.30 kms of forest roads, and2818.72 kms of inter-village roads. The mode of road transport in the district is purely private. By 2017-18, 1239 villages were covered with rural drinking water supply programme and of the 5047 habitations, 4507 were fully covered and 502 partially covered by LPCD drinking water.

3.3.1.5 Education

Balasore is one of the educationally most developed districts in the state. As per government records, the district had 1629 primary schools, 1462UP-Primary schools, 607 secondary schools and 167 general education colleges, 8 each Diploma Colleges and Technical Degree Colleges in 2017-18. The literacy rate in the district was estimated at 79.79 per cent in 2011 census.

3.3.1.6 Health

In 2017-18 the district had one medical college and hospital, 2 hospitals, 21 community health centres (CHCs)97 primary sub-centres and 22 private hospitals /nursing homes in the allopathic mode, 32 homoeopathic dispensaries and 25 ayurvedic dispensaries.

3.3.2 District Profile of Mayurbhanj (As per District Statistical Handbook Mayurbhanj-2018)

3.3.2.1 Location and geography

Mayurbhanj district is located between 850 40′ and 870 11′east longitude and between 210 16′ and 220 34′ north latitude. It is bounded by the Jharkhand state on the north, Balasore district on the south, West Bengal state on the east and Keonjhar district on the west. The general climatic condition of the district is hot with high humidity during April – May and cold during November-December. Normally, the monsoon breaks in the district during June.

The district has a geographical area of 10418 sq. kms with a forest cover of 4094.17 sq kms which accounts for 39.30 per cent of the total geographical area. The geographical area of the district is 6.69 per cent of that of the state territory. The district has 4 subdivisions, 26 blocks, 26 tehsils, 3950 villages and 472123 households.

3.3.2.2 Demography

The total population of the district as per 2011 census is 2519738 with SCs and STs accounting for 7.3 per cent and 58.7 per cent respectively. The district accounts for 6.0 per cent of the total population of the state and has a population density of 242 per sq.km. which is lower than that of the state (270). The worker to population ratio of the district has been estimated at 48.56 per cent. The average daily wage rate for different categories of workers are given at Rs.451.25 for carpenters, Rs 464.58 for masons, Rs.549.72 for tractor drivers, Rs.265.28 for male agricultural laborers and Rs 230.42 for female agricultural laborers.

3.3.2.3 Agriculture

The annual rainfall in the district in 2018 was 1654.3 mm as against the normal rainfall of 1600.6 mm and the yield rate of paddy, the principal crop of the district, was 30.65 quintals per hectare for 2017-18. The total production of paddy in the district was 9934143 quintals followed by 15999 quintals of potatoes, 9576 quintals of maize and7623 quintals of ground nuts in 2017-18. By 2017-18, the total irrigation potential created in the district stood at 148359 hectares and 78900 hectares during Kharif and Rabi seasons respectively.

3.3.2.4 Infrastructure

As in 2017-18, the district had 52 agricultural co-operative credit societies, 4 CARD, one central co-operative bank with branches, one urban co-operative bank,08 consumer cooperative societies, 6 specialized co-operative marketing societies, one co-operative cold storage, 712 post offices and 2724 villages electrified. It has 264.85 kms of national highway, 192.61 kms of state highway, 129.14 kms of major district roads, 937.79 kms of forest roads, 6058 kms of inter-village roads and 3465.96 kms of village roads. The mode of road transport in the district is purely private. Up to 2017-18, of the 8441 villages/hamlets in the district, 6923 were covered with rural drinking water supply programme and of the 10746 habitations, 9000 were fully covered and 1739 were partially covered under 40 LPCD drinking water scheme.

3.3.2.5 Education

As per government records, the district had 2890 primary schools, 1404UP-Primary schools, 750 secondary schools and 35 general education colleges, 37 Diploma Colleges and 3 Technical Degree Colleges in 2017-18. The literacy rate in the district was estimated at 63.17 per cent in 2011 census.

3.2.2.6 Health

In 2017-18, the district had 4 Government Medical College/ hospitals, 28 community health centers, 88 primary health center, and 589 sub-centres in the allopathic mode, 44 homoeopathic dispensaries and 44 ayurvedic dispensaries.

3.3.3 District Profile of Keonjhar

3.3.3.1 Location and geography

Keonjhar district is located in the northern part of the state. It lies between 850 11′ and 860 22′east longitude and between 200 1′ and 220 10′ north latitude. It is bounded by the Jharkhand state on the north, Jajpur district on the south, Anugul district on the east and Mayurbhanj district on the west. The climatic condition of the district is normally hot with high humidity during March to July and cold during November to February. Usually, the monsoon breaks in the district during June. The district has a geographical area of 8303 sq.kms with a forest cover of 3222.16 sq. kms accounting for 38.81 per cent of its area. The geographical area of the district is 5.33 per cent of that of the state. The district has 3 subdivisions, 13 blocks, 13 tehsils, 2137 villages and 403869 households.

3.3.3.2 Demography

The total population of the district as per 2011 census is 1801733 with SCs and STs accounting for 11.62 per cent and 45.45 per cent respectively. The district accounts for 4.29 per cent of the state's population and has a population density of 217 per sq. km. as against 270 persons per sq. km. of the state. The worker to population ratio in the district is estimated at 42.54 per cent. The average daily wage rates for different categories of workers are given at Rs.490.97 for carpenters, Rs.500.69 for masons, Rs.574.31 for tractor drivers, Rs.267.36 for male agricultural laborers and Rs 230.00 for female agricultural laborers.

3.3.3.3 Agriculture

The annual normal rain fall in the district is 1487.7 mm and the yield rate of paddy was 31.78 quintals per hectare as in 2017-18. The total production of paddy in the district was 598550metric tons, followed by 13220 metric tons of sugar cane and 69400metric tons of maize in the year 2017-18. By 2017-18, the total irrigated potential created in the district stood at 128209 hectares and 53235 hectares during Kharif and Rabi seasons respectively.

3.3.3.4 Infrastructure

The district had 41 agricultural co-operative credit societies, 8 non-agricultural co-operative credit societies, 2 specialized co-operative marketing societies, one central co-operative bank with 13 branches, 444 post offices and 1789 villages electrifiedin 2017-18. It has 341.30 kms of national highway, 52.74 kms of state highway, 34.29 kms of major district roads, 885.98 kms of other district roads, 249.88 kms of forest roads, 3912.49 kms of inter-village roads and 1945.9 kms of rural roads. The mode of road transportation in the district is both public and private. The railway route length in the district measures 158.06 km. As on 30 September 2019, 2067 revenue villages in the district in the district which constitute 97.4 per cent of the total revenue villages were electrified. Some villages in the district's mining region have been sucked dry and they do not have any source of safe drinking water.

3.3.3.5 Education

The district had 1779 primary schools, 1040UP Primary schools, 520 secondary schools and 54 Junior and 34 Degree Colleges imparting general education in 2017-18. The literacy rate in the district was estimated at 68.24 per cent as per 2011 census.

3.3.3.6 Health

In 2018-19, the district had 21 hospitals and community health centers and 65 primary health centers in the allopathic mode, 48 homoeopathic dispensaries and 34 ayurvedic dispensaries.

3.4 Profile of the Sample Blocks

The Socio-economic profiles of the sample blocks are discussed in this section

3.4.1 Block Profile of Nilagiri

Originally a princely state, Nilagiri was added as a part of Balasore district when it was merged into the state of Odisha on the 1st January 1948and was constituted into a regular Sub-Division of the district on the 15th December 1949.Nilagiri Sub-Division has two blocks namely, Nilagiri and Oupada.

3.4.1.1 Geography

Nilagiri is a Tribal Sub-Plan Block. It has a total geographical area of 245.2 sq.kms with forest cover of 9.77 sq.kms. The total geographical area of the block is 6.44 per cent of the district. The block has 158 villages and 31679 households.

3.4.1.2 Demography

The total population of the block as per 2011 census is 129360 with SCs and STs accounting for 9.86 per cent and 57.75 per cent of the population of the block respectively. The block accounts for 5.57 per cent of the total population of Balasore district. The worker-to-population ratio (WPR) for the block is estimated at 43.40 per cent as against the district figure of 41.8 per cent. This means that the WPR in the block is higher than that of the district. The average daily wage rates for different categories of workers have been assumed to be the same as in the district. The block has a population density of 528 per sq.km. which is lower than that of the district (610).

3.4.1.3 Agriculture

The annual rain fall in the block is 1943 mm and the yield rate of paddy is 34.22 quintals per hectare which is lower than the yield rate in the district (35.29) quintals. The total production of paddy in the block during 2017-18 was 564576 quintals.

3.4.1.4 Infrastructure

The block has two co-operative credit societies and 24 post offices. The mode of road transportation is private and the distance of the block from the district headquarters is 22 kms. The block is well connected with the district by all-weather roads.

3.4.1.5 Education

The block has 96 primary schools, 73Up schools, 35 secondary schools and 5 colleges. The literacy rate of the block is 65.33 per cent which is less than the district literacy rate (79.79 per cent). This speaks of the backwardness of the block.

3.4.1.6 Health

The block has one hospital, 5 CHCs and 32 primary health centres and other hospitals in allopathic mode. It has 3 homoeopathic and 2 Ayurvedic dispensaries.

3.4.2 Block Profile of Jashipur

Jashipur is a TSP block in Mayurbhanj district.

3.4.2.1 Geography

The total geographical area of Jashipur block is 443.12 sq. kms. The block has a forest cover of 113.23 sq. kms which constitutes 25.55 per cent of its total geographical area. The share of the block area is 4.25 per cent of the total area of Mayurbhanj district. The block consists of 228 villages and 23461 households.

3.4.2.2 Demography

As per 2011 Census the total population of the block is 101058 and it is 4.01 per cent of the district population. The population of SCs and STs categories account for 7.18 per cent and 69.78 per cent respectively of the total block population. The worker-to-population ratio for the block has been estimated at 52.81 per cent which is higher than the district rate (48.56 per cent). The average daily wage rates across categories of workers have been assumed to be the same as in the district. The population density in the block has been worked out at 228 per sq. km. as against the density of (242) in the district.

3.4.2.3 Agriculture

The average annual rain fall in the block is 1602.5 mm and the paddy yield rate is 27.82 quintals per hectare which is lower than that for the district (30.65 q/ha). Both the figures are lower than their respective district figures. The total production of paddy in the block during 2017-18 was 561035 quintals.

3.4.2.4 Infrastructure

In this block there are 2 co-operative credit societies and 12 post offices. The block is situated at a distance of 94 kms from the district headquarters and has all weather road connectivity with the district headquarters.

3.4.2.5 Education

There are 138 primary schools, 59 UP-primary schools, 30 secondary schools and 3 colleges in the block. The block has a literacy rate of 56.85 per cent and it is lower than the literacy rate for district (63.17 per cent) which shows its backwards.

3.4.2.6 Health

To cater to the health requirements of the people, there are two allopathic community health centers, three primary health centers, and 25 sub-centres in the block. In addition, there are three homoeopathic and two Ayurvedic dispensaries in the block.

3.4.3 Block Profile of Patna

Parna became a block of Keonjhar district on 1 April 1960. It is a TSP block.

3.4.3.1 Geography

The total geographical area of Patna block is 416. 32 sq. kms and it is 5.01 per cent of the total geographical area of Keonjhar district. The block has a forest cover of 47.97 sq. kms which constitutes 11.52 per cent of its total area. Patna block has 153 villages and 23630 households.

3.4.3.2 Demography

According to 2011 census the population of the block is 101518 and the shares of SCs and STs population in the total population are 8 per cent and 53 per cent respectively. The estimated worker–population ratio for the block is 50.45 per cent and it is higher than the district rate (42.54 per cent). The daily wage rates for both the skilled and unskilled worker categories are expected to be the same as in the district. The population density of the block is 244 per sq. km. which is much higher than that for the district (217).

3.4.3.3 Agriculture

The estimated average annual rain fall in the block is 1489.69 mm and the paddy yield rate is 71.78 quintals per hectare.

The figures compare favourably with those for the district.

3.4.3.4 Infrastructure

There are 2 agricultural co-operative credit societies and 28 post offices in the block. The block has private road transportation system. The distance of the block from the district headquarters is 49 kms and is well connected by all-weather roads.

3.4.3.5 Education

The numbers of primary schools, UP-primary schools, secondary schools and colleges in the block are 129, 72, 40 and 5 respectively. The block has a literacy rate of 58.64 which is close to that in the district.

3.4.3.6 Health

The total number of allopathic health units in the block is 6 consisting of onecommunity health centre and five primary health centres. Under the homeopathic and ayurvedic modes there are two dispensaries each.

3.5 Profile of the Sample Villages

It has already been indicated that two villages from each sample block have been randomly picked up for indepth enquiry. The profile of the sample villages is given in this section to highlight their peculiarities with respect to CPR forest resources. A clear understanding of these peculiarities can help to diagnose the research issues at the grassroots level.

3.5.1 Profile of Sample Villages of Balasore District

A brief outline of the population and land characteristics of the sample villages Tenda and Banthiapada of Sajanagarh grampanchayat of Nilagiri block in Balasore district are given in Table-3.3.

Table-3.3: Profile of the Villages Tenda and Banthiapada

DISTRICT-Balasore

BLOCK-Nilagiri

G.P.-Sajanagarh

Sl. No	*Village Profile*	*Tenda*	*Banthiapada*
1	Population	1275	451
2	Households	276	73
	No. of ST Households	276	73
	No. of Other Households (other than ST)	0	0
	Land (Acres)		
3	Agricultural Land	295.25 *(27.40)*	361.50 *(59.73)*
	Forest Land used by the villagers	170.49 *(15.82)*	84.34 *(13.93)*
	Village Forest	0	0
	Grazing Land	29.77*(2.76)*	31.01*(5.12)*
	Homestead Land	45.46 *(4.22)*	41.19 *(6.81)*
	Other Land	536.43 *(49.79)*	87.22 *(14.41)*
	Total Land Area	1077.40*(100)*	605.26 *(100)*
	Per household Availability of Agriculture Land	1.06	4.95
	Per household Availability of CPR Forest	0.62	1.16
	Per household Availability of Grazing Land	0.10	0.42
	Per household Availability of Homestead Land	0.16	0.56
	Per household Availability of Other Land	1.94	1.19

Source: R.I. Office, Nilagiri, Balasore

Note: Figures in parentheses indicate percentages to total land area.

It can be read off the table that Tenda and Banthiapada villages in the Balasore district have 276 and 73 households respectively. The population in both the villages are 1275 and 451 respectively. Both the villages are homogeneous in terms of social composition, i.e. all households belong to the ST category. The total agricultural land in Tenda is 295.25 acres and that of Banthiapada is 361.50 acres. They account for 27.40 per cent and 59.73 per cent of the total geographical area of the two villages respectively. Agricultural land per household is 1.06 acres for the village Tenda, 4.95 acres for Banthiapada and 1.88 acres for the two villages as a whole.CPR forest land per household works out to be 0.62 acre for Tenda, 1.16 acres for Banthiapada and 0.73 acre for the two villages taken together. At the household level, a 0.73 acre size of CPR forest land may be considered adequate.

Availability of total grazing land, homestead land and other lands for the village Tenda are, 29.77 acres (2.76 per cent), 45.46 acres (4.22 per cent) and 536.43 acres (49.79 per cent) acres respectively. For the village Banthiapada the figures are 31.01 acres (5.12 per cent), 41.19 acres (6.81 per cent) and 87.22 acres (14.41 per cent) acres respectively. The per household availability of grazing land, homestead land and other land for the village Tenda are 0.10 acre, 0.16 acre and 1.94 acres respectively. Similarly for the village Banthiapada the respective quantities are 0.42 acre, 0.56 acre and 1.19 acres.

3.5.2 *Profile of Sample Villages of Mayurbhanj District*

The population, household and land particulars of the sample Ramasahi and Mandam villages of Mayurbhanj district are presented in Table-3.4.

Table-3.4: Profile of the Villages Ramasahi and Mandam

DISTRICT-Mayurbhanj
BLOCK-Jashipur
G.P.-Baunsanali

Sl. No	*Village Profile*	*Ramasahi*	*Mandam*
1	Population	503	471
2	Households	64	60
	No. of ST Households	64	57
	No. of Other Households (other than ST)	0	3
	Land(Acres)		
3	Agricultural Land	243.98 *(43.80)*	195.99 *(54.47)*
	Forest Land used by the villagers	192.25 *(34.51)*	95.06 *(26.42)*
	Village Forest	35.87 *(6.44)*	17.98 *(5.00)*
	Grazing Land	32.06 *(5.76)*	15.52 *(4.31)*
	Homestead Land	12.29 *(2.21)*	8.88 *(2.47)*
	Other Land	40.63 *(7.29)*	26.39 *(7.33)*
	Total Land Area	557.08 *(100)*	359.82 *(100)*
	Per household Availability of Agriculture Land	3.81	3.27
	Per household Availability of CPR Forest	3.56	1.88

Per household Availability of Grazing Land	0.50	0.25
Per household Availability of Home Stead Land	0.19	0.14
Per household Availability of Other Land	1.57	2.27

Source: R.I. Office Bhanjakia Circle, Mayurbhanj

Note: Figures in parentheses indicate percentages to total land area.

The table reveals that the sample villages Ramasahi and Mandam in the Mayurbhanj district consist of 64 and 60 households respectively. The populations in the villages are 503 and 471 respectively. Both the villages are largely homogeneous in terms of social composition in the sense that all households in Ramasahi are ST households while 57 out of 60 households in Mandam belong to the ST category. The total agricultural land in Ramasahi is 243.98 acres and that in Mandam is 195.99 acres. The share of agricultural land in total village area for Ramasahi and Mandam are 43.8 per cent and 54.47 per cent respectively. Agricultural land per household is 3.81 acres in Ramasahi, 3.27 acres in Mandam and 3.55 acres for the two villages taken together. CPR forest land per household works out to be 3.56 acres for Ramasahi, 1.88 acres for Mandam and 2.75 acres for the two villages as a whole. This may be considered as quite reasonable for a household.

Availability of total grazing land, homestead land and other land types for the village Ramasahi are, 32.06 acres (5.76 per cent), 12.29 acres (2.21 per cent) and 40.63 acres (7.29 per cent) respectively. For the village Mandam the figures are 15.52 acres (4.31 per cent), 8.88 acres (2.47 per cent) and 26.39 acres (7.33 per cent) respectively. The per household availability of these three categories of land for Ramasahi have been estimated at 0.50 acre, 0.19 acre and 1.57 acres respectively. For the village Mandam the quantities are 0.25 acre, 0.14 acre and 2.27 acres in the same order.

3.5.3 Profile of Sample Villages in Keonjhar District

A brief description of population, household category and land particulars of the sample villages Ghatabalijodi and Tanda of Dumuria grampanchayat of Patna block in Keonjhar district is given in Table-3.5.

Table-3.5: Profile of the Villages Ghatabalijodi and Tanda

DISTRICT-Keonjhar

BLOCK-Patna

G.P.-Dumuria

Sl. No	*Village Profile*	*Ghatabalijodi*	*Tanda*
1	Population	450	522
2	Households	75	87
	No. of ST Households	45	60
	No. of Other Households (other than ST)	30	27
Land (Acres)			
3	Agricultural Land	343.99 *(53.60)*	601.77 *(66.09)*
	Forest Land used by the villagers	191.49 *(29.84)*	140.23 *(15.40)*
	Village Forest	-	-
	Grazing Land	28.60 *(4.46)*	67.60 *(7.42)*
	Homestead Land	29.29 *(4.56)*	24.65 *(2.71)*
	Other Land	48.45 *(7.55)*	76.34 *(8.38)*
	Total Land Area	641.82 *(100)*	910.59 *(100)*
	Per household Availability of Agriculture Land	4.59	6.92
	Per household Availability of CPR Forest	2.55	1.61
	Per household Availability of Grazing Land	0.38	0.78
	Per household Availability of Home Stead Land	0.39	0.28
	Per household Availability of Other Land	0.65	0.88

Source: R.I. Office Patna, Keonjhar

Note: Figures in parentheses indicate percentages to total land area.

The table shows that Ghatabalijodi has 75 households of which 45 are ST households and 30 are non-ST households. In village Tanda, there are a total of 87 households consisting of 60 ST households and 27 non-ST households. Thus, the villages are heterogeneous in terms of social composition. The total population in Ghatabalijodi is 450 and in Tanda the population is 522. The total agricultural land in Ghatabalijodi is 343.99 acres and that in Tanda is 601.77 acres. They constitute 53.6 per cent and 66.09 per cent of the total geographical area in the villages respectively. Agricultural land per household comes to 4.59 acres in Ghatabalijodi, 6.92 acres for Tanda and 5.84 acres for the two as a whole. The availability of total common property forest area in Ghatabalijodi and Tanda are 191.49 acres and 140.23 acres respectively. They constitute 29.84

per cent and 15.40 per cent of the total village area respectively. The per household availability of forest area has been found to be 2.55 acres for Ghatabalijodi, 1.61 acres for Tanda and 2.04 acres for the two villages taken together. At the household level, the afore mentioned size of forest area seems sufficient.

Availability of total grazing land, homestead land and other lands for the village Ghatabalijodi are, 28.60 acres (4.46 per cent), 29.29 acres (4.56 per cent) and 48.45 acres (7.55 per cent) respectively. For the village Tanda, the figures are 67.60 acres (7.42 per cent), 24.65 acres (2.71 per cent) and 76.34 acres (8.38 per cent) respectively. The per household availability of these three categories of land for Ghatabalijodi have been estimated at 0.38 acre, 0.39 acre and 0.65 acre respectively. For the village Tanda the respective quantities are 0.78 acre, 0.28 acre and 0.88 acre.

3.5.4 A Comparison Across Villages

A comparison of population, number and composition of households, and land categories in the sample villages reveals interesting facts. Social homogeneity of households is a common feature in the sample villages of Nilagiri and Jashipur blocks of Balasore and Mayurbhanj districts while heterogeneity is noticed in the villages of Patna block of Keonjhar. Per household availability of agricultural land is found to be the highest in the sample villages of Keonjhar followed by Mayurbhanj and Balasore. In terms of availability of CPR forest land, the sample villages in Mayurbhanj are at the top. Next in the ladder comes Keonjhar and Balasore is at the bottom.

4

Common Property Forest Dependency in Subsistence Economies

4.1 Introduction

Common property forest resources are vital to the life and economy of a vast majority of rural population. In rural Odisha, about 60 percent of villages are located on forest fringe areas. More than 15 million people residing in and around forest areas, most of them being poor and tribals, derive their livelihood from collection and /or marketing of forest produce. They collect and use roots and fruits as food; fuel wood and dry leaves for cooking and lighting; timber, bamboo and cane for house construction, fencing and stacking; medicinal plants and creepers as drugs against illness; green leaves and grass as fodder; streams for irrigating farm lands and vegetable fields; some dry leaves for smoking; and some flowers for brewing liquor and drinking. Besides, a good number of non-timber forest produce and some of the aforestated collections are sold by them in the market to obtain other household necessities with the help of the sales proceeds. Population pressure, lack of alternative gainful employment opportunities, poverty and distress are some of the compelling forces which make them critically dependent on common property forest resources. Forest dependency substantially reduces the expenses of households on items such as fuel wood, timber, fencing materials, house construction, crude agricultural implements, food and oil. This chapter discusses extensively, the results of the survey of the sample households' dependency on CPR forests in the state of Odisha.

4.2 Profile of Sample Households

For a comprehensive analysis of household level dependency on CPR forests it is imperative to study the basic characteristics of the sample households such as the composition of households, their land holding status, livestock position and level of income. A discussion of these aspects is made in this section.

4.2.1 Household Composition

The age and sex composition of sample households and household size are believed to have a bearing on CPR forest dependency. This relationship is analysed below with the help of relevant data given in Table-4.1.

4.2.1.1 Composition of sample households in Balasore district

The total number of persons in the surveyed households in Balasore district were found to be 360, of whom 114 were adult males, 107 were adult females and 139 were children. The average household size in the sample villages has been estimated at 5.14. At the household level the average size of adult males, adult females and children have been worked out to be 1.63, 1.52 and 1.98 respectively. The maximum and minimum household sizes were 10 and 2 respectively with a standard deviation of 1.61; the maximum and minimum number of adult males were found to be 4 and 0 respectively with a standard deviation of 0.90; for adult females, the respective figures are 6 and 1 with standard deviation 0.81; and for children the maximum, minimum and standard deviation figures are 5, 0 and 1.37 respectively.

4.2.1.2 Composition of sample households in Mayurbhanj district

In this district the total members in all the households surveyed were found to be 410 with 134 adult males, 123 adult females and 153 children. The average household size, adult males, adult females and children were estimated at 5.85, 1.91, 1.76 and 2.18. The maximum figures are 9, 4, 4, and 5 and the minimum figures are 2, 0, 1 and 1 respectively. The respective standard deviations are 1.73, 1, 0.89 and 1.45.

4.2.1.3 Composition of sample households in Keonjhar district

On the whole the 70 households surveyed in Keonjhar district have a total of 359 persons comprising 127 adult males, 122 adult females and 110 children. The average number of adult males, adult females and children come to 1.81, 1.74 and 1.57 respectively and the average household size in the sample is 5.12. The maximum numbers of adult males, adult females, children and household size in the sample have been found to be 4, 4, 5 and 16 respectively. Their respective minimum values are 0, 1, 0 and 2. The concerned standard deviations are estimated at 0.95, 0.71, 1.33 and 1.66.

4.2.1.4 Composition of sample households in the study area

Taking all the 210 sample households in the study area into consideration the population comes to 1129 persons, of which 375 are adult males, 352 are adult females and 402 are children. The average household size, adult males, adult females and children are 5.37, 1.78, 1.67 and 1.91 with standard deviations 1.69, 0.92, 0.75 and 1.40 respectively. The maximum figures for these variables are 10, 4, 6 and 5 and their minimum figures are 2, 0, 1 and 0 respectively.

Households own three categories of land such as agricultural land, homestead land and fallow land. Agricultural land is the fountainhead of income in the rural areas and land in general is the only asset for most of the households in hamlets and villages. Therefore, the size of land in general and that of agricultural land in particular, owned by a household can have a bearing on the share of income from forest sources in its total income. The land question is captured in *Table-4.2* and analysed in the context of the sample households.

4.2.2.1 Land holding status of sample households in Balasore district

The total amount of all land owned by the 70 sample households in Balasore district comes to 96.29 acres comprising agricultural land of 72.71 acres, homestead land of 15.81 acres and fallow land of 7.77 acres. The size of land per household has been estimated at 1.37 acre with 1.03 acres of agricultural land, 0.23 acre of homestead land and 0.11 acre of fallow land. The maximum amount of agricultural land, homestead land,

Table-4.1: Household Composition

STATISTICS	BALASORE				MAYURBHANJ				KEONJHAR				ALL HOUSEHOLDS			
	Adult Males	Adult Females	Children	Household Size	Adult Males	Adult Females	Children	Household Size	Adult Males	Adult Females	Children	Household Size	Adult Males	Adult Females	Children	Household Size
TOTAL	114.00	107.00	139.00	360.00	134.00	123.00	153.00	410.00	127.00	122.00	110.00	359.00	375.00	352.00	402.00	1129.00
AVERAGE	1.63	1.52	1.98	5.14	1.91	1.76	2.18	5.85	1.81	1.74	1.57	5.12	1.78	1.67	1.91	5.37
MAXIMUM	4.00	6.00	5.00	8.00	4.00	4.00	5.00	9.00	4.00	4.00	5.00	16.00	4.00	6.00	5.00	10.00
MINIMUM	0.00	1.00	0.00	2.00	1.00	1.00	0.00	2.00	0.00	1.00	0.00	2.00	0.00	1.00	0.00	2.00
STANDARD DEVIATION	0.90	0.81	1.37	1.61	0.89	0.71	1.45	1.73	0.95	0.71	1.33	1.66	0.92	0.75	1.40	1.69

Source: Primary Survey

Table-4.2: Land Status of Sample Households

(In Acres)

STATISTICS	BALASORE				MAYURBHANJ				KEONJHAR				ALL HOUSEHOLDS			
	Cultivated Land	Homestead Land	Fallow land	All land	Cultivated Land	Homestead Land	Fallow land	All land	Cultivated Land	Homestead Land	Fallow land	All land	Cultivated Land	Homestead Land	Fallow land	All land
TOTAL	72.71	15.81	7.77	96.29	170.60	26.91	33.19	230.70	151.52	16.91	27.79	196.22	394.83	59.63	68.75	523.21
AVERAGE	1.03	0.23	0.11	1.37	2.43	0.39	0.47	3.29	2.16	0.24	0.39	2.79	1.88	0.28	0.32	2.48
MAXIMUM	5.00	1.50	3.00	5.48	10.00	2.00	2.00	12.00	14.00	1.00	4.00	16.00	14.00	2.00	4.00	16.00
MINIMUM	0.00	0.01	0.00	0.05	0.00	0.03	0.00	0.10	0.00	0.01	0.00	0.06	0.00	0.01	0.00	0.05
STANDARD DEVIATION	1.08	0.23	0.41	1.24	2.08	0.42	0.67	2.44	2.12	0.23	0.67	2.54	1.92	0.32	0.62	2.30

Source: Primary Survey

fallow land and all land owned in the sample are found to be 5.0, 1.5, 3.0 and 5.48 acres respectively and their respective minimum values are 0.00, 0.01, 0.00, and 0.50 acre with standard deviations of 1.08, 0.23,0.41 and 1.24 acres in that order.

4.2.2.2 Land holding status of sample households in Mayurbhanj district

The total of all categories of land for the sample households in Mayurbhanj district is 230.70 acres consisting of 170.60 acres of agricultural land, 26.91 acres of homestead land and 33.19 acres of fallow land. The total land holding per household has been estimated at 3.29 acres which comprises cultivated land of 2.43 acres, homestead land of 0.39 acre and fallow land of 0.47 acre. The maximum amount of agricultural land, homestead land, fallow land and all land in the sample are estimated at 10.00, 2.00, 2.00 and 12.00 acres respectively and their minimum values are 0.00, 0.03, 0.00 and 0.10 acre with standard deviations 2.08, 0.42, 0.67 and 2.44 acres respectively.

4.2.2.3 Land holding status of sample households in Keonjhar district

For this district, the total amount of all land owned by all the sample households is196.22acres comprising agricultural land of 151.52 acres, homestead land of 16.91 acres and fallow land of 27.79 acres. The amount of land per sample household has been estimated at 2.79 acres of which agricultural land is 2.16 acres, homestead land is 0.24 acre and fallow land is 0.39 acre. The maximum amount of agricultural land, homestead land, fallow land and all categories of land are estimated at 14.00, 1.00, 4.00 and 16 acres respectively and the concerned minimum values are 0.00, 0.01, 0.00 and 0.06 acre with standard deviations 2.12, 0.23, 0.67 and 2.54 acres respectively.

4.2.2.4 Land holding status for all the sample households

For all the 210 sample households, the total land is found to be 523.21 acres with the breakup of agricultural land of 394.83 acres, homestead land of 59.63 acres and fallow land of 68.75 acres and the average figures are 2.48 acres, 1.88 acres, 0.28 acres and 0.32 acres respectively. The maximum figures are 16.00 acres, 14.00 acres, 2.00 acres and 4.00 acres respectively and the concerned minimum figures are 0.05, 0.00, 0.01 and 0.00 acres with the standard deviations 2.30, 1.92, 0.32 and 0.62 acres in that order.

4.2.3 Livestock Position of Sample Households

During the field survey it was observed that the sample households possess a variety of livestock such as bullocks, buffaloes, cows, calves, goats, sheep, pigs and hens. It can be reasoned that possession of livestock lowers the dependence on forest for livelihood. For they yield income and act as insurance against risk. But it is equally true that the households depend on common property forests to feed their livestock. The larger the number of livestock possessed by a household the greater can be its dependence on forests as the animal stock get much better-quality feed from CPR forests than village grazing lands. It has come out during the field survey that on the average the animals graze in the CPR forests for 6 to 8 hours every day round the year. It is thus possible to link the livestock held by the households and their dependence on common property forests. This dimension is discussed below in terms of *Table-4.3*.

4.2.3.1 Livestock position of sample households in Balasore district

The sample households in Balasore district as a whole possess bullocks, cows, calves, goats, pigs and hens and the total figures for each category are 91.00, 11.00, 13.00, 125.00, 2.00 and 9.00 respectively with maximum stocks 6.00, 2.00, 3.00, 20.00, 2.00 and 3.00 respectively and minimum values zero in all cases. The estimated standard deviations of different categories of livestock at household level are 1.36, 0.43, 0.57, 3.63, 0.23 and 0.53 respectively. The total number of all livestocks for the sample households in the district is 251.00.

4.2.3.2 Livestock position of sample households in Mayurbhanj district

On the whole the sample households in Mayurbhanj district have been found to have reared all livestock listed above at 4.2.3.1except pigs. Additionally, they possess buffaloes. The total of bullocks, buffaloes, cows, calves, goats, sheep and hens are found to be 81, 25, 65, 47, 165, 22 and 39 respectively. At

Table-4.3: Livestock Position of Sample Households

District	Statistics	Bullocks	Buffalo	Cow	Calf	Goat	Sheep	Pig	Hen	All
Balasore	**Total Livestocks**	**91.00**	**0.00**	**11.00**	**13.00**	**125.00**	**0.00**	**2.00**	**9.00**	**251.00**
	Average	1.30	0.00	0.15	0.18	1.78	0.00	0.02	0.12	
	Maximum	6.00	0.00	2.00	3.00	20.00	0.00	2.00	3.00	
	Minimum	0.00	0.00	0.00	0.00	0.00	0.00	0.00	0.00	
	Standard Deviation	1.36	-	0.43	0.57	3.63	-	0.23	0.53	
Mayurbhanj	**Total Livestocks**	**81.00**	**25.00**	**65.00**	**47.00**	**165.00**	**22.00**	**0.00**	**39.00**	**444.00**
	Average	1.15	0.35	0.92	0.67	2.35	0.31	0.00	0.55	
	Maximum	4.00	4.00	4.00	20.00	15.00	5.00	0.00	20.00	
	Minimum	0.00	0.00	0.00	0.00	0.00	0.00	0.00	0.00	
	Standard Deviation	1.21	0.99	1.18	2.51	3.11	1.01	-	2.60	
Keonjhar	**Total Livestocks**	**111.00**	**0.00**	**46.00**	**28.00**	**158.00**	**53.00**	**2.00**	**10.00**	**408.00**
	Average	1.58	0.00	0.65	0.40	2.25	0.75	0.02	0.14	
	Maximum	4.00	0.00	8.00	5.00	17.00	10.00	2.00	10.00	
	Minimum	0.00	0.00	0.00	0.00	0.00	0.00	2.00	0.00	
	Standard Deviation	0.89	-	1.30	0.93	3.43	2.03	0.23	1.19	

	Total Livestocks	**283.00**	**25.00**	**122.00**	**88.00**	**448.00**	**75.00**	**4.00**	**58.00**	**1103.00**
All Households	**Average**	1.34	0.12	0.58	0.41	2.13	0.36	0.02	0.27	
	Maximum	6.00	4.00	8.00	20.00	20.00	10.00	2.00	20.00	
	Minimum	0.00	0.00	0.00	0.00	0.00	0.00	0.00	0.00	
	Standard Deviation	1.18	0.50	1.09	1.58	3.39	1.34	0.19	1.68	

Source: Primary Survey

the household level the average holdings have been estimated at 1.15, 0.35, 0.92, 0.67, 2.35, 0.31 and 0.55 respectively and maximum figures 4.00, 4.00, 4.00, 20.00, 15.00, 5.00 and 20.00 respectively. The minimum is zero in all cases. Their standard deviations are 1.21, 0.99, 1.18, 2.51, 3.11, 1.01 and 2.60.The total of all categories of live stocks for the sample households in the district comes to 444.00.

4.2.3.3 Livestock position of sample households in Keonjhar district

The sample households for this district have been found to own bullocks, cows, calves, goats, sheep, pigs and hens with numbers 111, 46, 28, 158, 53, 2 and 10 respectively. The average holding at household level is 1.58, 0.65, 0.40, 2.25, 0.75, 0.02 and 0.14 respectively with standard deviations 0.89, 1.30, 0.93, 3.43, 2.03, 0.23 and 1.19 respectively. The maximum figures are 4.00, 8.00, 5.00, 17.00, 10.00, 2.00, and 10.00 respectively, the minimum being zero in all cases. For the whole sample of 70 households the estimated total livestock is 408.00.

4.2.3.4 Livestock position of all the sample households

For all the 210 sample households the total numbers of bullocks, buffaloes, cows, calves, goats, sheeps, pigs and hens have been 283.00, 25.00, 122.00, 88.00, 488.00, 75.00, 4.00 and 58.00 respectively with their average size 1.34, 0.12, 0.58, 0.41, 2.13, 0.36, 0.02, and 0.27 and maximum figures 6.00, 4.00, 8.00, 20.00, 20.00,10.00 2.00 and 20.00 respectively. The standard deviations in these cases are 1.18, 0.60, 1.09, 1.58, 3.39, 1.34, 0.19 and 1.68 respectively. For all the surveyed households covering three districts as a whole the total number of livestock is 1103.00.

4.2.4 Household Income and its Composition

The level and sources of income are an important indicator of economic status at the household level. It may be fairly argued that households with higher income depend less on common property forest resources than those with very low levels of income. This is because poor households collect a variety of materials from common forests for their livelihood and use forests as insurance against risk during worklessness, natural calamities, crop failure and other handicap situations compared to those with high income. It is, therefore, important to study the income aspect at the household level. This section delves into the income question. For simplicity we have made a twofold classification of income by sources. i.e., income from forest sources including imputed value of forest produce collected and used for household consumption and those from non-forest sources. Relevant data are presented in Table-4.4.

Table-4.4: Household Income by Source

(In Rupees)

District	*Statistics*	*Income from Non-Forest Source*	*Income from Forest Source*	*Income from All Sources*
Balasore	**Total**	**30,24,427.00**	**10,63,025.00**	**40,87,452.00**
	Average	4,3206.10	15,186.07	58,392.17
	Max	1,77,400.00	28.325.00	1,86,747.00
	Min	10,000.00	7,313.00	23,393.00
	Standard Deviation	30,446.74	4,397.00	30,683.84
Mayurbhanj	**Total**	**15,32,850.00**	**9,63,361.00**	**24,96,211.00**
	Average	21,897.85	13,762.30	35,660.15
	Max	3,20,000.00	29,100.00	3,41,100.00
	Min	3,000.00	6,590.00	11,900.00
	Standard Deviation	38,340.68	4,336.73	40,095.88
Keonjhar	**Total**	**19,13,215.00**	**8,76,519.00**	**27,89,734.00**
	Average	27,331.64	12,521.70	39,853.34
	Max	2,13,000.00	20,630.00	2,28,933.00
	Min	3,000.00	6,260.00	15,050.00
	Standard Deviation	31,617.34	3,360.41	32,376.53
All	**Total**	**64,70,492.00**	**29,02,905.00**	**93,73,397.00**
	Average	30,811.86	13,823.36	44,635.22
	Max	3,20,000.00	29,100.00	3,41,100.00
	Min	3,000.00	6,260.00	11,900.00
	Standard Deviation	34,691.62	4,184.92	35,856.50

Source: Primary Survey

4.2.4.1 Level and composition of household income of sample households in Balasore district

The annual total income of the sample households as a whole in Balasore district has been estimated at Rs 40, 87,452.00

of which the contribution of non-forest sources is Rs 30, 24, 427.00 and that of forest sources is Rs 10, 63, 025.00. The average annual income comes to Rs 58, 392.17 and the average annual income from the non-forest and forest sources are Rs 43,206.10 and Rs 15, 186.07 respectively. The maximum values for household total income, non-forest income and forest income are Rs 1,86, 747.00, Rs 1,77,400.00 and Rs 28, 325.00 respectively with their minimum values Rs 23,393.00, Rs 10,000.00 and Rs 7,313.00, and their standard deviations Rs 30, 683.84, Rs 30, 446.70 and Rs 4, 397.96.

4.2.4.2 Level and Composition of Household Income of Sample Households in Mayurbhanj District

In Mayurbhanj district the annual total income of the sample households is Rs 24, 96,211.00 consisting of Rs 15, 32,850.00 from non-forest sources and Rs 9, 63, 361.00 from forest sources. The average income is Rs 35, 660.15, with the average non-forest income of Rs 21, 897.85 and average forest income of Rs 13, 762.30. The maximum values of total income, non-forest income and forest income at the household level are Rs 3, 41, 000.00, Rs 3,20,000.00 and Rs 29, 100.00 respectively and their minimum values are Rs 11,900.00, Rs 3,000.00 and Rs 6,590.00 with standard deviations Rs 40,095.88, Rs 38,340.68 and Rs 4,336.73 respectively.

4.2.4.3 Level and Composition of Household Income of Sample Households in Keonjhar District

The annual total income of the surveyed households has been found to be Rs 27, 89,734.00 with the non-forest share of Rs 1913215.00 and forest share of Rs 8, 76,519.00. The average of these incomes are Rs 39, 853.34, Rs 27, 331.64 and Rs 12, 521.70 respectively. The maximum values of total, non-forest and forest incomes are Rs 2, 28, 933.00, Rs 2,13,000.00 and Rs 20, 630.00 and their minimum values are Rs 15, 050.00, Rs 3,000.00 and Rs 6,260.00 with standard deviations of Rs 32, 376.53, Rs 31, 617.34 and Rs 3, 360.41 respectively.

4.2.4.4 Level and Composition of Household Income for All Sample Households

For all the 210 sample households, the estimated annual

total income is Rs 93, 73, 397.00 of which the contribution of non-forest and forest sources are Rs 64, 70, 492.00 and Rs 29, 02, 905.00 respectively. The average of total, non-forest and forest incomes are Rs 44, 635.22, Rs 30,811.86 and Rs 13, 823.36 respectively. The maximum values of total income, non-forest income and forest income at the household level are Rs 3, 41, 100.00, 3, 20,000.00 and Rs 29,100.00 and their minimum values are Rs 11,900.00, Rs 3,000.00 and Rs 6,260.00 with standard deviations Rs 35,856.50, Rs 34, 691.62 and Rs 4, 184.92 respectively.

It is thus clear that forest sources are a significant contributor to household income, although their share is less in comparison to the non-forest sources in all cases. The same pattern is clearly visible in the sample districts and blocks.

4.3 Common Property Forest Dependency of Sample Households

We have seen above that the sample households derive their income from two sources- non-forest and forest sources. The share of the forest component gives a summary picture of the forest dependency of households in the study area. Decomposition of income from forest sources will show reasonable insights into such dependency. For analytical purposes we have divided income from forest sources into two broad groups on the basis of information collected during field survey. They are income from sales and imputed income. Income from sales are further subdivided into income from sales of NTFPs and products of forest-based activities (FBAs) while imputed income is decomposed into value of fuel wood, timber and bamboo collected from forests and used in the household. Table-4.5 shows sample households' forest dependency.

4.3.1 Common Property Forest Dependency of Sample Households in Balasore District

In the case of Balasore district income from non-forest sources constitutes 73.99 per cent and that from forest sources accounts for 26.01 per cent of the annual income of a household. Income from sales has a share of 8.66 per cent in household

Table-4.5: Common Property Forest Dependency of Sample Households

DISTRICT	Non Forest Source	Common Property Forest Source								Grand Total
		Income from Sales			Imputed Income				Total Forest	
		NTFP Sales	Products of Forest Based Activities	*Total*	Fuel Wood	Timber	Bamboo	*Total*		
BALASORE	***43206.10 (73.99)***	1628.01 (2.79) [10.72]	3427.71 (5.87) [22.57]	***5055.72 (8.66) [33.29]***	7785.26 (13.33) [51.27]	1772.55 (3.04) [11.67]	572.53 (0.98) [3.77]	***10130.34 (17.35) [66.71]***	***15186.06 (26.01) [100.00]***	**58392.16 (100.00)**
MAYURBHANJ	***21897.84 61.41)***	3467.81 (9.72) [25.20]	128.45 (0.36) [0.93]	***3596.26 (10.08) [26.13]***	7603.71 (21.32) [55.25]	2183.68 (6.12) [15.87]	378.62 (1.06) [2.75]	***10166.01 (28.51) [73.87]***	***13762.27 (38.59) [100.00]***	**35660.11 (100.00)**
KEONJHAR	***27331.60 (68.58)***	1984.07 (4.98) [15.85]	880.50 (2.21) [7.03]	***2864.57 (7.19) [22.88]***	8418.29 (21.12) [67.23]	1115.88 (2.80) [8.91]	122.88 (0.31) [0.98]	***9657.05 (24.23) [77.12]***	***12521.62 (31.42) [100.00]***	**39853.22 (100.00)**
ALL	***30811.85 (69.03)***	2360.00 (5.29) [17.07]	1478.90 (3.31) [10.70]	***3838.90 (8.60) [27.77]***	7935.75 (17.78) [57.41]	1690.70 (3.79) [12.23]	358.00 (0.80) [2.59]	***9984.45 (22.37) [72.23]***	***13823.35 (30.97) [100.00]***	**44635.20 (100.00)**

Note: Figures in ( ) indicate percentages in grand total.

Figures in [ ] indicate percentages in total forest income

Source: Primary Survey

income and as much as 33.29 per cent of the income derived from forest sources. Imputed value of produce collected from the forests and used in the household accounts for 17.35 per cent of annual household income and 66.71 per cent of its income obtained from forest sources. It can be seen from the table that the share of imputed income is double that of income derived from sales of forest produce. Again, in the category of income from sales of forest produce, FBAs have a share more than double that of NTFPs. In the imputed income group fuel wood has the highest share followed by timber and bamboo in that order. On the whole, fuel wood accounts for the highest percentage of total income as also of total forest income to a household during a year.

4.3.2 Common Property Forest Dependency of Sample Households in Mayurbhanj District

The situation is little different in the case of Mayurbhanj district. Here income from non-forest sources has a lower share (61.41 per cent) and that from forest sources a higher share (38.59 per cent) in the annual income of a household compared to Balasore district. Sales of NTFPs and products of FBAs account for 10.08 per cent of household income and 26.13 per cent of income obtained from forest sources. Imputed income from forest sources constitutes 28.51 per cent of annual income of a household and 73. 87 per cent of its income derived from forest sources. Imputed income is 2.8 times greater than forest income from sales. Within income from sales proceeds, FBAs have a very insignificant share and that from NTFPs is substantially very large. Unsurprisingly fuel wood has the highest share in the category of imputed income followed by timber and bamboo. It is also the single largest source of income for a household.

4.3.3 Common Property Forest Dependency of Sample Households in Keonjhar District

In Keonjhar district income from non-forest sources accounts for 68.58 per cent and that from forest sources constitutes 31.42 per cent of annual income of a household. Income from sales of NTFPs and output of FBAs has a 7.19

per cent share in household income and as high as 22.88 per cent of its income from forest sources as a whole. Imputed income from forests has a share of 24.23 per cent of annual household income and 77.12 per cent of that from common property forest resources. It is more than thrice the income from sales of NTFPs and products of FBAs. In the sales proceeds category NTFPs group has a far bigger share (15.85 per cent) than FBAs (7.03 per cent). In the category of imputed income, fuel wood dominates both as percentage of forest income and of total income of a household.

4.3.4 Common Property Forest Dependency of All Sample Households

A similar composition of annual income and forest dependency at the household level is observed for the sample as a whole. Share of non-forest income is 69.03 per cent and that of forest income is 30.97 per cent of the household annual income. Forest income from sales proceeds has a share of 8.60 per cent with NTFPs accounting for 5.29 per cent and FBAs, 3.31 per cent while that from imputed value of forest produce collected by and used in a household has a 22.37 per cent share comprising contributions from fuel wood (17.78 per cent), timber (3.79 per cent) and bamboo (0.80 per cent). Sales proceeds account for 27.77 per cent of total forest income with NTFPs constituting 17.07 per cent and FBAs 10.70 per cent but imputed income constitutes 72.23 per cent of forest income with fuel wood having the largest share (57.41 per cent) followed by timber (12.23 per cent) and bamboo (2.59 per cent).

It is thus clear that the share of forest sources in household annual income is very high (around 31 per cent) of which imputed value of forest produce used in a household has a lions share and direct sales are much less. Fuel wood is seen to be the single largest contributor to imputed income, all forest income and household income as a whole. This suggests that in the study area the households are critically dependent on common property forests. They earn direct income by sales of NTFPs, products of FBAs and livelihood by collecting fuel wood, timber and bamboo from the forests.

4.4 Heterogeneity and Common Property Forest Dependency

The literature on CPRs is quite large. Some of this literature have covered the relationship between CPRs and economic inequality. Income inequality can be taken as a proxy for economic inequality/heterogeneity and linked to common property forest dependency at the household level. This aspect is analyzed in terms of quintile and decile groups of income, and classification of sample households by BPL and non-BPL categories.

4.4.1 Common Property Forest Dependency by Quintile Groups

Classification of a sample by quintile groups reflects division of the sample into five classes having 20 percent of sample in each class. Analysis of data by quintiles captures the existence of inequality among the sample households and the relationship of such inequality with the variable. An attempt has been made here to examine common property forest dependency of sample households by quintiles and to assess the impact of economic inequality/heterogeneity on such dependency at the household level. Relevant data are presented in Table-4.6.

Table-4.6: CPR Forest Dependency by Quintile Groups
(In Rupees)

DISTRICT	*Quintile Groups in Ascending Order*	*Household Average Income from Non-Forest Source*	*HH Average Income from CPR Forest Source (Sales + Imputed)*	*HH Average Total Income*
BALASORE	1st	16342.15(52.38)	14855.43*(47.62)*	31197.57*(100.00)*
	2nd	27367.86(67.53)	13159.79*(32.47)*	40527.64*(100.00)*
	3rd	34451.93(68.27)	16008.79*(31.73)*	50460.71*(100.00)*
	4th	45654.29(77.37)	16569.57*(26.63)*	62223.86*(100.00)*
	5th	92214.28(85.74)	15336.79*(14.26)*	107551.07*(100.00)*
MAYURBHANJ	1st	7011.43(40.82)	10166.14*(59.18)*	17177.57*(100.00)*
	2nd	8950.72(41.50)	12619.57*(58.50)*	21570.29*(100.00)*
	3rd	13315(50.70)	12948.14*(49.30)*	26263.14*(100.00)*
	4th	20947.14(58.62)	14784.21*(41.38)*	35731.36*(100.00)*
	5th	59265(76.41)	18293.43*(23.59)*	77558.43*(100.00)*
KEONJHAR	1st	8360.71(44.78)	10311.29*(55.22)*	18672*(100.00)*
	2nd	12011.43(50.81)	11628.71*(49.19)*	23640.14*(100.00)*

3rd	16390(54.60)	13631*(45.40)*	30021*(100.00)*
4th	26948.22(66.74)	13431.71*(33.26)*	40379.93*(100.00)*
5th	72947.86(84.28)	13605.79*(15.72)*	86553.64*(100.00)*

Note: Figures in parentheses indicate percentages to respective row total

Source: Primary Survey

4.4.1.1 Dependency by quintile groups in Balasore district

The annual income of a household in the first, second, third, fourth and fifth quintiles in Balasore district have been found to be Rs 31,197.57, Rs 40,527.64, Rs 50,460.71, Rs 62,223.86 and Rs 1, 07,551.07 respectively. The share of non-forest income in household income in these quintiles have been 52.38 per cent, 67.53 per cent, 68.27 per cent, 73.37 per cent and 85.74 per cent respectively and that of forest component have been 47.62 per cent, 32.47 per cent, 31.73 per cent, 26.63 per cent and 14.26 per cent in that order. It is thus evident that the share of forest source in household income decreases as we move from the lowest (first) quintile to the highest (fifth) quintile suggesting that poor households are more dependent on common forests than their rich counterparts.

4.4.1.2 Dependency by Quintile Groups in Mayurbhanj District

For the sample households of Mayurbhanj district the annual income of a household in the first, second, third, fourth and fifth quintiles is estimated at Rs 17,177.57, Rs 21, 570.29, Rs 26,263.14, Rs 35,731.36 and Rs 77,558.43 with 40.82 per cent, 41.50 percent, 50.70 per cent, 58.62 per cent and 76.41 per cent shares of non-forest sources and 59.18 per cent, 58.50 per cent, 49.30 per cent, 41.38 per cent and 23.59 per cent shares of common property forest sources respectively. It is clear that the share of forest sources in a household's income varies inversely with its income from all sources indicating that for the poorer households forest dependency is higher than the richer households.

4.4.1.3 Dependency by Quintile Groups in Keonjhar District

The situation is not different in Keonjhar district in which the average total household income in the first quintile works out to Rs 18,672.00 with 44.78 per cent share of non-forest sources and 55.22 per cent share of forest sources. In the second quintile the respective figures are Rs 23,640.14, 50.81 per cent and 49.19 per cent; in the third quintile they are Rs 30,021.00, 54.60 per cent and 45.40 per cent; in the fourth quintile, they are Rs 40, 379.93, 66.74 per cent and 33.26 per cent; and in the highest (fifth) quintile, they are Rs 86,553.64, 84.28 per cent and 15.72 per cent.

In this district the share of forest sources in household income is the highest in the lowest (first) quintile followed by those in the second, third and fourth quintiles, and is the lowest in the highest (fifth) quintile. This shows the poorer a household in terms of the income parameter, the more dependent is it on common property forests and vice versa. It is no gainsaying then that a household's income position impacts on its dependence on common forests and that the dependency is higher in the case of the poorer households in comparison to the richer households.

4.4.2Common Property Forest Dependency by Decile Groups

Classification by deciles means division of a population in to ten classes with each class having ten per cent of the population in it. Data analysis in terms of deciles can show the extent of inequality/ equality among the population. We have attempted to examine the interlinkage between economic (income) heterogeneity (inequality) and dependence on common forests at the household level in the sample villages by looking at the decile groups. Quantitative information is given in Table-4.7.

Table-4.7: CPR Forest Dependency by Decile Groups (in Rupees)

Decile Groups in Ascending Order	*Non-Forest Source*	*HH Average Income from CPR Forest(Sales + Imputed)*	*HH Average Total Income*
1st	7081.90***(41.30)***	10063.71***(58.70)***	17145.62***(100.00)***
2nd	9338.58***(44.59)***	11606.86***(55.41)***	20945.43***(100.00)***
3rd	11931.43***(49.40)***	12218.9***(50.60)***	24150.33***(100.00)***
4th	14658.57***(52.00)***	13531.52***(48.00)***	28190.10***(100.00)***
5th	18184.28***(55.39)***	14642.57***(44.61)***	32826.86***(100.00)***

6th	23337.85*(62.01)*	14296.62*(37.99)*	37634.48*(100.00)*
7th	30446.04*(68.67)*	13890.19*(31.33)*	44336.24*(100.00)*
8th	36870.47*(69.79)*	15962.86*(30.21)*	52833.33*(100.00)*
9th	47769.52*(74.93)*	15980.29*(25.07)*	63749.81*(100.00)*
10th	108500*(87.12)*	16040.05*(12.88)*	124540.05*(100.00)*

Note: Figures in parentheses indicate percentages to respective row total Source: Primary Survey

It can be read off the table that non-forest sources dominate in the annual income of a household in the higher deciles while forest sources have a high share in the case of households in the lower deciles. The annual average income of a household in the first, second, third, fourth, fifth, sixth, seventh, eighth, ninth and tenth deciles have been estimated at Rs 17,145.62, Rs 20,943.43, Rs 24,150.33, Rs 28,190.10, Rs 32, 826.86, Rs 37,634.48, Rs 44,336.24, Rs 52,833.33,Rs 63,749.81 and Rs 1,24,540.05 respectively with shares of forest income at 58.70 per cent, 55.41 per cent, 50.60 per cent, 48.00 per cent, 44.61 per cent, 37.99 per cent, 31.33 per cent, 30.21 per cent, 25.07 per cent and 12.88 per cent, the balance being from non-forest sources in each case.

The findings are interesting. The households in the lowest income decile (first decile) with average income of Rs17, 145.62 have the highest share from forest sources (58.70 per cent) in their income and those in the highest decile (tenth decile) with average income of Rs 1, 24, 540.05 have the lowest share from forest sources (12.88 per cent) in their income. The same pattern is found when we move from the lower to the higher deciles. These results are in conformity with those obtained in the analysis by quintile groups i.e., the poorer households are more dependent on common property forest resources than the richer ones. Alternatively, economic heterogeneity impacts on the dependence on forests.

4.4.3 Common property Forest Dependency by Poverty Status

The foregoing analysis reveals that people with lower income are more dependent on common forests than those with higher income. Low level of income may mean poverty and the later can be linked to forest dependency. In India and in Odisha as well, poverty of a household is given an official status with issuance of a BPL card.

Table-4.8: CPR Forest Dependency of BPL and Non-BPL Categories *(In Rupees)*

Statistics	*BPL Households (152)*			*Non-BPL households (58)*		
	Income From			*Income From*		
	Non-Forest Sources	*Forest Sources*	*Total Income*	*Non-Forest Sources*	*Forest Sources*	*Total Income*
Total	4453402.00	2069084.00	6522486.00	2017090.00	833821.00	2850911.00
Percentage	68.28	31.72	100.00	70.75	29.25	100.00
Mean	29298.70	13612.40	42911.10	34777.41	14376.22	49153.63
Max	213000.00	28325.00	228933.00	320000.00	29100.00	341100.00
Min	3000.00	6260.00	11900.00	7000.00	7440.00	15440.00
Stdev.	28145.53	3880.83	29544.81	47876.93	4887.60	48714.28

Note: BPL-Below Poverty Line, APL-Above Poverty Line

Source: Primary Survey.

Using BPL card holding as an accepted indicator of poverty of a household we have attempted to discuss the linkage between poverty and common property forest dependency in the study area. For a comparative analysis we have divided all the sample households into BPL and non-BPL categories and their income into forest and non-forest sources. Data relating to this aspect is given in Table-4.8.

It can be seen from the table that the total income of all the 152 BPL households is Rs 65,22,486.00 consisting of Rs 44,53,402.00 (68.28 per cent) from non-forest sources and Rs 20, 69,084.00 (31.72 per cent) from forest sources. The respective mean values are Rs 42,911.10, Rs 29,298.70 and Rs 13,612.40; maximum values are Rs 2, 28,933.00, Rs 2, 13,000.00 and Rs 28,325.00; minimum values are Rs 11,900.00, Rs 3,000.00, Rs 6,260.00; and standard deviations are Rs 29,544.81, Rs 28,145.53 and Rs 3,880.83. For the non-BPL category of 58 households in the sample the total income is Rs 28, 50,911.00 having a non-forest source component of Rs 20, 17,090.00 (70.75 per cent) and a forest component of Rs 8, 33,821.00 (29.25 per cent). The mean of total income for this group of households is Rs 49,153.63, the mean income from non-forest sources is Rs 34,777.41 and from forest sources it is Rs 14,376.22. The maximum values of household income for the non-BPL sample is Rs 3,41,100.00, of which income from non-forest sources is

Rs 3,20,000.00 and from forest sources it is Rs 29,100.00. The respective minimum values are Rs 15,440.00, Rs 7,000.00 and Rs 7,440.00 and standard deviations of total income, income from non-forest sources and that from forest sources are Rs 48,714.28, Rs 47,876.93 and Rs 4,877.60 respectively.

Since BPL households obtain 31.72 per cent of their annual income from forest sources compared to 29.25 per cent of the non-BPL households, we can conclude the existence of a direct relationship between poverty and common property forest dependency.

4.5 Determinants of Common Property Forest Dependency

Analysis of field survey data thus far has clearly demonstrated that as we move from the highest income group to the lowest income group in the income distribution, household level dependency on CPR forests increases. This is indicative of the fact that households with lower incomes are more CPR forest dependent than those with higher incomes. Low household income, poor asset holding status, large household size and lack of adequate and gainful off forest employment opportunities may be the explanatory variables. In order to know the determinants of household level dependency on CPR forests, we have applied a regression model to the primary survey data. The model seeks to establish a linear functional relationship between the percentage of forest income to total household income in a year as the dependent variable (Y) and total annual household income (X1), household size (X2) and a household's possession of agricultural land (X3) as the independent variables.

A negative relationship is expected between the share of forest income in the total household income(Y) and total household income (X1). This is because higher income may be associated with a relatively greater contribution from off forest income yielding activities. A positive relationship between the percentage contribution of forest income to total household income (Y) and household size (X2) may be fairly expected. It can be reasoned that larger the household size greater will be the livelihood needs, more members from the household can be engaged in collection of materials from forests and higher may be the dependency on CPR forests. As has been discussed earlier, agricultural land is by far the most important form of asset for the rural households and for the vast majority of them it is the only asset and a predominant source of income. The possession of agricultural land (X3) is expected to be negatively related to the share of forest income in household income(Y). This means, households with larger amount of agricultural land are likely to depend less on CPR forest because they can be gainfully engaged in agricultural operations and derive a substantial amount of income from farming and vice-versa. Table-4.9 states the independent variables and their expected signs in relation to the dependent variable in the regression model.

Table-4.9: Determinants of CPR Forest Dependency and their Expected Signs in Relation to the Dependent Variable

Independent Variables (X)	*Expected Relationship with Dependent Variable (Y): Share of Forest Income in Total Income*
X_1= Total Household Income	Negative (-)
X_2= Household Size	Positive (+)
X_3= Agricultural Land	Negative (-)

The ordinary linear regression model may be specified as follows:

$$Y = \beta_o + \beta_1 X_1 + \beta_2 X_2 + \beta_3 X_3 + \varepsilon \quad (1)$$

$$\text{Or, } PercentageofForestincometototalHouseholdIncome = \beta_o + \beta_1 TotalHouseholdIncome + \beta_2 HouseholdSize + \beta_3 \text{ Size of } AgriculturalLand + \varepsilon$$

The coefficients explain the marginal effect of the three variables viz., total household Income, household size, and amount of agricultural land on a household's dependence on CPR forest. These coefficients (β_1, β_2 and β_3) are to be estimated from the data. The estimated regression equation may be written as

$$\widehat{Y} = \widehat{\beta}_o + \widehat{\beta}_1 X_1 + \widehat{\beta}_2 X_2 + \widehat{\beta}_3 X_3$$

Four regression equations have been estimated to study household level dependence on CPR forests-one each for the sample households in the three districts and one for the total sample of 210 households as a whole to capture the direction and effect of the determinants on household level forest dependency. The results of regression analysis have been given in Table-4.10.

Table-4.10: Regression Results

	Balasore		
R^2 =0.530	F= 24.781		Significance = 0.000
	Coefficient	*t-Statistic*	*Significance*
Intercept	40.994	9.064	0.000
Total Household Income	-0.0003	-7.364	0.000
Size of the Household	1.563	2.219	0.029
Agricultural Land	-8.069	-1.630	0.1077
	Mayurbhanj		
R^2 = 0.439	F=17.191		Significance = 0.000
Intercept	41.963	8.223	0.000
Total Household Income	-0.0002	-5.253	0.000
Size of the Household	2.494	3.183	0.002
Agricultural Land	-6.447	-2.048	0.045
	Keonjhar		
R^2 =0.547	F= 26.575		Significance = 0.000
Intercept	39.978	8.484	0.000
Total Household Income	-0.0004	-8.608	0.000
Size of the Household	3.152	3.679	0.000
Agricultural Land	-2.259	-0.365	0.716
	ALL		
R^2 =0.507	F= 70.49		Significance = 0.000
Intercept	40.096	13.667	0.000
Total Household Income	-0.0003	-12.996	0.000

Size of the Household	2.50	5.231	0.000
Agricultural Land	-2.710	-1.058	0.291

Source: Authors' Calculation

4.5.1 Regression Results for the Sample Households in Balasore District

A linear regression equation on the households' forest dependency has been estimated for the 70 sample households in Balasore district. The equation can be expressed as:

$$\hat{Y} = \mathbf{40.994 - 0.0003}X_1 + \mathbf{1.563}X_2 - \mathbf{8.069}X_3 .$$

The goodness of fit (R2) or the explanatory power of the linear regression model is 0.530. It indicates that 53 per cent of variation in the dependent variable (Y) can be explained by the three selected independent variables. The F-statistic of the regression model is also significant at 5 per cent level indicating overall significance of the regression model. The signs of the regression coefficients have appeared as expected. The total income (X1) is negatively related to the dependent variable (Y). The coefficient ($\hat{\beta}_1$ =0.0003) of X1 implies that a marginal increase in total income is likely to reduce the share of forest income in the total household income by 0.0003 per cent suggesting, as expected, that richer households are less forest dependent than the poorer ones. The coefficient ($\hat{\beta}_2$) of the independent variable X2 is estimated at 1.563 suggesting a direct relationship between the percentage share of forest income in the household total income and household size meaning that large sized households are more CPR forest dependent and vice versa. More particularly a marginal increase in household size will raise the share of forest income in a household's income by 1.563 per cent. As expected, the coefficient of X3 in the regression model has also taken a negative value ($\hat{\beta}_3$ =-8.069). This is indicative of the fact that higher agricultural land holding reduces household level CPR forest dependency and that a marginal increase in agricultural land holding will reduce the share of forest income in a household's income by 8.069 per cent. Except agricultural land the coefficients of total household income and household size are significant at 5 per cent level. This means that the model is a good fit.

4.5.2 Regression Results for the Sample Households in Mayurbhanj District

For the 70 sample households in Mayurbhanj district we have estimated a regression equation on the households' forest dependence. The equation is expressed as:

$$\widehat{Y} = 41.963 - 0.0002X_1 + 2.494X_2 - 6.447X_3 .$$

The goodness of fit (R2) or the explanatory power of the linear regression model is 0.439. It indicates that 43.9 per cent of the variation in the dependent variable (Y) can be explained by the three selected independent variables. The F-statistic of the regression model is found to be significant at 5 per cent level showing overall significance of the model. The signs of the regression coefficients have appeared as per our expectation. The total income (X1) is found to be negatively related to the dependent variable (Y). The coefficient (=0.0002) of X1 shows that a marginal increase in total income is likely to reduce the share of forest income in total household income by 0.0002 per cent. The coefficient () of the independent variable X2 has been found to be 2.494 indicating the existence of a direct relationship between the percentage share of forest income in a household's total income and household size. This means that large sized households are more CPR forest dependent than small sized ones and more particularly that a marginal increase in household size raises the share of forest income in a household's income by 2.494 per cent. The coefficient () of X3 in the regression model has also taken a negative value as expected and the same has been estimated at -6.447. This is indicative of the fact that higher agricultural land holding reduces CPR forest dependency at the household level and that a marginal increase in land holding lowers the share of forest income in household income by 6.45 per cent. The three coefficients () are significant at 5 per cent level. This suggests that the regression model is a good fit.

4.5.3 Regression Results for the Sample Households in Keonjhar District

A linear regression equation on household's forest dependency has been estimated for the 70 sample households of Keonjhar district. The estimated regression equation is

The goodness of fit (R2) or the explanatory power of the linear regression model is 0.547 showing that 54.7 per cent of the variation in the dependent variable (Y) is explained by the three selected independent variables. The F-statistic of the regression model is also significant at 5 per cent level. The signs of the regression coefficients have appeared as expected. The total income of a household (X1) is negatively related to the dependent variable (Y). The coefficient () of X1 implies that a marginal increase in total income is likely to reduce a households' share of forest income in its total income by 0.0004 per cent. The coefficient () of the independent variable X2 has an estimated value of 3.152 suggesting that there exists a direct relationship between the percentage share of forest income in a household's total income and household size which means that larger sized households are more CPR forest dependent. More particularly it means that a marginal increase in household size will raise the share of forest income in household income by 3.15 per cent. As expected, the coefficient () of X3 in the regression model has taken a negative value and the same has been estimated at -2.259 suggesting that larger the amount of agricultural land holding of a household, lesser will be its dependence on forests and vice versa. In strict quantitative terms a marginal increase in the size of agricultural land holding reduces the share of forest income in total income of a household by 2.26 per cent. Except the coefficient of agricultural land (, the other two coefficients () are significant at 5 per cent level implying that the model is a good fit.

4.5.4 Regression Results for All the Sample Households

The linear regression equation for all the 210 sample households has been estimated as

$$\widehat{Y} = 39.978 - 0.0004X_1 + 3.152X_2 - 2.259X_3 .$$

The goodness of fit (R2) of the linear regression model is 0.507. The R2 value indicates that 50.7 per cent of the variation in the dependent variable (Y) can be explained by the three independent variables which seem to be quite appealing. The F-statistic of the regression model is significant at 5 per cent level. Interestingly, the signs of the regression coefficients have appeared as expected. The total income (X1) is negatively related to the dependent variable (Y). The coefficient () of X1 has a value of -0.0003 and it indicates that a marginal increase in total income is likely to reduce a households' share of forest income in its total income by 0.0003 per cent. The coefficient () of the independent variable X2 with a value of 2.50 suggests that there exists a direct relationship between the per cent share of forest income in the household total income and household size indicating large sized households are more CPR forest dependent than the small sized ones. In quantitative terms a marginal increase in household size will tend to increase the share of forest income in a household's income by 2.50 per cent. As expected, the coefficient () of X3 in the regression model has a negative value of -2.710. This is indicative of the fact that higher agricultural land holding reduces a household's CPR forest dependency and a marginal increase in agricultural land holding of a household will lower the share of forest income in its annual income from all sources by 2.71 per cent. The regression model is a good fit.

4.6 Summary

The main findings of our primary survey relating to household level dependency on CPR forests in the villages of Odisha may be summarised as follows.

In Odisha, village level dependency on CPR forests is quite high and throughout the year the households are critically dependent on such resources for domestic use, livestock rearing and income generation.

Empirical findings evidence that for the sample households in the three selected districts of Odisha, CPR forest income constitutes 30.97 per cent of the total average annual household income. In the sample villages the share of CPR forest component in the households' annual average income have been estimated at 26.01 per cent, 31.42 per cent and 38.60 per cent in Balasore, Keonjhar and Mayurbhanj districts respectively. The results show that rural households are heavily dependent on CPR forest system. Fuel wood happens to be the single largest component of forest income and household income in all cases.

A direct relationship between the per household availability of CPR forest and the percentage share of CPR forest income in the households' annual average income has been found. But an indirect relationship is also observed between the population size of the village and the percentage share of the CPR forest component in the households' annual average income. People in villages with large population are more CPR forest dependent than those in villages having smaller population.

It is revealed that low income households are more CPR forest dependent than the high-income households. Analysis of field survey data suggests that the contribution of forest sources to household income is found to be the highest for the households in the lowest (first) quintile in income distribution followed by those in the second, third and fourth quintile groups. It is the lowest for the households in the highest (fifth) quintile. For the poorest 10 per cent of the sample households, CPR forest income constitutes 58.70 per cent of their total annual income. The share of this component decreases consistently as we move from the poorest decile to the richest decile. For the richest decile the income share is 12.8 per cent.

Our discussion of the relationship between official poverty status of households and their economic dependence on CPR forests yields similar results. It has been found that households falling under BPL category are more CPR forest dependent than those under the non-BPL category. The shares of CPR forest component in total household income for these two categories of households are estimated at 31.72 per cent and 29.25 per cent respectively.

Regression analysis shows that the household level dependency on CPR forest is negatively related to total household income and agricultural land holding, but directly related to household size. It points to the fact that both economic and demographic factors impact on the CPR forest dependence of the households. This proves our first hypothesis that dependence on common property forests is related directly to household size but inversely to the income and agricultural land holding status of the households. Hence the hypothesis is accepted.

5

Heterogeneity Collective Action and Management of Common Property Forests

5.1 Introduction

The consequences of overexploitation and poor management of natural resources including CPR forests are being manifested in serious environmental degradation and associated problems of climate change, deterioration in livelihood support systems and unsustainable economic growth. Renewable resources like forests, land and water are in fact declining at rates that threaten the basis of already fragile economies (Warford, 1989). The poor countries of the world which depend heavily on natural resource systems are the most vulnerable to damages caused by declining natural resource base. Their poor capital base (physical and human) and their limited ability to switch over to other off CPR gainful economic activities only intensifies the threat. People in the lower echelons of the economy in these countries are likely to suffer the most from the problems of commercial logging, reckless fuel wood harvesting and loss of forest cover; overgrazing, flooding, soil erosion, salinisation, sedimentation and land pollution; and loss of biodiversity which impact heavily on agricultural productivity and livelihood support systems. Efficient management of existing natural resources and CPRs are, therefore, highly essential from the standpoints of ecological balance, equity and sustainable economic growth.

5.2 The Costs of Overexploitation

Natural resources and CPRs in particular, perform very important functions of providing livelihood support, assimilating wastes, safeguarding intergenerational equity and promoting economic growth. But if the rate at which resources are extracted from the natural resource system exceeds their usual regeneration rate, then serious ecological and economic consequences are produced which impact negatively on the life of people and the society.

5.2.1 The Cost of Natural Resource Degradation

Ecology and economy are seen as interlinked and mutually reinforcing. Degradation of natural resource systems including CPRs not only have ecological consequences but also have serious economic implications. It is increasingly recognized by the developmental economists that the conventional measure of Gross National Product (GNP) per capita, provides misleadingly favourable estimates of economic wellbeing or growth of a nation as it disregards the drawing down of natural resource stock (both renewable and non-renewable) over time. Rough estimates show that in many tropical hard wood exporting countries the economic costs of unsustainable forest depletion range between 4 and 6 percent of GDP (Pearce, 1986). Poor and developing countries are characterized by widespread unemployment, under employment, acute poverty and poor quality of human capital. In these countries, natural resources including CPR systems play the role of a sheet anchor for the rural poor. Throughout the year they are directly and/or indirectly depend on such resources for their livelihood as well as supplementing their household income. Poor economic condition and absence of adequate and diverse gainful employment opportunities make the rural poor more dependent on CPRs leading to mounting pressure and depletion of these resource systems. Exploitation of these resources at a rate higher than their natural growth rate has serious negative effects on their livelihood and long-term economic growth. A careful investigation would reveal that many developing countries are experiencing high debt burden and deteriorating terms of trade conditions owing to growing imports to support livelihood in the face of natural resource degradation.

5.2.2 The Marginal Opportunity Cost (MOC) of Resource Depletion

Following Pearce and Markandya (1989) we may consider the use of the concept of marginal opportunity cost (MOC) to measure the economic effects of depletion of natural resources and focus on the need for rational extraction of such resources, their regulation and management and public investment in them. MOC has three elements such as marginal direct cost (MDC), marginal external cost (MEC) and marginal user cost (MUC). MOC=MDC+MEC+MUC. MDC is the cost incurred by the user for extracting the resource. MEC is the cost which the depletion inflicts on the efficiency of other related resources. MUC is the cost of reduced supply in future of the resource.

In the instant case of CPR forests the three elements of MOC of resource depletion or deforestation may be stated as follows. MDC consists of the labour and material costs of extracting forest resources; MEC measures the deforestation led soil erosion, siltation and loss of agricultural productivity; and MUC comprises the scarcity premium on the resource in terms of expected future demand, future supply and availability of substitute(s) of the forest resource.

Complex effects of resource degradation on income distribution, vulnerable groups such as indigenous people, irreversibility, genetic diversity and welfare of future generations etc. need to be taken into consideration for estimating the MOC. The concept serves as a benchmark to make judgements about the benefits of conservation and resource management, including investments, regulation and laws etc. It is extremely important to determine the appropriateness of investment decisions, policy measures and enforcement of various management regimes. The ideal situation for resource extraction calls for equality between MOC and the marginal benefits (MB) that users receive for resource depleting-activities. If MOC were greater than MB it suggests that resource systems are overexploited and signals the need for regulation and control on extraction. But if MOC were less than MB it justifies consumption. The basic problem is that individual/market centric extraction from forests considers only the MDC and overlooks MEC and MUC. As a result the resource gets overexploited and the system is in need of appropriate regulation and management.

5.2.3 Irreversible Effects and Future Generation

Some natural resources are renewable (water, forests etc.) while some others are non-renewable (coal, bauxite, iron ore etc.) Forest resources, though renewable, cannot be extracted limitlessly. Once extracted beyond a critical level, regeneration may not be compensatory and can be manifested in resource depletion and irreversibility. Such depletion may cause reduced availability for future generations and impact on intergenerational equity and human wellbeing.

5.2.4 Vicious Circle of Overexploitation

Environment and economy are not independent entities; they are interdependent in varied ways. The environment is the sole source of material supply for subsistence of life and economic growth as also the sink for assimilating wastes. Overexploitation of environmental resources creates hazards and can threaten life on this planet. The following chart presents an outline of a simple view of how the environment and the rural economy are interlinked with special reference to the problem of overuse of CPR forests. It shows the vicious circle of overexploitation and degradation of CPR forests.

As seen in the chart, overexploitation of CPR forests lowers resource availability leading to longer collection time and a greater distance to be covered than before for collecting materials both of which entail significant loss of labour. It also leads to fuel wood scarcity and the consequential diversion of dung and crop residues for cooking purposes resulting in reduced availability of fodder which impacts negatively on the growth of the livestock sector. A third way in which degradation of CPR forests can affect the economy is by causing increased runoff, soil erosion, siltation, sedimentation, salinity, warming, reduced water recycling and inadequate rains. These, in turn, reduce hydropower generation and supply, unfavourable monsoons, lesser irrigation and reduced soil fertility all of which culminate in loss of agricultural productivity. The diversion of crop residues for cooking causing

Chart 1: Vicious Circle of Overexploitation and Degradation of Forests

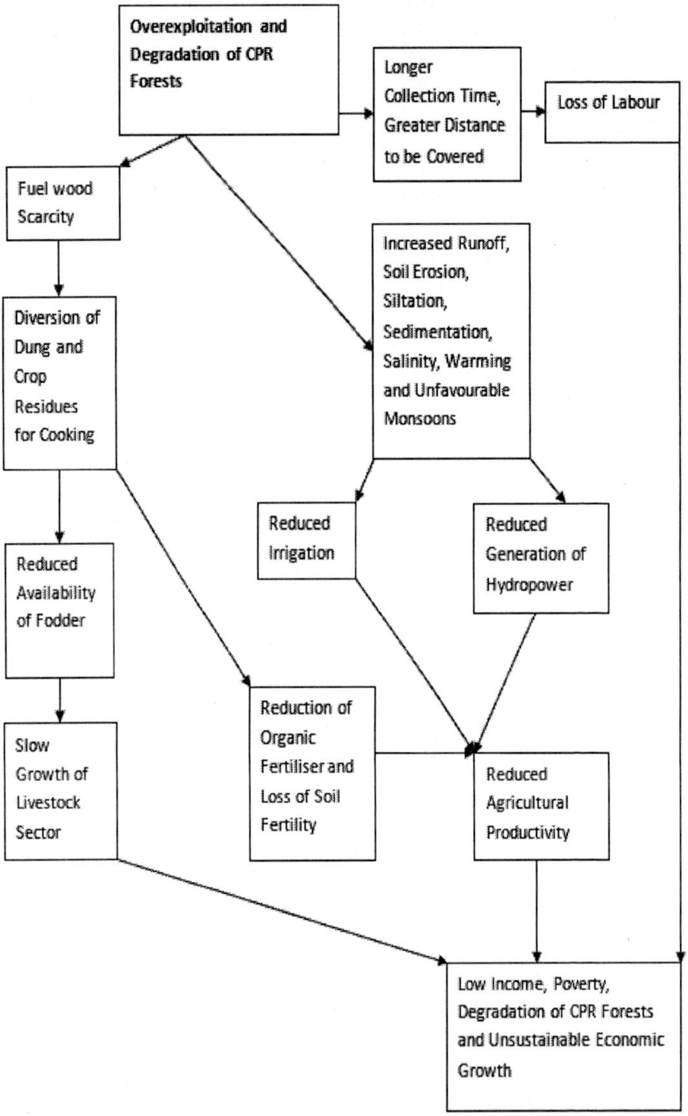

a reduction of organic fertiliser supply to agriculture only reinforces the loss in agricultural productivity. Finally, all three (i.e., slow growth of the livestock sector, agricultural stagnation, and reduced labour supply) result in low income generation and poverty which intensify the degradation of CPR forests and lead to slow and unsustainable economic growth and a vicious circle.

5.3 Open Acess CPR Vs Managed CPR

The problem with any type of CPR is that they turn to be open access resources in the absence of a management regime. However, their efficient utilization is possible under various regulatory regimes and credibility, mutual affection and pro-social disposition among the members of user group. The CPR model developed by Dasgupta (2005) suggests that with a very large user group, an unmanaged CPR approximates an open access resource owing to crowding externalities. To ensure efficient use of a piece of CPR he suggests determining the optimal user group size which calls for a regulatory regime.

His model describes that different regulatory regimes pressurize the user group to operate at their optimal size. Once the optimal user group size is determined, the next problem involves implementing that critical size by adopting an appropriate regulatory regime. The several management regimes may be quota restriction, imposition of entry tax, privatization and trust.

The essence of the model is that in the absence of regulatory mechanism, common ownership of renewable resources becomes the major cause of overexploitation which leads to resource degradation. The reason is; each user in the commonly used resource would always attempt to maximize his/her share/benefit at the expense of the other group members' share/benefit thereby diminishing the future potential of the resource body for all concerned. However, this possibility may not exist when there is a highly organized control over the use of a common property resource. In the absence of intervention in some or the other form i.e., quota restriction, entry tax, mutual agreements and community management etc., the status of resource becomes open access leading to overexploitation and resource depletion. The process becomes faster, with the introduction of technological and economic changes to the unmanaged CPR system.

5.4 Management of CPRs

CPRs are characterized by limited supply and community use. They are prone to free riding and overexploitation and the associated dangers of global warming, climate change and unsustainable economic growth. Therefore, their conservation and efficient management assume considerable significance. Unsurprisingly management of CPR has become a major subject of discourse among the academia and development planners in recent years. In view of the externalities resulting from individual actions in using common property resources their growing concerns focus on well defined property rights and appropriate management regimes for greater internalization of externalities and optimal husbanding of resources.

The vast literature relating to CPR management establish the superiority of decentralized collective management over other management systems for overcoming the tragedy of commons (Ostrom, 1990; Berkes, 1989; Wade, 1989; Jodha, 1986, Bromley, 1991). Common property management regimes in developing countries have shown that local level institutions have the capability to overcome management problems as well as achieve greater efficiency in the use of such resources. Participatory approach to CPR management in which promotion of community-based property rights is taken as one of the key thrust areas has received much attention following the Rio Earth Summit, where it was accepted as an integral part of the sustainable development process (Dearden et al., 1999). Although community control over natural resources is regarded as an effective mechanism for conservation of environment and local level development, empirical evidences on its livelihood and sustainability implications is rather mixed.

Experience from community forest programme in Nepal and in many other countries has indicated that poorer households are still marginalized even if resources are managed under community or group ownership. The reason is, economic and wealth status of individual users tends to affect leadership quality in the sphere of public decisions as well as the extent of resource exploitation and appropriation. There is considerable agreement among researchers on the issue that economic inequality in terms of social and physical capital among the members of a user group might be associated with different degrees of control and access over the local commons with heterogeneity negatively impacting on benefit sharing and adoption of sustainable management practices. To sum up the socio-economic status of community members may limit the opportunity available to weaker members to participate and benefit from community decision making. In such view of things, an appropriate management regime is highly essential for determining the optimal use pattern of common property resources to ensure equity and efficiency amongst the group members.

5.5 Forest Policies and Management

Odisha has got the dubious distinction of having high incidence of intense poverty in rural areas in general and tribal areas in particular. It is needless to say that the forest sector plays a crucial role in the lives of the rural poor and tribal communities of the state. Over the years, the actual forest cover of the state has been reduced to 30 per cent of its total geographical area due to population pressure and their mounting needs. This has adversely impacted on the livelihood conditions of the forest dependent population of the state. Degradation of forests, inadequacy of state policies in respect of the forestry sector and the conduct of stakeholders such as industrialists, mining interests, traders and forest mafias have further contributed to the deterioration of forest dwellers' livelihood conditions of the state. Since the rural poor and marginalized groups depend heavily on the forest resources of the state, it can be reasonably argued that the livelihood conditions of the people cannot be improved unless there is improvement in their access to forest produces and development of forest laws. This section discusses the prevailing forest policies and institutional arrangements in India and Odisha with regard to access to forest produce and management of forest resources in the state.

5.5.1 Forest Laws and Policies in India

In India the forest laws and policies are designed on the philosophy of conservation, livelihood concerns, participatory management and sustainable use of forests. The major forests and environmental laws in India are; Indian Forest Act, 1865 (Forests are considered as state property), Indian Forest Act, 1878 (Extension of Indian forest Act to all states), Indian Forest Act, 1927 (Relating to forests and forest produces), Wild life Protection Act, 1972 (Prohibition of hunting, collection of major forest produces and cultivation of certain species etc.), Indian Forest Act, 1980 (Prohibiting the use of forest land for non-forest purpose), National Forest Policy,1988 (Target of bringing one-third of the terrestrial area of the country under forests/ tree cover) and Biological Diversity Act, 2000 (Sustainable use of biodiversity, equitable sharing of benefits among the stakeholders and conservation of biodiversity).

5.5.2 Forest Laws and Policies in Odisha

The spirit of national forest policies has also been reflected in the state forest policies. The Odisha Forest Act, 1972 was enacted in line with the Indian Forest Act, 1927 and it makes provision for the reservation of trees and for the transit of timber. The Act also considers sandal trees as government property and imposes penalties for violation of the Act. The major laws on forest products and forest management in Odisha are; Odisha Grama Panchayat Act, 1964 (Ownership of minor forest products), Panchayat Act, 1996 (Management practices of community resource), Odisha Government Resolution, March 2000 (Grama Panchayat's ownership over 68 NTFP items) and Minor Forest Produce Administration Rules, 2002 (Grama Panchayat's power to regulate, procurement and trading of minor forest produce).

5.6 Forest Management in Odisha

In Odisha the management of forests is basically concerned with reforestation of degraded forests, controlling illegal exploitation of forest resources and encroachment of forest lands, nursery and plantation, protection of forests from forest fire, soil conservation and moisture conservation measures, construction of forest roads and coastal afforestation programmes. The Odisha Forest Department (OFD) is responsible for the protection and conservation of forest land in the state. The department plays the role of a regulator and enforcer of laws and acts relating to forest lands of the state. The OFD has three wings namely; Forest Wing, Kendu leaf Wing and Wildlife Wing. The administrative hierarchy of OFD in ascending order is; Beat (Managed by Forest Guard), Section (Managed by Forester), Range (Managed by Range Officer), Division (Managed by Division Forest Officer-DFO), Circle (Managed by Conservator of Forests-CF) and Headquarters (Managed by Principal Chief Conservator of Forest-PCCF). However, it is felt that there is a greater need of financial assistance, better facilities related to mobility and advanced communication and information technology to enhance the functional and administrative efficiency of the department.

5.7 Forest Management Institutions in Odisha

The primacy of an appropriate institutional framework for effective management of CPR forests is well established. A cursory look at the institutional arrangements for the promotion and development of forests in Odisha reveals a twofold system of management institutions operating in the state. They are: CFM and JFM. A brief description of these institutions and their functioning in respect of forest resources of the state is presented here.

5.7.1 Community Forest Management (CFM) in Odisha

Keeping in mind the importance of forests in the livelihood of rural poor, a large number of rural and tribal communities have evolved their own forest management mechanism to deal with the forest degradation situation in Odisha. The first ever recorded instance of voluntary forest protection committees or Community Forest Management (CFM) was formed in the year 1936 in the Lapanga village of Sambalpur district of Odisha. In subsequent periods the CFM institutions were formed in many villages of the Western and Central Odisha. At present the CFM institutions are operating in Nayagarh, Mayurbhanj, Keonjhar, Dhenkanal, Sambalpur, Balangir and Phulbani districts of the state. Presently around 8000 CFM institutions are engaged in protection and conservation of two million hectares of the state's forest. The CFM institutions are protecting different types of forests such as; bushy forest, degraded forest, open forest as well as forests which are not degraded. These institutions are engaged in controlling and managing forests irrespective of their legal status. The management practices followed by CFM institutions strike a balance between forest conservation and livelihood needs of the local communities.

5.7.2 Joint Forest Management (JFM) in Odisha

In realizing the need for community participation in forest protection, the Govt. of Odisha was the pioneer to adopt a policy of JFM even before implementation of National Forest Policy, 1988 (w.e.f. 2.10.1988) in the country and initiated a step to involve the people in protection of Reserved Forests adjoining their villages with assigning specific roles and in return granting certain concessions (under section 24 of the Odisha Forest Act1972) for meeting their bonafide requirement of firewood and small timbers through Resolution No. 10F (Pron) – 47/88/7240 FFAH dated 01 August 1988. The Resolution sought community participation for protection, regeneration and management of the forest wealth widening the scope of employment generation and social empowerment of the forest-fringe dwellers.

The forest department with the help of the villagers formed Village Forest Protection Committee (VFPC) in response to the resolution. The VFPCs were assigned the responsibilities of protecting the forests from fire, grazing, illegal felling of trees, theft etc. However, in the year 1993 a comprehensive resolution was adopted by the state government for involvement of local communities in the protection and management of state forests. The government coined a new term which is popularly known as Joint Forest Management (JFM) and the effort led to the constitution of Vana Sanrakhyana Samiti (VSS) around the degraded forests of the state. After the formulation of VSS, the VFPCs were declared null and void. The scope of the JFM was further extended to social forestry plantation and the VSS were given 100 per cent share over the forest products as well as the final harvest on the trees planted under the social forestry project.

With the changing scenario of forest management, increasing awareness among people and experiences gained from the past management practices, this resolution on JFM was revised and amended periodically. The latest revisions were effected on 2011 and 2015 respectively in adding several points, like inclusion of villages located within the National Park/ Sanctuaries as well as adjacent to the same for protection and management of the wildlife and habitat and covering the Reserve Forests and Protected forests, Village forests and Revenue forests having crown density of less than 40% under JFM, role of Palli Sabha, composition of members of Executive Body of Vana Surakshya samiti etc.

The two major objectives of JFM framework were involvement of local community in forest planning and management and equitable distribution of forest produces between the state and local stakeholders. Through the government resolution in 1993, the OFD delineated the guidelines on JFM as follows.

1. JFM institutions to operate in degraded reserved and protected forests.
2. It is to be operated only in the forest areas where the local people of the adjacent village or cluster of villages are willing to offer active co-operation in regeneration and protection of the forest tract.
3. The scheme allows a single village to manage and develop up to about 200 ha. of degraded forests.

The forest officials make due evaluation of the responses of the local community in relation to protecting and managing the forest areas and recommend the Grama Panchayat to constitute a VSS in the village. Then the VSS forms the Executive Committee (EC) for a term of two years with Naib Sarpanch of Gram Panchayat as the head. Subsequently, the VSS enters into a MoU with the concerned DFO for active participation in the programme designed by the JFM plan. The concerned forester of the Forest Department acts as the member secretary of the EC of VSS without voting power. The minimum participation of women in the General body and EC has been kept at 50 and 33 per cents respectively. The JFM has also been extended to less degraded forests. Both the forest department and the user group jointly participate in micro plans in JFM areas.

Over the years the JFM system has made rapid inroads into the management arena and is doing a good job for promoting the use and growth of forests in the state. Valuable information relating to the progress of JFM institutions in Odisha with special focus on the three sample districts as at the end of March, 2010 is presented in Table-5.1.

5.7.3 Problems of JFM institutions in Odisha

The JFM institutions in Odisha are confronted with the following problems.

1. Authority and Rights of VSS

Though the objective of JFM institutions is active participation of local communities in planning and management, in practice they enjoy minimal authority and rights. The foresters are left with almost all responsibilities relating to planning and management of the VSS.

2. Economic Viability of VSS

The VSS are operating with saddling supported by exclusive government funding. They are yet to be developed as an enterprise for their self-sustenance without public financial support.

3. VSS Management Manual

There are no detailed manuals for VSS management for use of VSS members and foresters. Arbitrary and discretionary actions of the foresters are very common.

4. Democracy and Cohesiveness within VSS

Normally the VSS leaders are nominated /selected by the forest officials. As a result the control and regulation of activities are concentrated in the hands of few VSS leaders and foresters. The influential groups of the village dominate the VSS management groups and the marginalized feels neglected.

Table-5.1: Progress of Joint Forest Management (VSS) by end of March-2021

District	Total number of VSS formed	Revenue village	Area under JFM of which				No. of families covered under JFM				No. of EDC
			RF (ha)	PRF/DPF (ha)	Other forests (ha)	Total (Ha)	SC	ST	GEN	All	
Balasore	183	276	4779.48	6438.20	4360.66	11547.68	6896	10761	18581	36238	12
Mayurbhanj	1067	1069	81586.79	11288.40	8018.38	100893.57	22423	96212	48536	167171	43
Keonjhar	836	826	47735.75	8493.16	14341.54	70570.45	29822	122947	65921	216690	11
Orissa	15689	15025	738419.00	369316.16	250698.49	1358433.65	326492	819111	730814	1876417	572

Source: Compiled from Records of the office of Principal Chief Conservator of Forest Odisha, Bhubaneswar.

The village women; the main collectors of forest resources, hardly participate in village meetings. Lack of transparency in opinion and fund utilization, and politicization and lack of awareness among the VSS members are the main reasons for functioning of VSSs in Odisha.

5. Micro Planning

In preparation of micro planning the forest officials play a predominant role. The local people remain as mere information providers with the overall control and implementation of plan resting with the forest department.

6. Status of VSS

The VSSs do not enjoy a legal status. They are yet to be registered as a society under the Society Registration Act to establish themselves as formal and legitimate institutions.

7. Relationship Between VSS and Panchayat Raj Institutions

The Grama Panchayat is hardy involved in the constitution of VSS. Hence such samities are participatory in form but bureaucratic in action.

5.8 Management of CPR Forests in the Sample Villages

Natural resource systems including CPR forests have been managed for centuries by communities across the globe (McKean, 1995). Although management of common property resources under community ownership has offered a stable form of resource management in many traditional societies, several studies have revealed that factors like population growth, user group characteristics in terms of economic condition and social status, motivational factors, cooperative efforts and political affiliations have considerably influenced their efficacy. In some cases political forces and socio-economic heterogeneity of members in the management have destabilized many of the existing viable local level institutions. In India, traditional village-based institutions regulate user's access to common property resources. These institutions enforce user groups' obligations relating to conservation, protection and development of village level common property resources such as land water and forests. The villagers make contribution both in terms of labour and funds to the upkeep of such resources. Any violation of restrictions is usually met with severe penalties.

Special emphasis has been put on the demographic (sex structure), economic (income including contribution of forest sources) and social (caste status) composition of the members of the management committee to ascertain the effectiveness of the existing mechanisms in ensuring equity in participation and sustainability of the management regime. It is revealed that the local level management institutions functioning in the villages covered under the study are in the JFM mode.

5.8.1 Village Level Forest Management in Balasore

Table-5.2 records the composition of the management committee in the sample villages Tenda and Banthiapada of Balasore district. The management institutions in these villages are Sinduragaura Jangal Surakshya committee in village Tenda and Banthiapada Jangal Surakshya committee in Banthiapada village. The major functions of the committees can be outlined as follows.

1. Protection and conservation of forests.
2. Preventing the forests from outsiders and illegal intruders by the 'Thengapali" approach. In the "Thengapali" system the management committee appoints a group of members to vigil the common property forest. It functions on daily basis and all the households are involved in the process by contributing manpower.
3. Bush cutting and cleaning activities in the forests to protect trees from fire and help them grow properly.
4. To prevent illegal hunting from the forest.
5. To clear trees that decay naturally.
6. To put control on logging activities.
7. To review households' needs and accordingly allot quota for harvesting timber from the forest.
8. However, in respect of fuel wood collection by individual households no restriction was imposed.

Table-5.2: Composition of Management Committees of Tenda and Banthiapada Villages in Balasore District

Balasore District		
Name of the Village	*Tenda*	*Banthiapada*
Name of the Committee	Sinduragaura Jangal Surakshya Committee	Banthiapada Jangal Surakshya Committee
Management Regime	VSS	VSS
Total Members	16	07
Male Members	11	07
Female Members	05	0
Maximum income in the group	Rs.1,00,000.00	Rs. 90,000.00
Minimum income in the group	Rs. 35,000.00	Rs. 32,000.00
Coefficient of Variation of income	37.79	38.84
Number of Scheduled Caste members	0	0
Number of Scheduled Tribe members	16	07
Others	0	0
Number of members earning more than half of annual household income from forest sources	10	04
Number of members earning more than half of annual income from non-forest sources	06	03

Source: Primary Survey

5.8.1.1 Sinduragaura Jangal Surakshya Committee

The Sinduragaura Jangal Surakshya committee has a total of 16 members with 11 males and 5 females. All the 16 members belong to the ST category. The maximum and minimum average annual income for the member households were found to be Rs. 1,00,000.00 and Rs.35,000.00 respectively with the Coefficient of Variation (CV) of 37.79. It can be seen that the 16-member committee is homogeneous with respect to social stratification but quite heterogeneous by the income parameter. The economic heterogeneity among the members has been captured by CV which with a value of 37.79 indicates wide economic disparity among the committee members. Members having higher household income were found to be dominating in the decision-making process, indicating concentration of power in the hands of the economically better off. In the management group, economically weaker members were found to be passive in participation and in the decision making as well. Considerable disagreement among the committee members over management issues were observed with the higher income group overpowering the members with lower income. Conflict in the committee was quite frequent and had not been resolved properly and women were passive. The functioning of the committee was found to be poor in terms of regularity in meetings, improving the condition of the forests, benefit sharing among users and their contribution to the quality of management practices followed.

5.8.1.2 Banthiapada Jangal Surakshya Committee

The seven-member Banthiapada Jangal Surakshya committee consists of only male members all of whom belonged to the ST category. The households' average annual income was found to vary between Rs.90, 000.00 and Rs. 32,000.00 with CV at 38.84. This management committee has also similar group characteristics as that of the management committee in the village Tenda. The group is homogeneous with respect to social stratification but highly heterogeneous by economic consideration. The high CV (38.84) is suggestive of presence of high disparity in the average annual income of the member households.

Here also the major decision-making authority lies with economically much better off group members and the rest of the group members remain as passive actors. The management committee is not functioning properly as in the village Tenda.

5.8.2 Village Level Forest Management in Mayurbhanj

The structure of the forest management committee in the two villages of Mayurbhanj district is given in a summary form in Table-5.3.

Table-5.3: Composition of Management Committee of Ramasahi And Mandam Villages in Mayurbhanj District

Mayurbhanj District		
Name of the Village	*Ramasahi*	*Mandam*
Name of the Committee	Ramasahi Jangal Surakshya Committee	Mandam Jangal Surakshya Committee
Management Regime	VSS	VSS
Total Members	12	07
Male Members	09	04
Female Members	03	03
Maximum income in the group	Rs.48,300.00	Rs. 42,000.00
Minimum income in the group	Rs. 40,000.00	Rs. 36,000.00
Coefficient of Variation of income	5.81	6.56
Number of Scheduled Caste members	0	0
Number of Scheduled Tribe members	12	07
Others	0	0
Number of members earning more than half of annual household income from forest sources	12	07
Number of members earning more than half of annual household income from non-forest sources	0	0

Source: Primary Survey

During field survey it was observed that in both the sample villages Ramasahi and Mandam, the peripheral common property forests are managed by the local community. The name of the management committees in the two villages are Ramasahi Jangal Surakshya committee and Mandam Jangal Surakshya committee respectively.

5.8.2.1 Ramasahi Jangal Surakshya Committee

Since the composition of the management institutions are crucial for ensuring effectiveness in their functioning and sustainable management practices, a further investigation has been made into the socio-economic profiles of the committee members and a link has been established between their composition and the effectiveness in CPR forest management.

The Ramasahi Jangal Surakshya committee consists of a total of 12 members of which 9 are males and 3 are females. The average annual household income of the committee members were found to range between Rs. 48,300.00 and Rs. 40,000.00 with a coefficient of variation (CV) of income of 5.81. Further all the group members belonged to the Scheduled Tribes (ST) category. For the households of all the members in the management committee forest sources contribute more than half of the annual household income. Interestingly the management group is homogeneous with respect to social stratification (all STs) and also near homogeneous in respect of their household annual income (CV=5.81). Moreover, all members including women members in the committee were active participant in the decision-making process. They were found working for sustainable use of forest resources and conservation of CPR forests. The committee is observed to be highly effective in managing the CPR forests.

5.8.2.2 Mandam Jangal Surakshya Committee

A similar observation was made in the case of Mandam Jangal Surakshya committee. The 7-member committee consists of 4 males and 3 females. At the household level the average annual incomes for all the 7 members were found to vary between Rs 42, 000.00 and Rs.36, 000.00 with a CV of 6.56. All the members belonged to the ST category. Thus, the committee members were found to be homogeneous both by social stratification and economic conditions. The very low CV (6.56) in the income suggests existence of economic homogeneity among the members in the management committee.

Hence, composition wise the management committees in the two villages were found to be fairly homogeneous in respect of both social and economic considerations. As in the case of Ramasahi all the members of the Mandam Jangal Surakshya committee reported to have derived more than half of the annual income of their respective households from forest sources. During interaction with the villagers and some of the members of the management committee it was found that in respect of functioning of the management institutions in both the villages, the local community is quite satisfied with the performance of the management committee.

In major decision making all the members were given fair chance to participate and free expression of their views. Further, the women members took active part in the decision making regarding the use and management of CPR forest. There have been no major conflicts in both the management committees for the last several years and the committees have been functioning smoothly. It was also observed that among the members the level of social capital such as trust, mutual affection etc. is quite high. The user group's attitude towards the members of the committee was found to be quite respectful. The user group contributes their labor for conservation and protection of CPR forests in both the villages. However, the local community feels that there is a greater need of funding from the state government for more effective management of CPR forests. On the whole, the management committees in the two villages are functioning pretty well as perceived by the user groups.

5.8.3 Village Level Forest Management in Keonjhar

Table-5.4 records the composition of the management committee in the villages Ghatabalijodi and Tanda of Keonjhar district.

Table-5.4: Composition of Management Committee of Ghatabalijodi And Tanda Villages in Keonjhar District

Keonjhar District		
Name of the Village	*Ghatabalijodi*	*Tanda*
Name of the Committee	Ghatabalijodi Jangal Surakshya Committee	Tanda Jangal Surakshya Committee
Management Regime	VSS	VSS
Total Members	15	15
Male Members	09	12
Female Members	06	03
Maximum income in the group	Rs.48,000.00	Rs. 56,000.00
Minimum income in the group	Rs. 42,000.00	Rs. 46,100.00
Coefficient of Variation of income	4.06	6.10
Number of Scheduled Caste members	0	0
Number of Scheduled Tribe members	10	09
Others	05	06
Number of members earning more than half of annual household income from forest sources	09	08
Number of members earning more than half of annual household income from non-forest sources	06	07

Source: Primary Survey

The management institutions in the villages of Ghatabalijodi and Tanda in the Keonjhar district are named after the respective villages as Ghatabalijodi Jangal Surakshya committee and Tanda Jangal Surakshya committee respectively. The roles and responsibilities of the institutions with respect to CPR forests are the same as discussed in the case of the villages in the Mayurbhanj district.

5.8.3.1 Ghatabalijodi Jangal Surakshya Committee

The Ghatabalijodi Jangal Surakshya committee has a total of 15 members comprising 9 males and 6 females. The maximum and minimum average annual household incomes of members in the committee are Rs. 48,000.00 and Rs.42, 000.00 with a CV 4.06. In terms of the social composition it was found that 10 members belong to the STs and 5 members belong to households other than STs. Here the management committee is quite homogeneous with respect to economic consideration as evidenced from the very low CV (4.06) of their household incomes. However, from the point of view social parameters, it appears to be heterogeneous. Hence, the management committee is characterized by economic homogeneity but social heterogeneity.

With regard to its functioning it was noticed that members belonging to higher social strata play a dominant role in major managerial decision making and women members were passive. The socially lower sections and women were not given adequate opportunity to participate in the decision-making process. Their participation is limited and they feel that they should have been given a more equitable treatment. Such unequal treatment led to conflicts among the members on various occasion in the past leading to poor outcomes in CPR forest management. The user group's perception about the functioning of the committee is not very satisfactory. Greater institutionalization, enforcement of equity in participation of the lower strata of the society and more public funding have been demanded for ensuring effectiveness and sustainability of CPR management.

5.8.3.2 Tanda Jangal Surakshya Committee

The Tanda Jangal Surakshya committee has 15 members

with the male and female member break up of 12 and 3 respectively. In the committee the maximum and minimum average annual household incomes of members were found to be Rs. 56,000.00 and Rs.46, 100.00 respectively with a CV of 6.10. The group consists of 9 members from the ST class and 6 members from other than ST.

An investigation into the group characteristics reveals that it is homogeneous with respect to economic consideration as indicated by the low CV (6.10) of incomes among the member households. But the group is heterogeneous in terms of social stratification as it consists of members belonging to both higher and lower strata.

This management committee is also dominated by members belonging to the higher strata and the members of the lower strata do not get ample scope to participate. The three women members never attended meetings. Major decisions pertaining to utilization of funds and CPR management are taken by the upper caste influential members. During discussion with the sample households it was noticed that their perception and attitude towards functioning of the local level management institution is not very satisfactory. It was felt that there is lack of both co-operation and proper co-ordination among the committee members towards management of CPR forest in the villages. Inequitable treatment may be the demotivating factor behind such non-cooperation which is consequential upon social heterogeneity in management. The management in this village was also found to be less effective compared to the management in the study villages of Mayurbhanj.

5.8.4 Participatory Management: An Overview

The results of the analysis of the functioning of participatory management in the sample villages are revealing.

Management institutions have been most effective in the villages of Mayurbhanj district, followed by those in Keonjhar and Balasore. The effectiveness of management institutions in respect of common property forest were observed to be determined by four conditions namely, social composition, economic condition of the members of the management committee and sex structure and nature of base level forest management organization. The management committees in the sample villages of Mayurbhanj were socio-economically homogeneous and women members in these committees were active in the managerial decision-making process. Besides, these committees were originally in the CFM mode with an inherent attitude of the users towards rational use of forest resources and their sustainable management. Obviously, the management is highly effective. In Keonjhar district the management committees are characterized by economic homogeneity but social heterogeneity and women members were passive actors. The village forest management committee in the sample villages of Balasore are found to be economically heterogeneous and socially homogeneous with women being noncommittal. It is revealed that economic heterogeneity is a predominant factor determining the efficacy of forest management committees as compared to social heterogeneity for which the management is moderately effective in Keonjhar but less functional in Balasore.

5.9 Sustainability of Forest Management Institution

During the last two and half decades, economists, social scientists, planners and policy makers have been obsessed with issues of sustainability. Sustainable management practices are a pre-condition for intergenerational equity in resource allocation. Keeping this in view we have attempted to examine the sustainability of CPR forest management institutions operating in the study area on the basis of user group's perception of the functioning of these institutions. The respondents of sample households in the villages were asked to give their response on seven selected indicators on a five point scale (1-5) with one, indicating the lowest value and five, the highest. The seven indicators used for the purpose are: 1. User groups' assessment of management system, 2. Behaviour towards users, 3. Equity consideration, 4. Resource conservation/regulation, 5. Promptness in decision making, 6. Strict adherence to rules, and 7. Provision to check illegal logging/intrusion. On the five-point scale, 1 indicated the lowest and 5 indicated the highest. For each indicator, the index has been calculated using the formula as follows.

Index= (Average-Min)/ (Max-Min).

Finally, for each districts the composite index has been calculated taking the arithmetic average of the indices for the seven indicators stated above. Composite index with a value exceeding 0.60 is accepted to suggest high sustainability. A value within the range 0.50-0.59 is assumed to indicate medium sustainability. Low sustainability is indicated by a value of less than 0.50. Relevant information is presented in Table-5.5.

Table-5.5: User Groups' Perception of Functioning of Management Institutions

Sl. No.	*Indicators*	*Districts*		
		Mayurbhanj	*Keonjhar*	*Balsore*
1	User groups' assessment of management system	0.785	0.570	0.392
2	Behaviour towards users	0.820	0.470	0.392
3	Equity consideration	0.730	0.600	0.427
4	Resource conservation/regulation	0.700	0.505	0.412
5	Promptness in decision making	0.470	0.655	0.305
6	Strict adherence to rules	0.520	0.612	0.495
7	Provision to check illegal logging/intrusion	0.827	0.702	0.780
8	Composite Index	0.693	0.587	0.457
9	Sustainability	High	Medium	Low

Source: Authors' Calculation using Primary Data

5.9.1 Management Sustainability: The Case of Balasore

The composite index for the Balasore district has been estimated at 0.457. The indices for the seven indicators are 0.392, 0.392, 0.427, 0.412, 0.305, 0.495 and 0.780 respectively in the same order as given in the table. The index of the indicator "provision to check illegal logging/intrusion" has taken the highest value (0.780) and the lowest score has been observed for the indicator "promptness in decision making" with a value 0.305.

5.9.2 Management Sustainability: The Case of Mayurbhanj

The estimated value of the composite index for the Mayurbhanj district has been 0. 693.The index for "Provision to check illegal logging/intrusion" was found to be the highest (0.827) followed by the index for "Behaviour towards users" (0.820). The indices for "User groups' assessment of management system"," Equity consideration", "Resource conservation", "Promptness in decision making" and "Strict adherence to rules" are found to be 0.785,0.730, 0.700, 0.470 and 0.520 respectively. It can be observed that except for the indicators "Promptness in decision-making" and "Strict adherence to rules", the remaining five indicators have taken values 7.00 or more. The higher values for most of the indicators suggest that the users are satisfied with the functioning of the village level forest management institutions and that it is sustainable. This reaffirms our finding in the preceding section.

5.9.3 Management Sustainability: The Case of Keonjhar

The composite index for management sustainability for Keonjhar district was found to be 0.587. The user groups' ratings for the seven indicators are 0.570, 0.470, 0.600, 0.505, 0.655, 0.612 and 0.702 respectively in the same order as has been recorded in the table. The highest and the lowest values are found against the indices "Provision to check illegal logging" with score 0.702 and "Behavior towards users" with index=0.470.

5.9.4 Comparison of Management Sustainability across the Districts

A comparative analysis of the composite index score of management sustainability indicators for the three districts suggest that community management is highly sustainable (Index=0.693) in Mayurbhanj district followed by Keonjhar with medium sustainability (Index=0.587) and Balasore where sustainability is low (Index=0.457).This is in conformity with the results relating to the extent of effectiveness of village level management institutions obtained in section 5.8. Amongst the individual indicators, the indicator, "Provision to check illegal logging/intrusion" has taken the highest value in all the districts.

5.10 Summary

Overexploitation of CPR forests has serious implications for livelihood security and intergenerational equity. Hence rational use of forest resources and sustainable management practices assume considerable significance. People living near forest areas and collecting materials from forests for their subsistence, employment and earning are traditionally inclined to limit their collections as per need and to take steps for the regeneration of exploited materials with a view to promoting the growth of forests. In the sample villages the CPR forests are being managed by the JFM kind of institutions although in some parts of the state CFM type management is still functional.

Social, economic and demographic heterogeneity of the members of the management committee are the crucial factors affecting the effectiveness of management mechanisms and institutional stability. Management is found to be more effective and sustainable where there is socio-economic homogeneity among the members of the management committee and active participation of women in the decision-making process. On the other hand, socio-economic heterogeneity among the committee members has a negative bearing on the effectiveness and sustainability of management. Thus, our hypothesis that heterogeneity among the members of the management committee is an important determinant of the effectiveness of collective action in managing common property forest resources stands valid and is accepted. Another factor which influenced the working of the management mechanism is the kind of forest management institution that was working initially. In villages where CFM was practised initially but later a switch over to JFM system was effected, the effectiveness of the present organization is high. It is thus clear that left to themselves, forest dwellers can take steps for the promotion of forests. Creation of awareness and provision of motivations will contribute to their effort.

6

Sustainability of Common Property Forest Resources

6.1 Introduction

'A woman can either be beautiful or faithful but not both' goes the adage. It illustrates the tendency to create boxes. In the realm of environment-economy interdependence it may be indicative of a conflict between rapid economic growth, and quality and quantity of environmental resources- we can either have rapid economic growth or sustainable natural resource system but not both. Contemporary development economies, notably China and India have experienced unprecedented economic growth with even higher rates of growth at the sub-national level. For instance, the growth rate of GSDP in Odisha is higher than the national rate. Environmentalists, social activists, economists, political heavyweights and media unequivocally view such phenomenal growth achievements as the concomitant, among other things, of environmental degradation and depletion of CPR forests. Everybody is used to be a huge fan of the ecological movement arguing strongly for environmental clearances in major industrial and other development projects. Rational extraction of materials from forests and product management of the forest system are considered vital for a sustainable resource base with a view to achieving higher economic growth at the present without compromising the development requirements of the posterity. The strategy of development is now increasingly focusing on forests as a sector of development and on how best we can make productive use of forest resources in order to further human wellbeing now and forever. This has come to be widely known as the environmental basis of sustainable development.

6.2 The Case for Sustainable Forest Resources

The need for sustainable forest resource systems in poor and developing states is well established. They are the primary producers with large subsistence sectors depending heavily on their natural resources like forests, land and water. High population growth, acute poverty, widespread unemployment and unskilled nature of human resources make people critically dependent on CPR forests for their livelihood. Overexploitation of CPR forest resources and their depletive uses causes a collapse of the resource system and will cease their main livelihood support opportunities as well as the environmental basis of economic growth leading to poverty and overexploitation and hence perpetuation of the vicious circle. All of us must, therefore, be sensitive to forests, especially with the rapid degradation of forest cover and forest resources. We must no longer sacrifice the forests for the sake of economic growth and shift focus from growth per se to the sources and quality of growth.

6.3 The Requirement of Sustainable Forestry

The social, ecological and economic basis of sustainable forest resources is well taken on grounds of ensuring a non-reducing supply of forest resources, a non-declining consumption rate, a non-diminishing per capita level of utility, per capita welfare, and a non-deteriorating average quality of life for both the present and future generations. The goal involves both equity and efficiency issues. It involves both intra- and inter-generational equity in resource allocation and optimality of resource use. Achieving a sustainable forest resource system is contingent upon fulfilling the following conditions or rules.

1. The use of common property forest resources be designed and directed in such a way that the harvest rate (h) does not exceed the normal regeneration rate (r). i.e., h d″ r.
2. The waste flows (w) to the CPR forests be such as not to exceed the assimilative capacity (a). i.e., w d″ a.

3. Since population growth is the principal cause of poverty and degradation of forests the growth rate of number (p) be limited to the minimum possible level. i.e., p d" pmin.
4. The basic characteristics of a common pool resource are that it is limited in supply and is accessible to a user group. In the process of using the resource each user, with a view of maximizing his utility function inflicts some negative externalities on the other and causes degradation/depletion and the subsequent collapsing of the resource base. It is therefore necessary to keep such negative externalities (e) at their minimum (emin) level. i.e., e d" emin.

6.4 Sustainability of Forest Resources in the Sample Villages

In our study on CPR forest dependency of the rural households it was found that the sample households are heavily dependent on CPR forests for making their livelihoods, household enterprises and incomes. Irrespective of the district characteristics, the degree and extent of dependency was found to be very high across all the six sample villages. Colossal poverty, widespread unemployment and lack of adequate gain full employment opportunities were the important determining factors for such high dependency.

During the survey it was revealed that almost all the sample households were dependent on CPR forest some way or the other way round throughout the year. Heavy dependency in terms of resource use and extraction may pose serious threat to the long-run sustainability of the CPR forest resources in the area. The per household availability of common property forest resources for the sample villages in the study districts Balasore, Mayurbhanj and Keonjhar were estimated at 0.73, 2.75 and 2.04 acres respectively. CPR forest area per household was found to be the highest in the sample villages of Mayurbhanj (2.75), followed bythose ofKeonjhar (2.04) and Balasore (0.73) in that order. This indicates that among the sample villages there is remarkable variation in per household availability of the CPR forests. The village profiles suggest that such variation exists owing to two important factors i.e., the amount of total CPR forest area at village level and the number of households in the sample villages. However, at the aggregate households level the average CPR forest area of 1.32 acres may be considered to be quite substantial. For the 210 samples the percentage share of households' forest income in the annual average income was found to be 30.97 per cent. The highest contribution of the forest income in total household income has been observed for the Mayurbhanj district (38.59 per cent), followed by Keonjhar (31.42 per cent) and Balasore (26.01 per cent). However, such a high degree of dependency on CPR forest resources may put a big question mark on intergenerational resource allocation and resource sustainability in the state. An attempt has been made here to study the sustainability aspects of common property forest resources in the study area.

6.4.1 Resource Sustainability by Qualitative Indicators

In order to know sustainability of the common property forest resources in the study area, the survey schedule was designed with some indicators for obtaining information from the sample respondents as questions on resource sustainability. The sample households were asked to give a comparative picture of the current state of CPR forests in qualitative terms in respect of four indicators such as Total Area, Density, Collection Quantity and the Quality of the Produce. The responses were collected for three points of time i.e., as on date of survey, five years back and ten years preceding the survey and recorded in Table-6.1.

Table-6.1: Respondents' Perception of Resource Sustainability

District	*Indicators*	*Number of Households Reporting*			
		No Change	*Moderate Decline*	*Substantial Decline*	*Total*
Balasore	Area	0(0.00)	60(85.71)	10(14.29)	70(100.00)
	Density	0(0.00)	11(15.71)	59(84.29)	70(100.00)
	Collection	0(0.00)	48(68.57)	22(31.43)	70(100.00)
	Quality	0(0.00)	42(60.00)	28(40.00)	70(100.00)
Mayurbhanj	Area	3(4.30)	63(90.00)	4(5.70)	70(100.00)
	Density	2(2.85)	40(57.15)	28(40.00)	70(100.00)

	Collection	4(5.70)	53(75.70)	13(18.6)	70(100.00)
	Quality	3(4.30)	59(84.30)	8(11.40)	70(100.00)
Keonjhar	Area	2(2.80)	62(88.60)	6(8.60)	70(100.00)
	Density	2(2.80)	25(35.70)	43(61.50)	70(100.00)
	Collection	1(1.40)	51(72.90)	18(25.70)	70(100.00)
	Quality	1(1.40)	47(67.20)	22(31.40)	70(100.00)
All	Area	5(2.40)	185(88.10)	20(9.50)	210(100.00)
	Density	4(1.90)	86(41.00)	120(57.10)	210(100.00)
	Collection	5(2.40)	152(72.40)	53(25.20)	210(100.00)
	Quality	4(1.90)	148(70.50)	58(27.60)	210(100.00)

Source: Primary Data

6.4.1.1 Households' response on resource sustainability in Balasore

It may be noted that none of the respondents in the selected villages of Balasore district reported no change in forest area during the last ten years. 60 households (85.71 per cent) indicated that the area has reduced moderately and ten households (14.29 per cent) viewed the decline as substantial. Thus, the majority view ran in terms of a moderate decline in forest area over the last ten-year period. For the sustainability indicator density of the CPR forest 11 households (15.71 per cent) have reported the density to have moderately decreased and 59 sample households (84.29 per cent) reported that it has decreased substantially. Thus, majority of the sample households were alarmed at the substantial decline in the density of forest area. This seems to be quite grave situation for sustainability of CPR forests. When the sample households were asked about their experience on collection of produces of any kind from CPR forests 48 households (68.57 per cent) responded that the collection has gone down moderately and 22 households (31.43 per cent) reported that it has decreased substantially. For this sustainability indicator the majority view ran in terms of moderate reduction of collection of materials from CPR forests per person and per annum. Similar responses were obtained in regard to the quality of produce collected from forests with 42 households (60 per cent) collected and the balance 28 households (40 per cent) indicating a substantial quality deterioration.

6.4.1.2 Households' response on resource sustainability in Mayurbhanj

In the case of Mayurbhanj district the situation is comparatively better. For the indicator forest area only 03 households (4.30 per cent) indicated no change in area during the last ten years, 63 households (90 per cent) indicated the area to have decreased moderately and 04 households responded (5.7 per cent) reported that the area has decreased substantially. Thus, a vast majority of the households' response was in terms of a moderate decline in forest area. With respect to density indicator only 2 households (2.85 per cent) reported no change in density of forests while 40 households (57.15 per cent) indicated a moderately decline and 28 sample households (40 per cent) have reported that the density of CPR forests has decreased substantially. It paints a grave situation for the future sustainability of CPR forests in the sample villages of Mayurbhanj. The sample households were also asked about their experience on collection of produces from CPR forests. On this issue 04 households (5.70 per cent) indicated no change, 53 households (75.7 per cent) responded the collection to have gone down moderately and the balance 13 households (18.6 per cent) reported the collection to have reduced substantially. For this sustainability indicator majority of the sample households indicated a moderate decline in collection. In respect of the indicator quality of produce 03 households (4.30 per cent) reported no change in quality of collection from forests, 59 households (84.30 per cent) indicated a moderate deterioration and 08 households (11.40 per cent) viewed the quality deteriorated as substantially. On this score also, the major response has been in terms of a moderate deterioration.

6.4.1.3 Households' response on resource sustainability in Keonjhar

A summary picture of the responses of sample households on the indicators of sustainability of CPR forests for Keonjhar district is presented in Table-6.4. Keonjhat lies in between Mayurbhanj and Balasore. With regard to the area indicator 2 households (2.8 per cent) indicated no change, 62 households (88.60 per cent) reported moderate decline and 6 households (8.60 percent) have shown it to have declined substantially.

Thus the majority of households have reported a moderate decline in forest area during the last ten years. As regards the density parameter only 2 households (2.8 per cent) have reported no change, 25 households (35.70 per cent) indicated a moderate decline and 43 sample households (61.50 per cent) have reported the density of CPR forest land to have declined substantially. In respect of sustainability of CPR forest land the situation is very grave in the sample villages of Keonjhar. The sample households' response on collection of produces from CPR forests shows that only one household (1.4 per cent) reported no change while 51 households (72.90 per cent) indicated that the collection has gone down moderately and 18 households (25.70 per cent) reported it to have decreased substantially. For this sustainability indicator the majority response indicated a substantial decline. On the issue of quality of produce only one household (1.40 per cent) indicated no change as against 47 households (67.20 per cent) reporting moderate decline in quality of product and 22 households (31.40 per cent) pointing to a substantial quality deterioration.

6.4.1.4 Households' response on resource sustainability (All Households)

As in the earlier cases responses are basically households' perceptions about the selected indicators. With regard to the indicator common property forest area 05 sample households (2.40 per cent) reported no change during the last ten years, 185 households (88.10 per cent) indicated a moderate decline and for 20 households (9.50 per cent) the decline has been substantial. Hence majority of sample households' response was a moderate decline in area under CPR forests used for the villagers. In respect of the density indicator 04 households (1.90 per cent) indicated no change, 86 households (41 per cent) a moderate decline and 120 households (57.10 per cent) reported the density to have reduced substantially. Thus majority of respondents indicated a substantial decline in density of forests which is quite threatening. As to the collection from CPR forests, 05 households (2.40 per cent) indicated no change, 152 households (72.40 per cent) reported a moderate decline and 53 (25.20 percent) have viewed decline as quite substantial. The majority viewed the reduction in collection of materials from forests as moderate. In terms of the quality of produce indicator, 04 households (1.90 per cent) indicated no change, 148 households (70.50 per cent) viewed that quality of produce collected from forests has deteriorated moderately. However, 58 households (27.60 per cent) reported the deterioration of quality to be substantial.

A comparison across districts reveals that Mayurbhanj district exhibits higher sustainability of common property forest resources as measured by qualitative indicators in comparison to the two other districts. A close look at Table-6.1 indicates that in terms of all the indicators the percentage of respondents reporting substantial decline is the lowest in this district followed by Keonjhar and Balasore. The threat to resource sustainability is the least for Mayurbhanj, highest for Balasore and Moderate for Keonjhar. Our results hence confirm to those obtained in the preceding chapter on effectiveness and sustainability of management institutions.

6.4.2 Resource Sustainability by Quantitative Indicators

As a useful supplement to our analysis of sustainability of common property forest resources presented in the previous section, we have considered the information provided by the respondents of the sample households in terms of six other selected indicators. They are : (i) the distance to be covered for collection of NTFPs and fuel wood, (ii) the number of days in a month the household goes to the forest for collecting materials, (iii) income from sale of NTFPs collected per year, (iv) quantity fuel wood collection per month, (v) average age of plants cut and (vi) average number of hours required to collect a bundle of fuel wood. The respondents were asked to furnish information relating to these indicators for three points of time i.e, the year of survey, five years preceding the year of survey and ten years preceding the year of survey-the last of these being taken as the reference point to find out the change. To make the data compatible distance was measured in kms, value of NTFPs were estimated at the current price, fuel wood collection was measured in kgs and life of plants cut was taken in years.

6.4.2.1 Resource sustainability in Balasore district

Table-6.2 summarizes response of the sample households in Balasore district.

Table-6.2: Resource Sustainability by Quantitative Indicators in Balasore District

Sustainability Indicators (Sample Average)	*10 Years Back*	*5 Years Back*	*Now*
Distance to Forest for Collection of Materials (Kms)	0.46(100.00)	0.68(145.00)	0.75(164.30)
No. of days an Average Person Engaged in Collection of Material from Forest	22.1(100.00)	15.53(70.30)	13.30(60.20)
Annual Income from Sale of NTFPs (Rs.)	3342.29(100.00)	2082.24(62.30)	1628.01(48.70)
Quantity of Fuel wood Collection per Month (in K.g)	362.71(100.00)	232.96(64.23)	211.80(58.40)
Average Age of Plant Cut (Years)	14.12(100.00)	9.62(68.20)	8.41(59.60)
Average Time Spent to Collect a Bundle of Fuel Wood (Hours)	1.52(100.00)	2.43(160.00)	2.70(178.00)

Source: Primary Data

It can be seen from the table that a person now travels 0.75 km to collect materials as against 0.46 km ten years hence and 0.68 km five years back suggesting a 64.30 per cent increase in distance to forests over a ten year period. For collecting materials, a person is found to be going to the forest on 13.30 days per month now as against 22.10 days before ten years and 15.53 days five years back. This shows a 40 per cent decline in the number of days a person is engaged in collection of materials from forests probably because of a reduction in availability of such materials. Income from NTFP collections from forests have reduced sustainability from Rs. 3342.29 ten years back to Rs 2082.24 five years hence to Rs.1628.01 now- a decline by 51.30 per cent over the last ten years. Reduced availability and collection per man day may be a valid reason for this situation. Similarly, quantity of fuel wood collected per month has fallen from 362.71 kgs to 232.96 kgs to 211.80 kgs during the period indicating a decline by 41.60 per cent due to the same reason. At the present an average plant is cut at 8.41 years of age as against 9.62 years five years back and

14 12 years ten years hence. It shows a reduction in age at felling by 40 per cent because of quantity deterioration and falling tree cover. On an average 2.70 hours are now required to collect a bundle of fuel wood against 1.52 hours ten years back and 2.43 hours five years before sharing an increase in collection time by 78.00 per cent over a period of ten years.

6.4.2.2 Resource sustainability in Mayurbhanj District

Information relating to households' perception on sustainability indicators in the sample villages of Mayurbhanj presented in Table-6.3.

Table-6.3: Resource Sustainability by Quantitative Indicators in Mayurbhanj District

Sustainability Indicators (Sample Average)	*10 Years Back*	*5 Years Back*	*Now*
Distance to Forest for Collection of Materials (Kms)	0.69(100.00)	0.87(126.00)	1.08(156.60)
No. of days an Average Person Engaged in Collection of Material from Forest	28.96(100.00)	24.47(84.50)	20.80(71.82)
Annual Income from Sale of NTFPs (Rs.)	6312.50(100.00)	4811.23(76.21)	3467.81(54.90)
Quantity of Fuel wood Collection per Month (in K.g)	473.07(100.00)	366.64(77.50)	318.21(67.26)
Average Age of Plant Cut (Years)	29.45(100.00)	22.63(76.84)	20.21(68.62)
Average Time Spent to Collect a Bundle of Fuel Wood (Hours)	1.00(100.00)	1.40(140.00)	1.52(152.00)

Source: Primary Data

It can be read off the table that a person travels 1.08 kms now to collect materials from forests which is substantially greater than 0.69 km travelled ten years before and 0.87 km covered five years back indicating an increase of 56.60 per cent in distance to forests over a ten-year period. The number of days per month a person goes to the forests for collecting forest produce has fallen from 28.96 days ten years hence to 24.47 days five years back to 20.80 days now showing a decrease by 20.00 per cent. This may be due to reduced availability of materials in the forests. Income from sales of NTFPs collected from forests have registered a decline by 45.00 per cent over a ten years period from Rs. 6312.50 ten years before to Rs. 4811.23 five years back to Rs. 3467.81 now for a similar reason. The quantity of fuel wood collected per month by a household from 473.07 kgs ten year back to 366.64 kgs five years hence to 318.21 kgs now indicating a 33.00 per cent decline during the last ten years probably because of the same reason. The average age at which a plant is cut has also reduced phenomenally from 29.45 years to 22.63 years to 20.21 years now showing a 33.40 per cent decline. This means that a plant is cut at a far lower age now than before due to reduction in tree cover. The average number of hours required to collect a bundle of fuel wood has increased from one hour before ten years to 1.40 hours before five years to 1.52 years now indicating an increase in collection time by 52.00 per cent.

6.4.2.3 Resource sustainability in Keonjhar district

Table-6.4 presents a brief account of the respondents' views regarding the sustainability of forest resources in Keonjhar district.

Table- 6.4: Resource Sustainability by Quantitative Indicators in Keonjhar District

Sustainability Indicators (Sample Average)	*10 Years Back*	*5 Years Back*	*Now*
Distance to Forest for Collection of Materials (Kms)	0.78(100.00)	1.02(132.00)	1.25(160.20)
No. of days an Average Person Engaged in Collection of Material from Forest	25.00(100.00)	19.60(78.30)	16.98(67.90)
Annual Income from Sale of NTFPs (Rs.)	3772.00(100.00)	2576.30(68.30)	1984.07(52.60)
Quantity of Fuel wood Collection per Month (in K.g)	404.40(100.00)	283.92(70.21)	253.96(62.80)
Average Age of Plant Cut (Years)	38.84(100.00)	27.88(71.80)	24.74(63.70)
Average Time Spent to Collect a Bundle of Fuel Wood (Hours)	1.92(100.00)	2.78(145.00)	3.03(158.30)

Source: Primary Data

As can be seen from the table a person travels 1.25 kms now to collect materials from the forest as against 0.78 km ten years before and 1.02 kms five years hence indicating a 60.00

per cent increase in distance to forests over a decade. For collecting forest produce a person is found to be going to forest on 16.98 days per month now. He was going on 25 days before ten years and 19.60 days before five years. This shows that there has been a reduction in the number of days a person goes to the forest to collect materials by around 32.00 per cent over the last ten years. Reduced availability of materials may be the main reason for this reduction. Income from sale of NTFPs collected from forests have fallen phenomenally from Rs. 3772.00 ten years back to Rs. 2576.30 five years hence to Rs. 1984.07 now registering a decline by little more than 47.00 per cent over a decade. Similarly, the quantity of fuel wood collected per month has fallen from 404.40 kgs to 283.92 kgs to 253.96 kgs or by more than 37.00 per cent over ten years. At the present an average plant is cut at 24.74 years of age as against 27.88 years before five years and 38.84 years before ten years from now showing a reduction in age at felling by 36.30 per cent. On the whole it takes 3.03 hours to collect a bundle of fuel wood now against 2.78 hours five years hence and 1.92 hours ten years back indicating an increase by 58.30 per cent. Increase in distance to forests and collection time, and the decline in the number of days a person goes to forest for collection of materials, income from sales of NTFPs, collection of fuel wood per month and average life of plant at felling can be explained by reduction in forest cover and tree cover, and reduced availability of materials in forests.

6.4.2.4 Resource sustainability- all districts

Table-6.5: Resource Sustainability by Quantitative Indicators - All Districts

Sustainability Indicators (Sample Average)	*10 Years Back*	*5 Years Back*	*Now*
Distance to Forest for Collection of Materials (Kms)	0.64(100.00)	0.85(132.80)	1.02(159.37)
No. of days an Average Person Engaged in Collection of Material from Forest	25.35(100.00)	19.86(78.34)	17.02(67.14)
Annual Income from Sale of NTFPs (Rs.)	4475.50(100.00)	3156.59(70.53)	2359.90(52.73)

Quantity of Fuel wood Collection per Month (in K.g)	413.39(100.00)	294.50(71.24)	261.32(63.21)
Average Age of Plant Cut (Years)	27.47(100.00)	20.04(72.95)	17.78(64.72)
Average Time Spent to Collect a Bundle of Fuel Wood (Hours)	1.48(100.00)	2.20(148.60)	2.41(162.80)

Source: Primary Survey

The findings of the study on resource sustainability derived on the basis of information provided by all the 210 selected respondents are summarized in Table-6.5. It can be read off the table that the distance to be covered to collect materials from forests has increased from 0.64 km before ten years to 0.85 km five years hence to 1.02 km now or by 59.37 per cent over a decade. The number of days a person is engaged in a month to collect produce from forests has reduced from 25.35 days to 19.86 days to 17.02 days registering a decline by about 37.00 per cent during the last ten years. Income from sales of NTFPs collected from forests has fallen drastically from Rs. 4475.50 to Rs. 3156.59 to Rs. 2359.90 i.e. by 47. 27 per cent during the last decade. The amount of fuel wood collected has also fallen from 413.39 kgs to 294.50 kgs to 261.32 kgs or by 36.79 per cent and average life of a plant cut has a lowered by 35.28 per cent or from 27.47 years to 20.04 years to 17.78 years a ten-year period. The time taken for collecting a bundle of fuel wood has increased from 1.48 hours to 2.20 hours to 2.41 hours during the said period.

Resource sustainability differs across space. In terms of all six quantitative indicators of sustainability of common forests, the sample villages in Mayurbhanj show better results as compared to those in Keonjhar and Balasore in that order. These results corroborate those obtained with regard to management sustainability and qualitative indicators of resource sustainability.

6.5 Summary

The results obtained from the responses of the sample respondents on the issue of sustainability of common property forests are revealing. They show a substantial reduction in status relating to forest area, density of forest, collections and quality of forest produce over time. This means that sustainability of common forest resources has been affected negatively in the process of extraction of materials from forests and implementation of development projects which use forest materials one way or the other. However, the reduction in status of area, density, collections and quality are not uniform across space. The decline is reported to be the lowest or alternatively, the threat to resource sustainability is the least in Mayurbhanj followed by Keonjhar and with Balasore at the end of the ladder.

The findings based on quantitative indicators also indicate increase in the distance to be travelled to collect materials and time required to collect a given amount of produce from forests, and decline in the number of days per month a person is engaged in collecting materials, income from sales of NTFPs, fuel wood collection per month and average age of plant cut. These results show that sustainability of common property forest resources has reduced phenomenally over the years. Unsurprisingly, the impact has been non-uniform across areas. Among the three selected districts, the situation is the best in Mayurbhanj, worst in Balasore with Keonjhar in the moderate path on the sustainability scale.

Difference in initial endowments, mode of forest management practised in the past and present, and attitude of the users towards conservation and use of forests are the factors responsible for the perceived differences in resource sustainability among the districts surveyed.

It is thus amply clear that the common property forest resources are undergoing degradation and depletion over time. This proves our hypothesis that "Common property forest resources are becoming less sustainable over the years".

Another aspect of the finding of the study is that common forest resources are less unsustainable in villages having more effective and sustainable management practices compared to those with less effective and less sustainable management institutions. This proves our hypothesis that "The greater the sustainability of the management institutions the higher is the prospect of sustainability of the common property forest resources and vice versa."

7

Summary of Findings and Policy Implications

7.1 Introduction

About 85 per cent of the total population of Odisha live in the villages. A substantial proportion of them are poor, unemployed and victims of the prevailing economic and social systems. Common property resources (CPRs) such as forests, water and land play a vital role in the life and economy of this segment of the population in the state. Common pastures and grazing lands, village ponds, rivers, and forests and mangroves are the important sources of their livelihood and income generating activities. For example: fuel wood and dry leaves collected from the CPRs are used for cooking and heating purposes, grass and shrubs are used as fodder, timber and bamboo are used for construction of houses, and a large variety of fruits collected from forests and fish caught from village ponds, tanks, rivers and canals are used for sustenance of livelihood. CPRs also serve as insurance against risk for the rural poor of the state, particularly during the lean seasons of the year when wage employment is not available.

7.2 The Research Problem

In the ongoing process of liberalisation, privatisation and globalization, new markets are opening up, urbanization is expanding and production and demand patterns are changing very fast even in the rural sector of the state. The process has implications for availability and depletion of CPRs and dependence of the population on these resources. It is possible that CPRs are overexploited and have suffered a quality deterioration affecting the rural people in general and the rural poor in particular by causing further worsening off of their resource position and economic status. Problems of dependence, depletion, sustainability and management of these resources can be other possible outcomes. Degradation and mismanagement of common property resources impact heavily on the poor. in this backdrop we have drawn the boundaries of our research along three lines viz., dependence, heterogeneity and collective action, resource sustainability and their interlinkages in the villages of Odisha.

7.3 Significance of the Study

Keeping in mind the importance of common property resources, the present study has attempted to investigate into the role of common property forest resources in the rural livelihood support systems in villages of Odisha. We have tried to capture the broad issues outlined above with the help of a primary survey. At policy level, the research is expected to contribute significantly to governmental and non-governmental efforts towards micro level management of threatened ecological resources (forest) through institutions that are stable and equitable.

7.4 Objectives of the Study

The following are the objectives of the study.

1 To study the dependence of rural households on CPRs, compute the rate of their depletion and workout their current status at the national level.

2 To estimate the levels and extent of dependence of households on common property forest resources in relation to their economic heterogeneity in villages of Odisha.

3 To examine the role of socio-economic heterogeneity in the existing institutions and incentives for collective action and participatory management of common property forest resources in villages of Odisha.

4 To identify the trends in status of common property

forests and their sustainability in Odisha at the village level.

5 To derive lessons from the survey and suggest appropriate policy measures that can facilitate sustainability of common property forest resources, their use and management.

7.5 Hypotheses

The hypotheses tested in the present research are the following

1 Dependence on common property forests is related directly to household size but inversely to the income and agricultural land holding status of the households.

2 Socio-economic heterogeneity among the members of the management institutions has a negative bearing on its effectiveness in managing common property forests.

3 Common property forest resources are becoming less sustainable over the years.

4. The greater the sustainability of the management institutions the higher is the prospect of sustainability of the common property forest resources and vice versa.

7.6 Methodology

The investigation has been conducted on the basis of a four stage sample survey of six villages in three districts of Odisha. The survey districts are Balasore, Mayurbhanj and Keonjhar. The selection of districts was made on the basis of the classification of districts in to different agro-climatic zones by the NSSO 54th Round Survey on Common Property Resources in India. The sample villages from the Balasore district are Tenda and Banthiapada under Nilagiri Block. The two villages from Mayurbhanj district are under Jashipur block are Ramasahi and Mandam. From Keonjhar district the two villages Tanda and Ghatabalijodi come under the patna block.

On the whole 210 households were surveyed from all the six villages with 35 households randomly selected from each village. The random approach was adopted to minimize the bias factor in data collection and in quest of better results. Primary data were collected during April and May, 2010.

Standard statistical techniques have been applied to study household level dependence on CPR forest. Regression analysis has been conducted to ascertain the intensity of linkages between household level dependency on common property forests and its determinants such as household size, income, and agricultural land holding status.

Village level dependency on CPRs has been examined in relation to variables such as the status of CPRs, size of population, and degree of social and economic heterogeneity among users. Both quantitative and qualitative analysis have been carried out to assess future sustainability of CPR forests in the sample villages.

7.7 Dependency, Depletion and Current Status of CPRs in India

The study based on NSSO 54th Round data at the national level reveals that rural households are critically dependent on CPRs. Their collections from CPRs bear a direct relation with the size and consumption expenditure of households. A majority of rural households collect fuel wood from CPR forests and use them for cooking. Fuel wood collections were higher for larger population size class of villages. a direct relationship between availability and dependence was observed in the case of CPRs. A heartbreaking conclusion of the macro level study is that the CPR base of the country is depleting at an alarming rate and if appropriate corrective measures were not taken at the right earnest, they can prove fatal to the survival of life on the earth.

7.8 Socio-Economic Profile of the Study Area

It is correctly said that Odisha is a rich state inhabited by poor people. The state is endowed with vast tracts of fertile farm land, huge amount of mineral deposits, a long coast line, large amount of water resources, abundant forest resources, large livestock population and it enjoys a population dividend in terms of a large number of persons in the working age group. But the per capita income in the state is one of the lowest in the country and it is the most poverty stricken of all states. There is enough scope for expanding industries in the state and initiatives are on in this direction. Establishment of large plants is likely to cause serious damage to forests in the state for which environmentalists, economists and policy thinkers are organizing moments to save forests and displacement of population. The sample villages are inhabited by indigenous people with low income and are critically dependent on forests.

In terms of social composition both the villages in the Balasore district were homogeneous comprising only of STs. Similarly, in the Mayurbhanj district both the sample villages were observed to consists of ST population hence are homogeneous in terms of social stratification. However, the study villages in the Keonjhar district have heterogeneity in terms social composition and consisted of ST and non-ST population.

7.9 Common Property Forest Dependency

Investigation in respect of dependency of households on common property forests reveals very unsurprising results.

1. It shows that households in rural areas, particularly those living near the forests, are heavily dependent on CPR forests. They collect a variety of materials from forests for use in their households, livestock rearing and income generation.
2. Income from forest sources (i.e. value of NTFPs, FBAs, fuel wood, bamboo, timber) constitutes a significant proportion of aggregate income of the households. It accounts for 26.01 per cent of household income in Balasore, 38.59 per cent in Mayurbhanj and 31. 42 per cent in Keonjhar. Fuel wood has the commanding heights in the collection constitution 17.78 per cent of income from forest sources and 57.41 per cent of income from all sources at the aggregate level.
3. Villages endowed with greater amount of CPR forests per household are found to be those in which contribution of CPR forests to household income is higher compared to villages having relatively smaller amount of CPR forests per household.

4. For large population size class of villages the percentage share of forest income in total household income is observed to be higher in comparison to small size class of villages. this means that households in large population size class of villages are more CPR forest dependent and vice versa.
5. It is evidenced that households with comparatively lower income are more dependent on CPR forests than those with relatively higher income. The share of forest sources in total household income is found to be the highest for the households in the first quintile and first decile in income distribution and lowest for those in last quintile and last decile class. Similarly, BPL households are observed to be more CPR forest dependent than non-BPL households.
6. The results of regression analysis on the impact of economic heterogeneity on dependence of households on common property forests is noteworthy. It shows that large sized households depend more and households with relatively higher income and comparatively more amount of agricultural land depend less on CPR forests than those having less members, lower income and smaller amount of agricultural land. This establishes and proves our hypothesis that "dependence on common property forests is related directly to household size but inversely to the income and agricultural land holding status of the households".

7.10 Heterogeneity, Collective Action and Management

Our study on collective action and management of CPR forests and their relationship with socio-economic heterogeneity yields interesting results.

1. Forest dwellers and those living around forests have an inherent tendency to manage forests themselves through conventional methods of preventing cutting of immature plants and illegal felling of trees, using forests as per needs rather than wants, and taking steps for regeneration of forests. In the sample villages, forests are being managed by the JFM system although in

Mayurbhanj district CFM system was in vogue earlier.

2. Social, economic and demographic homogeneity / heterogeneity among the members of the forest management committee exert considerable influence on the effectiveness and sustainability of management institutions. Management is more effective and sustainable if there is social and economic homogeneity among the committee members and if women members play active roles in the decision-making process. But where there is social and economic heterogeneity among members and women are passive, management is less effective and less sustainable.

This proves our second hypothesis that "Socio-economic heterogeneity among the members of the management institutions has a negative bearing on its effectiveness in managing common property forests".

7.11 Resource Sustainability

The study on sustainability of common property forest resources in the study villages yields similar results. The sample respondents were asked to reveal their perceptions about both qualitative and quantitative indicators of resource sustainability. The qualitative indicators were area under forests, forest density, collection of materials from forests and quality of materials collected. The respondents indicated significant decline in area under forests, reduction in forest density, fall in quantity of collections per person per unit of time and deterioration in quality at the present compared to their status ten years preceding the survey and five years before the survey. Among the quantitative indicators, distance to forests, dependence on forests in number of days per month, income from sale of NTFPs, collection of fuel wood per month, average age of plant cut, time required to collect a given quantity of materials from forests figured. Increase in distance to forests and in time required to collect a given amount of materials were observed while a reduction in the number of days of dependence on forests, in income from sale of NTFPs, quantity of fuel wood collection per month and average age of plant cut was reported. The results obtained on the basis of both the qualitative and quantitative indicators point to phenomenal reduction in sustainability of common property forest resources. Thus the hypothesis that common property forest resources are becoming less sustainable over the years is proved.

However, falling resource sustainability has not been uniform across the districts covered under the study. The decline in sustainability is found to be the lowest in Mayurbhanj district and highest in Balasore district with Keonjhar lying in between. Differences in the initial resource endowments, mode of forest management practised in the past and present, and attitude of the users towards conservation and extraction across areas explain such spatial variations. Spatial variations in resource sustainability also bear a close link with such variations in effectiveness of management mechanisms operating in respective areas. It is observed that the districts where management is more sustainable are the districts where resources are less unsustainable and vice versa. This proves our hypothesis that Socio-economic heterogeneity among the members of the management institutions has a negative bearing on its effectiveness in managing common property forests.

7.12 Conclusion

The following are the main conclusions of our study

1 The rural households in Odisha are critically dependent on CPR forests. The results of sample survey results indicate that the share of CPR forest in total household income is very high at about 30 per cent.
2 The share of CPR forest income (direct and indirect) in the households' total income depends on the village level availability of CPR forests, population size of the village and scope for off-forest income. The share of CPR forest income in relation to households' total income is directly related to village level availability of CPR forest and inversely related to population of the village and opportunity to earn income from non-forest sources.
3 Low income households are more CPR forest dependent than relatively high-income households. The share of the CPR forest income in households' annual income increases as we move from the richest 10 percentage to

the poorest 10 percentage of the households in the income distribution and when we move from the first quintile to the fifth quintile in the income distribution.

4 Regression analysis suggests that the percentage share of CPR forest income in households' total income is directly related to household size and negatively related to households' economic condition measured by income and agricultural land holding status.

5 In Odisha the current pattern of resource use poses serious threats to future sustainability of CPR forest resource systems in the state. The CPR forest has deteriorated in terms of area, density, collection quantity and quality of produce compared to the status 10 years back and that five years hence.

6 In respect of the sustainability indicators such as, number of days households are engaged in collecting materials from CPR forests, income from sales of NTFPs, quantity of fuel wood collection at household level and average age of plant cut, it was observed that the same have decreased remarkably compared to the position 10 and five years back. Distance to CPR forest and collection time to make a bundle of fuel wood have gone up substantially compared to those 10 years and five years back.

7 In all the six sample villages the CPR forests are managed by village level formal management institutions and the role of those institutions are mostly confined to

a) Protection of CPR forest.

b) Bush cutting and clearing activities.

c) Saving trees from fire and helping them to grow properly.

d) To catch thieves and illegal intruders to the CPR forest.

e) To prevent illegal haunting.

f) To clear the trees decaying naturally and to put control over logging activities.

g) Reviewing households' requirement of timber for house construction, fencing and household enterprises and accordingly allotting quota.

8 Institutional stability as well as their effective functioning largely depend on group characteristics such as socio-economic heterogeneity and attitude of committee members towards promotion of forests. Group homogeneity brings stability of the management institutions and ensures sustainable management of common property forest resource systems. This is evidenced from the two sample villages in Mayurbhanj. In both these sample villages, management committees are homogeneous in respect of social stratification and economic status. The committees exist for the last 20 years and are free from any major conflicts among the members.

Group heterogeneity in terms of both social stratification and economic condition have destabilized the management institutions, causing laxity in management of CPR forest. This has been evidenced from the four sample villages in Keonjhar and Balasore districts.

7.13 Policy Implications

It has been observed that dependence and pressure on the existing common property forest resource system is higher than the acceptable level. The extraction of materials from forest is too high and management is too inadequate to pose serious threats to the future sustainability of existing management mechanisms and resource systems. In the interests of providing livelihood support to the forest dwellers, indigenous tribal communities and households living close to the forest areas as also of ensuring sustainability of forest resources, conservation and promotion of common forests assumes priority significance. It is imperative to take initiatives at local, sub-national and national levels by indigenous people, government administration, non-governmental organizations and the civil society at large to conserve, protect and facilitate growth of the forest resource system. The findings of the study and observations made above have significant implications for corrective and promotive policy.

1. Lack of off-forest income earning opportunities tend

to put heavy pressure on common property forest resources leading to unsustainable use of forests, degradation and quality deterioration. Appropriate measures need to be taken to provide off-forest employment opportunities in the village areas. Expansions of educational avenues have a vital role in this respect. Education can be a deterrent to manual labour for exploiting forests; it can also make them aware of the dangers of overexploitation and the need of planting trees and creating social forestry.

2. The existing legal system is prohibitive rather than promotive. It tries to prevent the entry of people into protected and reserved forests, let alone extracting materials from them. History teaches us that restrictionism is a new form of the Raj and it promotes piracy, pilferage and corruption. Our experience with the forest laws and their implementation only reaffirms this. What is needed is to allow people to collect low-priced regenerative fuel wood and other NTFP kind of requirements by the people but prohibitive restrictions on overextraction of less regenerative high-priced forest products by the privileged minority. Administration of controlled harvesting of these resources through government outlets will address both equity and resource sustainability.
3. The indigenous people have an undeclared and unwritten right over common forests. They have a tendency for controlled extraction and the motivation for facilitating regeneration. The JFM form of participatory management system, though devised to ensure broad based participation in the management decision making process, has not proved successful. It achieved neither joint management nor participatory management. The officials of the forest department still hold the key and operate the management system to their own advantage through a handful of village level power elite with others being passive actors in the process. While forming village level institutions due care need to be taken to take members from all social

strata, economic background, sex and ages. The official functionaries should provide funds and act as facilitators for forest promotion activities.

4. Big industrial and development projects are a major cause of degradation and depletion of forests. It is definitely immoral to prevent the establishment of these projects as they would slow growth and increase poverty, but it is certainly rational to establish them on barren and waste lands. By taking little care in granting location sites to these projects the government can achieve both high economic growth and sustainability of common property forest resources.

Nature has given us enough to meet our needs but at the same time it is very niggardly when it comes to satisfy our wants. We can create jobs and wealth, enhance our capabilities and livelihood support systems even without undermining the common property forest resource base.

7.14 The Six Global Forest Goals

The United Nations Strategic Plan for Forests 2017-2030 (UNSPF), created by the Member States of the United Nations Forum on Forests (UNFF) to provide a global framework for action at all levels to sustainably manage all types of forests and trees outside forests, and to halt deforestation and forest degradation, has six Global Forest Goals and 26 associated targets (UN, 2021). All these goals and targets are voluntary and universal. The Goals fully encompass and build on the foundation of the four Global Objectives on Forests of the United Nations Forest Instrument (UNFI) which was adopted by the United Nations General Assembly (UNGA) in 2007. The Six Goals are to:

1. Reverse the loss of forest cover worldwide through sustainable forest management, including protection, restoration, afforestation and reforestation, and increase efforts to prevent forest degradation and contribute to the global effort of addressing climate change.
2. Enhance forest-based economic, social and environmental benefits, including the livelihoods of forest-dependent people.

3. Increase significantly the area of protected forests worldwide and other areas of sustainably managed forests, as well as the proportion of forest products from sustainably managed forests.
4. Mobilize significantly increased, new and additional financial resources from all sources for the implementation of sustainable forest management and strengthen scientific and technical cooperation and partnerships.
5. Promote governance frameworks to implement sustainable forest management, including through the United Nations forest instrument, and enhance the contribution of forests to the 2030 Agenda for Sustainable Development.
6. Enhance cooperation, coordination, coherence and synergies on forest-related issues at all levels, including within the United Nations system and across member organizations of the Collaborative Partnership on Forests, as well as across sectors and relevant stakeholders.

The Report has made three observations-based recommendations as under:

i. Sustainably resourced and managed forests can bolster employment, disaster risk reduction, food security and social safety nets, for starters.
ii. Safeguarding and restoring forests are among the environmental actions that can reduce the risk of future zoonotic disease outbreaks and help promote global health.
iii. The future course of action should include greater sustainability and a greener and more inclusive economy to tackle the threats of Covid-19, climate change and the biodiversity crisis faced by forests.

8.15 Scope for Further Research

Over the years considerable interest has developed in research on common property forest resource system. Expectedly, many of these researches including the present one have attempted to fill up the research gaps in the field, but gaps do still exist.

This study concentrates on dependency on forests of the villages living in or around forest areas, management mechanisms operating in those villages and resource sustainability issues as perceived by them. There are other users of forest, other uses of forest produce, other management mechanisms and other forest regions even within Odisha. Researches on these issues will have a rich pay off.

Bibliography

Adhikari, B. (2000): Property Rights and Natural Resources: Socio-economic Heterogeneity and Income Distribution in Common Property Resource Management in Nepal. *Paper Presented in Beijer.*

Adhikari, B. (2001): Literature Review on the Economics of Common Property Resources.*Report Prepared for NRSP Project R7857.*

Adhikari, B. and J. Lovett. (2006): Institutions and collective action: Does heterogeneity matter in community-based resource management? *Journal ofDevelopment Studies* 42(3):426-45.

Agarwal, A. (2007): Forests Governance and Sustainability: Common Property Theory and its Contributions. *International Journal of the Commons,* Vol-1, No-1.

Agrawal, A. (1996): The Community versus the Market and the State. *Journal of Agricultural and Environmental Ethics* 9(1):1-15.

Agrawal, A. (2001): Common Property Institutions and Sustainable Governance of Resources. *World Development* 29(10): 1649-1672.

Agrawal, A. (2003): Sustainable Governance of Common-pool Resources: Context, Methods and Politics. Annual Review of Anthropology, 32: 243-62.

Agrawal, A. (2005):*Environmentality: Technologies of Government and the Making of Subjects.* Durham, NC, Duke University Press.

Agrawal, A. and A. Chhatre (2006): Explaining success on the commons: Community forest governance in the Indian Himalaya. *World Development* 23(1):149-66.

Agrawal, A. and G. Yadama (1997): How do social institutions mediate market and population pressures on resources?

Forest Panchayats in Kumaon India. *Development and Change* 28: 435-65.

Ali,T, M. Ahmad, B. Shahbaz and A. Suleri (2007): Impact of Participatory Forest Management on Financial Assets of Rural Communities in Northwest Pakistan. *Ecological Economics*, 63:588-593.

Ameha, A., Larsen, H.O. & Lemenih, M. (2014). Participatory Forest Management in Ethiopia: Learning from Pilot Projects. Environmental Management, **53:** 838–854.

Andelson, R. V. (1991): *Commons without Tragedy: The Congruence of Garrett Hardin and Henry George,* in R. V. Andelson (Eds): Commons without Tragedy: The Social Ecology of Land Tenure and Democracy, Centre for Incentive Taxation, London.

Anderson, J. M. (1977):*A Model of the Commons,* in Hardin, G. J. Baden (eds.): Managing the Commons, W. H. Freeman, San Francisco.

Andersson, K. P, C.C. Gibson and F. Lehoucq (2006): Municipal politics and forest governance: Comparative analysis of decentralization in Bolivia and Guatemala. *World Development* 34(3): 576-95.

Anitha, V. & Muraleedharan, P.K. (2007). Economic Valuation of Ecotourism Development of a Recreational Site in the Natural Forests of Southern Western Ghats. Kerala Forest Research Institute (KFRI) Research Report No. 288.

Anitha, V. & Muraleedharan, P.K., (2002). Study on Social and Economic Dependencies of the local communities on Protected Area- A case of Peechi Vazhani and Chimmony Wildlife Sanctuaries. Kerala Forest Research Institute (KFRI) Research Report No.240.

Antinori, C. and D. B. Bray (2005): Community Forest Enteprises as Entreprenuerial Firms: Economic and Institutional Perspectives from Mexico. *World Development* 33(9): 1529-43.

Arnold, J. E. M. (1990): Common Property Management and Sustainable Development in India. *Working Paper No. 9,* Forestry for Sustainable Development Program, Department of Forest Resources, University of Minnesota, St. Paul, MN.

Arnold, J. E. M. (1998):*Managing Forests as Common Property.* FAO Forestry Paper 136. Rome: FAO.

Arnold, J. E. M. and W. C. Steward (1991): Common Property Resource Management. *Tropical Forestry Paper No. 24*, Oxford Forestry Institute, University of Oxford, Oxford.

Axelrod, R. (1981): The Emergence of Co-operation among Egoists. *American Political Science Review*, 75, pp.306-318.

Axelrod, R. (1984):*The evolution of cooperation*. Basic Books, New York.

Axelrod, R. and D. Dion (1988): The further evolution of cooperation. *Science* 242.4884, 1385-90.

Babu, P. V., S. Chandra and J. B. Dent (1996): Common Property Resource Management in Haryana State, India: A Success Story of the Rehabilitation of Degraded Village Common Lands. Presented at "Voices from the Commons", *the sixth annual conference of the International Association for the Study of Common Property (IASCP), Berkeley,* CA, June 5-8.

Babu, PV.S.C (1998): Common Property Resource Management in Haryana State, India: Analysis of the impact of Participation in Management of Common Property Resources and the Relative Effectiveness of Common Property Regimes. *Paper presented at the IASCP Conference, 1998-10-14 June,* Vancouver, Canada.

Baden, J. A., and D. S. Noonan (1998):*The Federal Treasury as a Common-Pool Resource: The Predatory Bureaucracy as a Management Tool,* in J. A. Baden and D.S. Noonan, (eds.), Managing the Commons, Indiana University Press, Bloomington:

Baland, J. M. and J. P. Platteau (1998): Division of the Commons: A Partial Assessment of the New Institutional Economics of Land Rights. *American Journal of Agricultural Economics* 80 (3): 644-650.

Baland, J.M and J.-P. Platteau (1996): *Halting Degradation of Natural Resources: Is there a Role for Rural Communities*, Clarendon Press, Oxford.

Baland, J.M. and J.-P. Platteau (1996-A): Inequality and Collective Actions in the Commons. *Paper Presented* at Amherst, May 1996.

Balasubramanian, R. and K.N. Selvaraj (2003): Poverty, Private Property and Common Pool Resource Management: The Case of Irrigation Tank in South India. *SANDEE working paper, No. 2-03.*

Ballabh, V., K. Balooni and S. Dave (2002): Why Local Resource Management Institutions Decline: A Comparative Analysis of *Van* (Forest) Panchayats and Forest Protection Committees in India. *World Development*, 30(12): 2153-2167.

Bardhan, P. (1984): *Land, Labor and Rural Poverty*, New York, Columbia University Press.

Bardhan, P. (1993): Symposium on management of local commons. *The Journal of Economic Perspectives* 7(4).

Bardhan, P. and J. Dayton-Johnson (2000): Heterogeneity and Commons Management. *Draft Paper Prepared for the National Research Council's Institutions for Managing the Commons Project*. Department of Economics. University of California, Berkeley, USA.

Bardhan, P., M. Ghatak and A. Karaivanov (2002): Inequality and Collective Action.

Bardhan, Pranab K., (ed.) (1989): *The Economic Theory of Agrarian Institutions*, Oxford, Clarendon Press.

Bardhan, Pranab. (2000): Irrigation and Cooperation: An Empirical Analysis of 48 Irrigation Communities in South India. *Economic Development and Cultural Change*, 48(4): 847-865.

Beck, T., Ghosh and G. Madan (2000): Common property resources and the poor: findings from West Bengal. *Economic and Political Weekly* 35(3): 147-153.

Beckley, T. M. (1998). The nestedness of forest dependence: a conceptual framework and empirical exploration

Behera, B. (2008): Institutional Dynamics and Natural Resource Management: A Study of JFM in AP. *Journal of Rural Development*. 27(4).

Berkes, F. (ed.) (1989): *Common Property Resources: Ecology and Community Based Sustainable Development*. Belhaven Press, London.

Bhandari D.&Jianhua, Z. (2017) Household Dependency on Buffer Zone Community Forest and its Implication for Management of Chitwan National Park, Nepal. International Journal of Sciences, 6 (3): 68-80.

Bon. E. (2003): Common Property Resources at the Interface of Agriculture and Forest policies; before and after 1988. *Tropical Ecology* 44 (1).

Bousquet, F. et al., (1996): Tragedy of the commons, game theory and spatial simulation of complex systems. *Ecological Economics* 1(8).

Box, T. W. (1995): A viewpoint: range managers and the tragedy of the commons. *Rangelands* 17: 83-84.

Boyce, J. (1988): Technological and Institutional Alternatives in Asian Rice Irrigation. *Economic and Political Weekly* 26 March, A6-A22.

Boyce, J.K. (1994): Inequality as a cause of environmental degradation. *Ecological Economics*, 11:169-178.

Branney, P. and K.P. Yadav (1998): Changes in Community Forest Condition and Management 1994-1998: Analysis of Information from Forest Resource Assessment Study and Socio-Economic Study in the Koshi Hills. *Project Report G/ NUKCFP32 NUKCFP, Kathmandu*.

Bray, D.B., C. Antinori, and J.M. Torres-Rojo (2006): The Mexican model of community forest management: The role of agrarian policy, forest policy and entrepreneurial organization. *Forest Policy and Economics* 8(4): 470-84.

Bromely, D. (ed.), (1992): *Making the Commons Work: Theory, Practice and Policy*. Institute for Contemporary Studies Press, San Francisco, CA.

Bromley, D. W. (1991): *Environment and Economy: Property Rights and Public Policy*. Oxford, UK, Oxford University Press.

Bromley, D. W. (1992): The commons, common property and environment policy. *Environmental and Resource Economics* 2(1): 1-17.

Brooks, J.S., M.A. Franzen, C.M. Holmes, M.N. Grote, and M. Borgerhoff Mulder (2006): Testing hypotheses for the success of different conservation strategies. *Conservation Biology* 20(5): 1528-38.

Burger, J. and M. Gochfeld (1998): The tragedy of the commons thirty years later. *Environment40*: 4-27.

Calvert, R.L. (1995): Rational actors, equilibrium and social institutions. In J. Knight and I.Sened (eds.), *Explaining social institutions*, University of Michigan Press, Ann Arbor.

Campbell J.Y. (1992): Joint forest management in India. *Social Change*, 22(1):36-53.

Campbell, B., A. Mandondo, N. Nemarundwe, B. Sithole, W. de Jong, M. Luckert and F. Matose (2001): Challenges to proponents of common property resource systems: despairing voices from the social forests of Zimbabwe. *World Development* 29(4):589-600.

Campbell, B.M., S. Jeffrey,M. Luckert, M.Mutamba, and C. Zindi (2002):*Household livelihoods in semi-arid regions: options and constraints.* Center for International Research, Bogor, Indonesia.

Cavendish, W. (1998): The Complexity of the Commons: Environmental Resource Demands in Rural Zimbabwe. Centre for the Study of African Economies, Institute of Economics and Statistics, University of Oxford, Oxford, UK, *(Working Paper no. 8).*

Cavendish, W. (1999): Poverty, inequality and environmental resources: quantitative analysis of rural households. *Working Paper Series 99-9,* Centre for the Study of African Economies, Oxford.

Cavendish, W. (2000): Empirical regularities in the poverty-environment relationship of rural households: evidence from Zimbabwe. *World Development,* 28(11) pp 1979-2003.

Chambers, A. (1991): The Paradox of the Commons. *Presented at the second annual conference of the International Association for the Study of Common Property (IASCP),* Winnipeg, Manitoba, September 26-29.

Charnley, S., Kelly, E. C. & Fischer, A. P. (2020). Fostering collective action to reduce wildfire risk across property boundaries in the American West. Environmental ResearchLetters, 15(2). Open Access Retrieved from https://iopscience.iop.org/article/10.1088/1748-9326/ab639a on 25.07.2021.

Cheung, S.N. (1970): The Structure of a Contract and the Theory of a Non-exclusive Resource. *Journal of Law and Economics,* Vol.13, pp.49-70.

Chisika, S. N. & Yeom, C. (2021). Enhancing Ecologically Sustainable Management of Deadwood in Kenya's Natural Forests. Hindawi International Journal of Forestry Research, Volume 2021, Article ID 6647618, 20 pages,

Chopra K., G.K. Kadekodi and M.N. Murty (1990) *Participatory Development: People and common property Resources, studies in economic development and Planning, No.52,* Institute of Economic Growth, Delhi, Sage Publication.

Chopra, K. and G. K. Kadekodi (1991): Participatory institutions: the context of common and private property resources. *Environmental and Resource Economics,* 1:353-372.

Chopra, K., C. Kadekodi and M. Murthy (1989): People's Participation and Common Property Resources. *Economic and Political Weekly,* Vol (24) pp: A.189-A.195.

Chopra, K., G. K. Kadekodi and M. N. Murty (1988): Economic Evaluation of People's Participation in the Management of Common Property Resources. *Working Paper, no. 3,* National Institute of Public Finance and Policy, New Delhi, India.

Ciriacy, W., S. V. and R. C. Bishop. (1975): Common property as a concept in natural resource policy. *Natural Resources Journal* 15: 713-727.

Cornes R. and T. Sandler (1989):*The Externalities, Public Goods and Club Goods,* Cambridge University Press, Cambridge.

Cornes, R. and T. Sandler (1983): On commons and tragedies. *American Economic Review* 83: 787-792.

Damodaran, A. (1991): Tragedy of the commons and comedy of common property resources. *Economic and Political Weekly* 26(38): 2213-2215.

Dana, D. (1997): Overcoming the political tragedy of the commons: lessons learned from the reauthorization of the Magnuson Act. *Ecology Law Quarterly* 24: 833-ff.

Dasgupta P. (1982): *The Control of Resources,* Basil Blackwell, Oxford.

Dasgupta, P. (2005): Common Property Resources: Economic Analytics. *Article based on Lecturers* at the May 2004 workshop at the SANDEE in Bangalore.

Dayton-Johnson, J. (2000): Determinants of Collective Action on the Local Commons: A Model with Evidence from Mexico. *Journal of Development Economics,* Vol. 62, pp: 181-208.

Dearden, P.M. Carter, R. Kowalski, M. Surridge (1999): ICITRAP- An Experimental Training Exercise for Examining Participatory Approaches to Project Management. *Public Administration and Development,* Vol.19, pp.93-104.

Demsetz, H. (1967): Towards a Theory of Property Rights. *American Economic Review,* Vol.52, No.2, pp: 347-379.

Dietz, T., E. Ostrom, and P. Stern (2003): The struggle to govern the commons. *Science* 302: 1907-12.

Duraiappah A.K. (1998): Poverty and Environmental Degradation: a review and analysis of the nexus. *World Development,* 26(12): 2169-2179.

Dutta, P. K. and R. K. Sundaram (1993): The tragedy of the commons? *Economic Theory* 3: 413-426.

Easter K. W. And K. Palanisami (1986): Tank irrigation in India: an example of common Property resources management. In: National Research Council, Proceedings of the Conference on common property Resource Management, National Academy Press, Washington D.C.

Economics and Statistics, Odisha, Bhubaneswar.

Economics and Statistics, Odisha, Bhubaneswar.

Edney, J. J. (1981): Paradoxes on the commons: scarcity and the problem of inequality. *Journal of Community Psychology* 9: 3-34.

Edney, J. J. and C. S. Harper (1978): The commons dilemma: a review of contributions from psychology. *Environmental Management* 2: 491-507.

Eggertsson, T. (1990): *Economic Behaviour and Institutions*. Cambridge, UK, Cambridge University Press.

Ellickson, R.C. (1991): *Order without law: how neighbors settle disputes*. Harvard University Press, Cambridge.

Elliott, H. (1997): A general statement of the tragedy of the commons. *Population and Environment*18: 515-ff.

Feeny, D. et al., (1998):*The Tragedy of the Commons: Twenty-Two Years Later*, in J. A. Baden and D. S. Noonan, eds., Managing the Commons, Indiana University Press, Bloomington.

Fisher, M., (2004): Household welfare and forestry dependence in Southern Malawi. *Environmental and Development Economics* 9 (2004) 135-154.

Fisher, M., M. Chaudhury and B. Mccusker (2010): Do Forest Help Rural households Adapt to Climatic Variability? Evidence from Southern Malawi. World Development.38(9): 1241-1250.

Flanery, A., Mbatu, R., Johns, R. & Stewart, D. (2020). Heterogeneity and Collective Action: Community Integration Appraisal for REDD+Forest Management Implementation. Small-scale Forestry, **19 (1)**: 1–17.

Fortmann, L., Sohngen, B. & Southgate, S. (2017). Assessing the Role of Group Heterogeneity in Community Forest Concessions in Guatemala's Maya Biosphere Reserve. Land Economics, 93 (3): 503–526.

Gautam, K.H. (2006) Forestry, politicians and power—Perspectives from Nepal's forest policy, Forest policy and economics, 8 (2): 175-182.

Gehrig, S., Schlüter, A. & Hammerstein, P. (2019). Sociocultural heterogeneity in a common pool resource dilemma. PLoS ONE 14(1): e0210561. https://doi.org/10.1371/journal.pone.0210561. Open Access Article Retrieved on 25.07.2021.

Gibson, C., E. Ostrom, and J.T. Williams. (2005): Local enforcement and better forests. *World Development* 33(2): 273-84.

GoI (2012). India State of Forest Report (ISFR)- 2012. Forest Survey of India (FSI), Ministry of Environment & Forest (MoEF), Government of India.

GoI (2019). Population Projections for India and States 2011 – 2036, Report of The Technical Group on Population Projections. National Commission on Population, Ministry of Health & Family Welfare, Government of India.

GoI (2020). India State of Forest Report (ISFR)- 2019. Forest Survey of India (FSI), Ministry of Environment, Forest & Climate Change (MoEF&CC), Government of India.

Goldman, M. (1998):*Inventing the Commons: Theories and Practices of the Commons' Professional*, in Goldman, M. (Ed.): Privatizing Nature: Political Struggles for the Global Commons, Rutgers University Press, New Brunswick, NJ.

Gordon, H.S. (1954): The Economic Theory of a Common Pool Resource: The Fishery. *Journal of Political Economy*, Vol. 62, pp: 124-42.

Government of India (2001): Basic Rural Statistics, Ministry of Rural Development, Government of India, New Delhi.

Government of India (2010): Economic Survey, 2009-10. Ministry of Finance, Government of India New Delhi.

Government of Odisha (2018): Odisha Economic Survey 2017-18

Government of Odisha (2007): District statistical hand book Balasore. Directotate of

Government of Odisha (2008): Odisha agricultural statistics, 2006-07. Directorate of Agriculture and Food Production Odisha, Bhubaneswar.

Government of Odisha (2010): Economic Survey, 2009-10. Planning and Co-ordination Department, and Directorate of Economics and Statistics, Government of Odisha, Bhubaneswar.

Government of Odisha (2018): District statistical hand book Balasore. Directotate of Economics and Statistics, Odisha, Bhubaneswar.

Government of Odisha (2018): District statistical hand book Keonjhar. Directotate of

Government of Odisha (2018): District statistical hand book Mayurbhanj. Directotate of Economics and Statistics, Odisha, Bhubaneswar.

Grafton, R. Quentin (2000): Governance of the Commons: A Role for the State? *Land Economics* 76(4): 504-17.

Guha, R. (1989):*The Unquiet Woods: Ecological Change and Peasant Resistance in the Himalaya.* New Delhi: Oxford University Press.

Hanna, S. (1992): *Lessons from Ocean Governance from History, Ecology and Economics.* In B. C. J. N., D. W. Cicin-sain (eds.) Ocean Governance: A New Vision. Center for the Study of Marine Policy, Graduate College of Marine Studies, University of Delaware, Newark.

Hanna, S. and M. Munasinghe (1995): *An Introduction to Property Rights and the Environment.* In S. Hanna and M. Munasinghe (eds.) Property Rights and the Environment: Social and Ecological Issues. The Beijer International Institute of Ecological Economics and The World Bank.

Hardin G. (1968): The tragedy of common. *Science*, 162:1243-1248.

Hardin, G. (1991): *The Tragedy of the Unmanaged Commons: Population and the Disguises of Providence,* in R. V. Andelson, eds., Commons Without Tragedy, Barnes and Noble, Savage, MD.

Hardin, G. (1992): *The tragedy of the commons,* in A. Markandya and J. Richardson, eds., Environmental Economics: A Reader, St. Martin's, New York, NY.

Hazlett, D. (1997): A common property experiment with a renewable resource. *Economic Inquiry* 35: 858-861.

He, J., Martin, A., Lang, R. &Gross-Camp, N. (2021). Explaining success on community forestry through a lens of environmental justice: Local justice norms and practices in China. World Development, 142, June 2021

Heltberg, R. (2001): Determinants and impact of local institutions for common resource management. *Environment and Development Economics* 6: 183-208.

Herr, A. R. (1996): Appropriation Externalities in the Commons: Theory and Experimental Evidence: Ph.D. Dissertation, Indiana University.

Honneland, G. (1999): Interaction of research programmes in social science studies of the commons. *Acta Sociologica*, 42: 193-205.

Hopa, N. and A. Cheater (1996): Trusteeship and Maori Commons. presented at "Voices from the Commons," *the sixth annual conference of the International Association for the Study of Common Property (IASCP)*, Berkeley, CA, June 5-8.

Horsfall, J. G. (1972): Agricultural strategy in the tragedy of the commons. *Agricultural Science Review* 10: 17-22. https://doi.org/10.1155/2021/6647618. Retrived on 05.08.2021.

Hung, N. M. and Y. Richelle (1997): Trade gains, paretian transfer and the tragedy of the commons. *Economic Studies Quarterly* 48: 213-ff.

Inoni, O.E. (2009): Effects of Forest Resources Exploitation on the Economic Well-being of Rural Households in Delta State, Nigeria. *Agricultura Tropica et Subtropica*, Vol.42 (1).

Iqbal, T., Slathia, P. S., Peshin, R., Sehgal, S., Sharma, M., Kour, K. & Kumar, R. (2021). Perception Towards Joint Forest Management Programme in Conservation of Forest Resources in Jammu Division. Indian Journal of Extension Education, 57(1): 67-72.

Iyengar, S. (1988): Common property land resources in Gujarat: Some findings about their size, status, and use. Working paper no. 18, Gujarat Institute of Development Research, Ahmedabad, India.

Jain, P. & Sajjad, H. (2016). Household dependency on forest resources in the Sariska Tiger Reserve (STR), India: implications for management. Journal of Sustainable Forestry, 35 (1): 60-74.

Janvry, D. A., N. McCarthy and E. Sadoulet (1998): Endogenous provision and appropriation in the commons. *American Journal of Agricultural Economics* 80:658-664.

Jayaraman, T.K. (1981): Farmer's Organization in surface irrigation projects: two Empirical studies from Gujurat . *Economic and Political Weekly*, 16(39):A89-A98.

Jodha, N. S. (1985): Population growth and decline of common property resources in Rajasthan, India. *Population and Development Review 11(2).*

Jodha, N. S. (1986): Common property resources and rural poor in dry regions of India. *Economic and Political Weekly*, 21(27):1169-1181.

Jodha, N. S. (1990): Rural common property resources: contributions and crisis. *Economic and Political Weekly*, 25(26): A65-A78.

Jodha, N. S. (1992): Common property resources: A missing dimension of development Strategies, *World Bank Discussion Papers*, No. 169, World Bank Washington D. C.

Jodha, N. S. (1994): 'Management of Common Property Resources in selected dry areas of India', in Kerr, John et al., *op cit*, pp. 339-361.

Jodha, N. S. (1995): Common property resources and the dynamics of rural poverty in India's dry regions. *Unasylva 46(1):* 23-29.

Johnson, O.E.G. (1972): Economic Analysis, the Legal Framework and Land Tenure Systems. *Journal of Law and Economics*, Vol.15, pp.259-276.

Joshi, B.K. (2006): Common Property Resources Synergy and Perspectives of Sustainable Management in Garurganga watershed, Indian Central Himalaya.

Jumbe, B.L, et al. (2005): Contribution of Dry Forests to Rural Livelihoods and National Economy of Zambia.

Kadekodi, G.K. (1995): Operationalising Sustainable Development: Ecology – Economy Interactions at a Regional level, Institute for Environmental Studies, The Netherlands.

Kalaba, F.K., Quinn, C.H. & Dougill, A.J. (2013). Contribution of forest provisioning ecosystem services to rural livelihoods in the Miombo woodlands of Zambia. Population and Environment, 35 (2): 159-182.

Kanbur, R. (1992): Heterogeneity, Distribution and Cooperation in Common Property Resource management, Policy Research Working Papers, WPS 844, World Bank, Washington D. C.

Kant, S. (2000): A Dynamic Approach to Forest Regimes in Developing Economies. *Ecological Economics*. 32, pp: 287-300.

Klooster, D. and O. Masera (2000): Community Forest Management in Mexico: Carbon Mitigation and Biodiversity Conservation through rural Development. *Global Environmental Change*, 10: 259-272.

Kumar, S. (2002): Does "Participation" in Common Pool Resource Management Help the Poor? A Social Cost-Benefit Analysis of Joint Forest Management in Jharkhand, India. *World Development*, 30(5):763-782.

Kumar, S. K. and D. Hotchkiss (1988): Consequences of Deforestation for Women's Time Allocation, Agricultural Production and Nutrition in the Hills of Nepal, *IFPRI Research*

Report No.69, International Food Policy Research Institute, Washington D. C.

Lemos, M.C. and A. Agrawal (2006): Environmental governance. *Annual Review of Environment and Resources* 31: 297-325.

Libcap , G.D. (1995): The Conditions for Successful Collective Action. *In Local Commons and Global Interdependence: Heterogeneity and Cooperation in Two Domains*, ed.Robert, O. Keohane and Elinor Ostrom. 161-90. London: Sage.

Libecap, G. D. (1989): Distributional Issues in Contracting for Property Rights. *Journal of Institutional and Theoretical Economics* Vol. (145), pp: 6-24.

Lise, W. (2000): Factors Influencing People's Participation in Forest Management in India. *Ecological Economics*, 34: 379-392.

Luswaga, H. &Nuppenau, E. (2020). Participatory Forest Management in West Usambara Tanzania: What Is the Community Perception on Success?*Sustainability*, 12(3): 921. Retrived on 05.08.2021.

Mahanty, S., J. Fox, L. McLees, M. Nurse and P. Stephen (2006): Introduction: Equity in Community-based Resource Management. In: Mahanty, S., J.Fox, M. Nurse, P. Stephen and L. McLees. (Eds), *Hanging in the Balance: Equity in Community Based Natural Resource Management in Asia*. RECOFTC andEast-West Center.

Malla, Y.B. (2000): Impact of Community Forest Policy on Rural Livelihood and Food Security in Nepal. *Unasylva* 202, Vol.51.

Mallik, R.M. (1994): *Study of Some Minor Forest Produces in Odisha: An Empirical Investigation*. Nabakrushna Choudhury Centre for Development Studies (NCDS), Bhubaneswar, Odisha.

Mallik, R.M. (1996): Procurement and Marketing of Kendu Leaves in Odisha: An Empirical Investigation, NCDS, Bhubaneswar, Odisha.

Mallik, R.M. (2000): Sustainable Management of Non-Timber Forest Products in Odisha Some Issues and Options. *Indian Journal of Agricultural Economics*, 55(3):384-397.

Mallik, R.M. and N. Panigrahi (1998): *Study of Domestic and Commercial Use including marketing of NTFPs*, Research Report Submitted to SCC, SANDIACONSULT NATURA, Sweden.

Markandya, A. (2001): Poverty Alleviation and Sustainable Development: Implications for the Management of Natural Capital, **SANDEE** Research and Training Workshop, New Delhi.

Marothia, D.K. (2010): Decentralisation of Natural Resource Management in India: An Institutional perspective. *Indian Journal of Agricultural Economics*, Vol.65, No.1, Jan-Mar.

Matta, J.M. and J.R.R. Alavalapati (2006): Perceptions of Collective Action and its Success in Community Based Natural Resource Management: An Empirical Analysis. *Forest Policy and Economics*, 9: 274-284.

McCarthy, N. (2004): Local-level public goods and collective action. In *Collective action and property rights for sustainable development*. Focus 2020, 11. Ed. R. S.Meinzen-Dick, and M. Di Gregorio. Washington DC: International Food PolicyResearch Institute.

McKean, M.A. and E. Ostrom (1995): Common Property Regimes in the forest: Just a relic from the past. *Unasylva* 180, Vol 46, 3-14. FAO, Rome.

Meinzen-Dick, R. et al. (2006): SECURING THE COMMONS, *Policy Brief No-4, May-2006.*

Mishra, A. (2020). Poverty, Forests and Livelihoods: A Study of Three Villages in Odisha, India. SSRN Electronic Journal · July 2020.

Mishra, D. and S. Kant (2004): Production Analysis of Collaborative Forest Management Using an Example of Joint Forest Management from Gujarat, India. *Forest Policy and Economics*, 6:301-320.

MoEF (2010). Report to the People on Environment and Forests 2009–2010. Ministry of Environment and Forests (MoEF), Government of India.

Mohanty, P.C. (2006): Role of Community Participation through JFM for Rural Development in India. Small scale forestry and rural development: the intersection of ecosystems, economics and society.

Mukhija, V. (2005): Collective Actions and Property Rights: A Planner's Critical Look at the Dogma of Private Property. *International Journal of Urban and Regional Research*, Vol.29, No.4.

Mukul, S.A., Rashid, A. Z. M. M., Belal Uddin, M. & Khan, N.A. (2016) Role of non-timber forest products in sustaining forest-based livelihoods and rural households 'resilience capacity in and around protected area: a Bangladesh study. Journal of Environmental Planning and Management, 59 (4): 628-642.

Murty, M. N. (1994): Management of Common Property Resources:

Limits to voluntary Collective action. *Environmental and Resource Economics*, 4(6): 581-594.

Nagendra, Harini (2011). Heterogeneity and Collective Action for Forest Management. United Nations Development Programme Human Development Reports Research Paper 2011/02 November 2011.

Negi, S., Pham, T. T., Karky, B & Garcia, C. (2018). Role of Community and User Attributes in Collective Action: Case Study of Community-Based Forest Management in Nepal. Forests, 9(3): 1-20.

Netting, R. Mc C. (1976): What Alpine peasants have in common? Observations on communal tenure in a Swiss village. *Human Ecology* 4(2): 135-46.

Neupane, H. (2003): Contested impact of community forestry on equity: Some evidence from Nepal. *Journal of Forest and Livelihood* 2(2): 55-61.

Ninan, K.N. & Inoue, M. (2013a) Valuing forest ecosystem services: what we know and what we don't, Ecological Economics, 93: 137-149.

Ninan, K.N. & Inoue, M. (2013b) Valuing forest: case study of a forest reserve in Japan, Ecosystem Services, 5: 78-87.

Ninan, K.N. & Kontoleon, A. (2016) Valuing forest ecosystem services and disservices – Case study of a Protected Area in India, Ecosystem Services, 20: 1-14.

Norgaard, R. B. (1989): The case for methodological pluralism. *Ecological Economics*, 1:37-57.

NSSO, (1999): *Common Property Resources in India*, 54th Round, Report No. 452 (54/31/4).

Nygren, A. (2005): Community-based forest management within the context of institutional decentralization in Honduras. *World Development* 33(4): 639-55.

Ojha. N (2006): Report on Difficulties in JFM/CFM affecting forest dependent communities in Odisha.N-4/144, IRC Village, Bhubaneswar, Odisha.

Okumu, B. & Muchapondwa, E. (2017). Determinants of Successful Collective Management of Forest Resources: Evidence from Kenyan Community Forest Associations. ERSA working paper 698. Economic Research Southern Africa,

Olson, M. (1965): *The Logic of Collective Action: Public Goods and the Theory of Groups*. Cambridge: Harvard University Press.

Ostrom E. (1990): *Governing the Commons: The Evolution of*

Institutions for Collective Action. Cambridge University Press, Cambridge.

Ostrom, E. (1998): A Behavioural Approach to the Rational Choice Theory of Collective Action. *American Political Science Review*, 92(1).

Ostrom, E. (1999): Self Governance and Forest Resources. *Occasional Paper No.20,* Center for International Forestry Research, Bogor, Indonesia.

Ostrom, E. (2000): Collective Action and the Evolution of Social Norms. *The Journal of Economic Perspectives*. 14(3).

Ostrom, E. (2000): Type of Good and Collective Action. Paper Presented at the University of Maryland, Collective Choice Centre and IRIS.

Ostrom, E. (2005): *Understanding Institutional Diversity*. Princeton University Press.

Ostrom, E. (2009): A General Framework for Analyzing the Sustainability of Social-ecological Systems. *Science*, 325(5939).

Ostrom, E. (2010): Beyond Markets and States: Polycentric Governance of Complex Economic Systems. The Nobel Foundation's Year Book. *Les Prix Nobel*.

Ostrom, V., D. Fenny and H. Pitch (1988): *Rethinking Institutional Analysis Development: Issues. Alternatives and Choices*. ICEG, Panama.

Pathania, M. S., G D. Vashist, KD Sharma and H. Lal (2010): Livelihood Dependence on Common Property. Land Resources-A Field Study in Himachal Pradesh. *Journal of Rural Development*. 29(2): 125-139.

Pathania, M.S., K.D. Sharma and H. Lal (2008): System Synergy of Farming System and Common Property Resources in Mountain Regions: A Case Study of Himachal Pradesh. *Agricultural Economics Research Review*, Vol.21, January-June, pp 99-108.

Pearce, D. (1986): The Economics of natural Resource Management. Projects Policy Department, *World Bank*, Washington, D.C.

Pearce, D.W. and R.K. Turner (1990): *The Economics of Natural Resources and the Environment*, London: Harvester-Wheatsheaf.

Pearce, D.W. (2001) Economic Value of forest Ecosystem. Ecosystem Health, 7 (4): 284-296.

Peluso, N.L. (1992): *Rich Forests, Poor People*. Berkeley: University of California Press.

Peters, P. E. (1987): *Embedded systems and rooted models: the grazing lands of Botswana and the commons debate*. In: McCay B.J. and Acheson J.M. (Eds.), The Question of the commons, The University of Arizona Press, Tuscon: 171-194.

Poffenberger, M. and C. Singh (1991): Emerging directions in Indian forest policy: the Legal framework for joint forest management of forestlands, working paper 14, Ford Foundation, New Delhi.

PoI (2019). Status of Forests in India. Report No. 324, Parliament of India (PoI)- Rajya Sabha, Rajya Sabha Secretariat, New Delhi.

Poteete, A. R. & Ostrom, E. (2004). Heterogeneity, Group Size and Collective Action: The Role of Institutions in Forest Management. Development and Change, 35(3):435 – 461.

Pradhan, A. K. & Patra, R. (2020). Common Property Forest Resources and Participatory Management: Issues in Heterogeneity and Sustainability. Journal of Rural Development, 39(2):

Raj, K. (2006): Common Property Resources Synergy and Prospects of Sustainable Management: Garurganga watershed, Indian Central Himalaya; *J. Hum. Ecol.*, 20(1).

Ramachandra, T.V., Soman, D., Naik, A.D. & Chandran, S.M.D. (2017) Appraisal of Forest Ecosystems Goods and Services: Challenges and Opportunities for Conservation, Journal of Biodiversity, 8 (1): 12-33.

Randall, A. (1983): The problem of market failure. *Natural Resources Journal*, 23(1): 131-148.

Reddy, S.R.C., S. P. Chakravarty (1999): Forest Dependence and Income Distribution in a Subsistence Economy: Evidence from India. *World Development* 27(7): 1141-1149.

Reddy, V.R, B. Behera and D.M. Rao (2001): Forest degradation in India: Extent and Determinants. *IndianJournal of Agricultural Economics*, 56(4):630-651.

Repetto, R. (1986): *World Enough and Time*. New Haven, Conn.: Yale University Press.

Ribot, J. (2002): Democratic decentralization of natural resources: Institutionalizing popular participation. *Working Paper*, Washington: World Resources Institute.

Ribot, J.C. (1999): Decentralization, participation, and accountability in Sahelian forestry: Legal instruments of political-administrative control. *Africa* 69(1):23-65.

Rishi, P. (2007): Joint Forest Management in India: An Attitudinal Analysis of Stakeholders. *Resources, Conservation and Recycling*, 51: 345-354.

Saha, D. &Agarwalla, S. (2021). People's Forest Dependence: A Case Study of Similipal Biosphere Reserve, India. Review of Developmentand Change, 26 (1): 63-82.

Samal, K.C. (2009): Liberalization, Deforestation and Dependence on Forest. *Social Action, Vol.59, Jan-Mar*.

Sandee Policy Brief (2004): Tank Degradation and Poverty Reduction- The importance of Common Property Resources in Sustaining the Rural Poor.

Sapkota, I.P and P. C. Odën (2008): Household Characteristics and Dependency on Community Forests in TERAI Nepal. *International Journal of Social Forestry* (IJSF), 1(2):123-144.

SAPROF TEAM (2005): Special Assistance for Project Formation (SAPROF) for Odisha Forestry Sector Development Project. Final Report Vol.1.

Sarap, K and T.K. Sarangi (2010): An Analysis of Working of Forest Institutions in Odisha. *Journal of Social and Economic Development*, 12(2): 192-210.

Sarap, K. (2004): Participatory Management in ODISHA: A Review of Policies and Implementation.

Saravanan, V.S. (2002): Institutionalizing Community Based Watershed Management in India: Elements of Institutional Sustainability. *Water Science and Technology*, Vol.45, No.11.

Sarker, D. (2009): Sustainable Rural Livelihoods Under Joint Forest Management (JFM) Programme: Some Evidence from West Bengal, India, *Artha Vijnana*, Vol.LI, No.1, pp.59-84.

Sarker, D. and N. Das (2006): Social Capital and Joint Forest Management Programme: A Comparative Study of Female Headed and Joint Forest Protection Committees in West Bengal. *Journal of Rural Development*. 25(4): 537-563.

Sathyapalan, J. (2005) Households' Dependence on Protected Forests: evidence from the Western Ghats, Indian Journal of Agricultural Economics, 60 (1): 60-70.

Saxena, N. C. (1993): Social forestry and panchayats. *Seminar*, 406, June.

Schramm, G and J.J. Warford (1989): Environmental Management and Economic Policy in Developing Countries, *Environmental Management and Economic Development*: The Johns Hopkins Press.

Seeland, K. (1991): Sanskritization and environmental perception among Tibeto-burman Speaking groups. *Presented in the International Seminar Anthropology of Tibet and The Himalayas,* 21-28 September 1990 at the Ethnographic Museum of the Univ. of Zurich.

Sekar.C (2001): Externality Effects of Common Property Resource Degradation. *Indian Journal of Agricultural Economics,* 56(3):346-358.

Sen, A. (1977): Rational fools. *Philosophy and Public Affairs* 6.4, 317-44.

Sengupta, R. (2001): *Ecology and Economics: An Approach to Sustainable Development,* Oxford University Press.

Sikka, A.K. et al. (2002): Land and water care through participatory watershed management in India: An Overview. Presented at 12th ISCO Conference Beijing 2002.

Smith, R. (1981): Resolving the Tragedy of the Commons by Creating Private Property Rights in Wildlife. *CATO Journal,* Vol (1), pp.439-468.

Society & Natural Resources, 11 (2): 101-120.

SOFO (2014). Enhancing the Socioeconomic Benefits from Forests. State of the World's Forests (SOFO). Food and Agriculture Organization of the United Nations.

SOFO (2016). Forests and Agriculture: land-Use Challenges and Opportunities. (SOFO). Food and Agriculture Organization of the United Nations.

Soman, D. & Anitha, V. (2020). Community dependence on the natural resources of Parambikulam Tiger Reserve, Kerala, India. Trees, Forests and People, Volume 2. Open Access Article Retrieved on 30 May 2021.

Somanathan, E., Prabhakar, R. & Mehta, B.S. (2002). "Collective action for forest conservation: Does Heterogeneity matter?" Discussion Papers 02-01, Indian Statistical Institute, Delhi.

Somanathan, E., Prabhakar, R. & Mehta, B. S. (2007). Collective Action for Forest Conservation: Does Heterogeneity Matter? Chapter- 9 in Somanatban, E., Prabhakar, R. & Mehta, B. S. (Eds.) Inequality, Cooperation, and Environmental Sustainability. Princeton University Press 2007.

Somanathan, E., R. Prabhakar, and B Singh Mehta (2005): Does decentralization work? Forest conservation in the Indian Himalayas. *Discussion Paper 05-04.* New Delhi: Indian Statistical Institute.

Sonak.S, S.Kazi, M.Sonak and M. Abraham (2006): Why was traditional common property resource management system more successful in the coastal wetlands of Goa?

Srigiri, S.R., R.Chennamaneni and K. Hagedorn (2003): Equity and Poverty Issues in Watershed Development Projects – A Case Study of Impact Assessment on Marginal Farmers and the Landless. *Paper Presented at the Conference on International Agricultural Research for Development*, Gottingen.

Srinivasan, J.T. (2005): The Differential Impact of User Heterogeneity in Resource Management: A case study from Kerla. *Working paper No.66.*

Stevenson, G.G. (1991): *Common Property Economics: A General Theory and Land Use Application*. Cambridge University Press.

Sugden, R. (1986): *The economics of rights, co-operation, and welfare*. Blackwell, Oxford.

Sullivan, A., York, A. M., White, D. D., Hall, S. J. &Yabiku, S. T. (2017). De jure versus de facto institutions: trust information and collective efforts to manage the invasive mileaminute weed (*Mikania micrantha*). International Journal of the Commons, 11 (1): 171–199.

Sundar N. (2001): Is Devolution Democratization? World Development, 29(12): 2007-2023.

Tábara, J.D. and C. Pahl-Wosti(2007): Sustainability Learning in Natural Resource Use and Management, Ecology and Society 12(2).3.

Tacconi, L. (2007): Decentralization, Forests and Livelihoods: Theory and Narrative. Global Environmental Change, 17: 338-348.

Tang, S.Y. (1991): Institutional arrangements and the management of common-pool resources. *Public Administration Review*, 51(1): 42-51

Tang, S.Y. (1992): *Institutions and collective Action: Self-governance in Irrigation Systems*. ICS Press, San Francisco.

Tiwari, M. (2010): Operationalization of Village Forest Committees: Some Hypothesis and Their Verification.*Indian Journal of Social Development*, 10 (1): 47-58.

Tiwari, M. (2010-A): Joint Forest Management and Rural Development in Jharkhand. *Journal of Rural Development*. 29(4): 479-492.

Turkelboom, F., T.R. Gurung and D. Dupka (2001): Role and Use of Common Property Resources (CPRs) in Bhutan

Himalayas: Between Tradition and Globalization. *Paper presented at the Inaugural Pacific Regional Meeting for Common Property Resources at Brisbane,* Sept.2-4, 2001.

Uberhuaga, P., Smith-Hall, C. & Helles, F. (2012) Forest income and dependency in lowland Bolivia. Environment, Development and Sustainability: A Multidisciplinary Approach to the Theory and Practice of Sustainable Development, Springer, 14(1): 3-23.

UN (2021). The Global Forests Goals Report. United Nations Department of Economic and Social Affairs, United Nations.

Vemuri, A. (2008): Joint Forest Management in India: An Unavoidable and Conflicting Common Property Regime in Natural Resource Management. *Journal of Development and Social Transformation,* Vol.5, Nov.

Verma, D., Negandhi, C., Khanna, A., Edgaonkar, A., David, A., Kadekodi, G., Costanza, R. & Singh, R. (2015). Economic Valuation of Tiger Reserves in India: A Value+ Approach. Indian Institute of Forest Management, Bhopal, India.

Verma,M., Tiwari, C., Anand, S., Edgaonkar, A., David, A., Kadekodi, G., Ninan, K.N., Sharma, P., Panda, P. & Thatey, Z. (2019). Economic Valuation of Tiger Reserves in India: Phase II. Indian Institute of Forest Management, Bhopal, India.

Vinodan, A. & Manalel, J. (2011). Local Economic benefit of ecotourism: a case study of Parambikulam Tiger Reserve in Kerala. *South Asian Journal* of Tourism and *Heritage,* 4 (2): 93-109.

Vondal, P.J. (1987): *The common swamplands of southeastern Borneo: multiple use, management and conflict.* In:McCAY. B.J. and Acheson J.M. (Eds), The Questions of the common, The University of Arizona press, Tuscon: 231-249.

Wade, R. (1987): The Management of Common Property Resources: Collective Action as an Alternative to Privatisation or State Regulation. *Cambridge Journal of Economics,* Vol (11) pp: 95-106.

Wade, R. (1988): *Village Republics: Economic conditions for collective Action in South India.* Cambridge University Press, Cambridge.

Wade, R. (1994): *Village Republics: Economic Conditions for Collective Actions in South India.* Oakland: ICS Press.

Wittman, H. and C. Geisler (2005): Negotiating locality:

Decentralization and communal forest management in the Guatemalan highlands. *Human Organization* 64(1): 62-74.

World Commission on Environment and Development (1987): *Our Common Future*, Oxford: Oxford University Press.

(SLRM501)http://india.gov.in/allimpfrms/alldocs/10523.pdf (UOH-1998- 322)http://dspace.vidyanidhi.org.in:8080/dspace/bitstream/2009/4353/3/UOH-1998-320-2.pdf (Pepfarstatesorr)http://newdelhi.usembassy.gov/pepfars/pepfarstatesorr.pdf

Glossary of Terms

Canopy (or Crown): The cover of branches and foliage formed by the crown of trees.

Canopy Density: Percent area of land covered by the canopy of trees. Also referred to as "Crown Density".

Crown Area: The area of crown of individual trees computed by measuring the width of the horizontal projection of tree crown on the ground.

Dense Forest: All lands with a forest cover with canopy density of 40 percent and above.

Farm Forestry: The practice of planting/cultivating and managing trees on farms or agricultural lands. Forest Area: Geographic areas recorded as forests in Government records. It is also referred to as "recorded forest area".

Forest Cover: All lands, more than one hectare in area, with a tree canopy density of more than 10 percent. Such lands may not be statutorily notified as forest area.

Forest fringe village: a village located nearby a forest area whose population draw their livelihood and derive ecological services from forest and other associated natural assets.

Forest Inventory: The measuring and describing the quantity and quality of forest crop and many other characteristics of the land area upon which forest crop is growing.

Geographic Area: The total physical area within the boundaries on a map. (The geographic area of India includes area that is under illegal occupation of Pakistan and China).

Geographic Information System (GIS): A system for capturing, storing, checking, manipulating, analysing and displaying data that are spatially referenced to the earth.

Growing Stock: The sum-total of all the trees, by number or volume or biomass, growing within a particular area of interest.

Joint Forest Management: Joint Forest Management refers to partnerships involving the state/government and the local people working for conservation, protection and development of forests; the local people are usually those living in forest fringe villages.

Land Cover: Broad land use classes interpreted from satellite data. The land cover classes used in this report are dense forest, open forest, scrub and non-forest.

Mangroves: Salt tolerant forest ecosystem found mainly in tropical and sub-tropical coastal and/or inter-tidal regions.

Mangrove Cover: Area covered under mangrove vegetation as interpreted digitally from remote sensing data. It is classified into dense mangrove cover (canopy density over 40 percent) and open mangrove cover (canopy density from 10 to 40 percent).

Net Change (in Forest Cover) : The sum-total of positive and negative changes in forest cover within a given region that took place during the period of two assessments. Non Forest Area: Geographic area outside recorded forest area.

Non-Forest: Lands without any forest cover. Open Forest: All lands with a forest cover with a canopy density of 10 to 40 percent.

Protected Forest: An area notified under the provisions of the Indian Forest Act or other State Forest Acts, having limited degree of protection. In Protected forest all activities are permitted unless prohibited.

Physiographic Zone: A physiographic zone constitutes geographical areas that exhibit broad similarities in factors responsible for the growth of tree vegetation. Physiographic zones have been used as strata for assessing tree cover in the country.

Recorded Forest Area: Same as "forest area"; i.e., geographic areas recorded as forests in Government records.

Reserved Forests: An area so constituted under the provisions of the Indian Forest Act or other State Forest Acts, having full degree of protection. In Reserved forests all activities are prohibited unless permitted.

Scrub: All lands, generally in and around forest areas, having bushes and/or poor tree growth chiefly of small or stunted trees with canopy density less than 10 percent.

Tree: Tree denotes all perennial woody vegetation (including bamboos, palms, coconut, neem, peepal, fruit trees, etc.). It excludes non-perennial non-woody species (e.g., banana) and tall shrubs or climbers (e.g., lantana or canes). For the purpose of assessing tree cover, only those trees having diameter of 10 cm or more at breast height (1.37 m) have been considered. In case of trees having multiple branches below breast height, the individual stems with diameter over 10 cm at breast height have been considered as individual trees.

Tree Cover: The term used in this report refers to the notional area covered by crown of trees that is too small to be delineated by digital interpretation of remote sensing data used for forest cover delineation. Trees Outside Forests: Tree wealth existing outside recorded forest areas. These include trees in towns, cities, on farms, along roads and railway lines, and in many other places which are by definition not forests.

Unclassed Forests: An area recorded as forest but not included in reserved or protected forest category. Ownership status of such forests varies from state to state.

Village Woodlot: Naturally growing trees (sometimes supplemented with tree plantations) growing on village community land or panchayat land.

Index